The Public Management and Leadership series

Series Editor: Paul 't Hart, Utrecht University & Netherlands School of Public Administration

Editorial Advisory Group

John Alford (University of Melbourne & Australia and New Zealand School of Government)

Michael Barzelay (London School of Economics and Political Science)

Geert Bouckaert (K.U. Leuven)

Joanne B. Ciulla (Jepson School, University of Richmond)

Jean Hartley (Open University Business School)

Werner Jann (University of Potsdam)

Per Lægreid (University of Bergen)

Mark H. Moore (Harvard University)

Jon Pierre (University of Gothenburg)

Donald J. Savoie (Moncton University)

Mark van Twist (Netherlands School of Government & Erasmus University)

Zeger van der Wal (National University of Singapore)

Kai Wegrich (Hertie School of Governance)

Public management and, more recently, public leadership have over several decades emerged as increasingly central elements in the study and practice of governance, public administration and public policy.

Around them have developed important new strands of research, debate, education and professional formation. And these in turn have informed a wide range of initiatives in many parts of the world to 'modernize', 'reform', 'innovate', 'de-bureaucratize' and 'professionalize' existing institutions and practices.

The Public Management and Leadership series aims to provide a set of key texts to meet the changing needs of the growing range of graduate and post-experience courses in this area as well as concise and accessible reading for busy practitioners.

Genuinely international in scope and conception, accessible in style and presentation, and drawing on empirical information and illustrations from a wide variety of jurisdictions and policy sectors, each title offers an authoritative review of the state of theory and practice in its respective field, and identifies the key challenges and the most promising conceptual and practical tools to tackle them.

D0160853

The Public Management and Leadership series

Series Editor: Paul 't Hart, Utrecht University & Netherlands School of Public Administration

The Public Management and Leadership Series
Series Standing Order ISBN 978–0–230–23657–8 hardback
Series Standing Order ISBN 978–0–230–23658–5 paperback

(outside North America only)

You can receive future titles in this series as they are published by a placing a standing order. Please contact your bookseller or, in the case of difficulty, write to us at the address below with your name and address, the title of the series and an ISBN quoted above.

Customer Services Department, Palgrave Macmillan Ltd,
Houndmills, Basingstoke, Hampshire RG21 6XS, England, UK

Rethinking Public Strategy

Sean Lusk

and

Nick Birks

First published 2014 by
PALGRAVE MACMILLAN

Palgrave Macmillan in the UK is an imprint of Macmillan Publishers Limited, registered in England, company number 785998, of Houndmills, Basingstoke, Hampshire RG21 6XS.

Palgrave Macmillan in the US is a division of St Martin's Press LLC, 175 Fifth Avenue, New York, NY 10010.

Palgrave Macmillan is the global academic imprint of the above companies and has companies and representatives throughout the world.

Palgrave® and Macmillan® are registered trademarks in the United States, the United Kingdom, Europe and other countries

ISBN 978-1-137-37757-9 hardback
ISBN 978-1-137-37756-2 paperback

This book is printed on paper suitable for recycling and made from fully managed and sustained forest sources. Logging, pulping and manufacturing processes are expected to conform to the environmental regulations of the country of origin.

A catalogue record for this book is available from the British Library.

A catalog record for this book is available from the Library of Congress.

Typeset by Cambrian Typesetters, Camberley, Surrey, England, UK

Printed in China

For Sally

Contents

List of Illustrative Material

Figures

Tables

Boxes

Preface

We came to write this book as two practitioners in the field of public strategy who were frustrated by how little sound advice and guidance existed for those who work in the field. There are many thousands of books describing both the theory and practice of corporate strategy, and some contain material useful to practitioners in government and public organizations. But very few describe the distinctive world of strategy-making in the public sphere in a useful way. One of the defining features of public strategy is that organizational success is – or should be – subordinate to the achievement of the outcomes the organization exists to achieve. Success for a public agency might be to achieve its aims so well that it can 'go out of business'; yet public bodies often thrive and grow while achieving too little in terms of publicly valuable outcomes.

In our respective roles – one of us heading the strategy and leadership faculty in the UK Government's civil service training college (at the time called the National School of Government), the other Head of Strategic Insight and Horizon Scanning at a large agency of central government – we were meeting colleagues from across the public sector, as well as academics and colleagues from other countries who repeatedly asked us two questions: do we understand how strategic thinking improves policy-making and successful public service delivery? And where is strategy made most successfully, and what makes it a success?

In our quest to find answers to these two questions we interviewed many hundreds of practitioners and academics and conducted a five year long research programme, testing ideas in a range of organizations in the UK and elsewhere. This book offers our answers to both questions, showing how strategic thinking can improve the quality of policy and make implementation effective and sustainable.

We live in an era when (it is often argued) the role of governmental action is circumscribed by the forces of international capital markets. The authority and legitimacy of governments is called into question by the increasing ability of networked populations to marshal political power through social media. It can be a challenge for government at all levels – city, regional, national and supranational – to understand how they can do the things that governments are supposed to do. How can governments continue to lead, shape and influence the direction of their societies and their economies? While there is nothing new about strategy, the circumstances in which strategy must be applied have changed, and this book is set in that context.

We include case studies from many countries showing who has succeeded in making strategy 'stick' and who has failed. Sometimes success comes down to the little things – the right people in the right place at the right time and to trusting relationships between elected politicians and unelected officials who then work successfully together. Sometimes it's the big things that make the difference – for instance, a strong public appetite for change or a crisis that makes the existing state of affairs untenable.

Much also comes down to a desire to understand the future, a willingness to embrace uncertainty and complexity, a spirit of curiosity, the ability to make sense of emerging patterns that others miss, the leadership to build a compelling vision of something new and better and the courage to see ideas through to their realization. In one sense, the set of skills and qualities required in rethinking public strategy is what outstanding public service is all about. Our hope is that this book is useful to those who are interested in making public service as good as it can be.

The book's structure

The first half of the book – Chapters 1 to 4 – sets the conditions for strategy. In these chapters we describe some of the problems in thinking and acting strategically and some of the benefits that good strategy can bring. In the second half of the book we offer some practical advice on how to think, act and deliver using strategic approaches. The final chapter is a consideration of the role of imagination and judgement in strategy.

Chapter 1 considers the overuse of the word 'strategy' and the need to rethink and restate the case for strategy in a world where the role of government is challenged by the power of international markets and by populations connected, and often mobilized, by social technologies. We examine the benefits of strategy and the cyclical appetite for it. The chapter examines whether the pace of change is relevant and concludes by looking at the importance of using strategy in the right place and at the right time.

Chapter 2 explains in more detail definitions of strategy and the relationship between strategy, policy and delivery. It describes what strategy is not as well as what it is, and makes clear why defined desired outcomes are so integral to the creation and execution of successful public strategy. It contrasts the strategic approach with narrow problem-solving approaches, and concludes with a brief exploration of the importance of different conceptualizations of the future for strategy work.

Chapter 3 examines the fundamental distinctions and similarities between strategy in the private domain, where the focus is on the ability of the organization to generate profit in the medium and long term, and in the public domain, where the focus is on creating civic goods that are of value to groups of citizens. We consider the theory of public value, the importance of legitimacy and the extent to which public engagement and accountability generate that legitimacy. We explore what – if anything – is equivalent in the public domain to the role that profit performs in the private domain. We examine the role of strategy in creating organizational resilience and the important distinction in the respective roles of the organization between the public and private domains. We consider the significance of co-production and the treatment of citizens primarily as consumers of public services.

Chapter 4 considers why it can be so difficult to think strategically, including the problems of 'lens of now' thinking, of groupthink, expert bias and short-termism. It also looks at the tendency to 'muddle through', and why that can sometimes be the right thing to do, and at the political and institutional context, and how this can sometimes constrain strategic approaches to policy formation and implementation.

Chapter 5 takes the reader through a strategic thinking process, beginning with ways to open-up thinking and 'crack the lens of now' and proceeding through a series of strategic thinking techniques from drivers for change to scenario-building. We look at the importance of systems thinking and consider sources of evidence and ways of applying evidence in a future-focused context.

Chapter 6 begins by looking at the need to build appetite to work strategically, considering how leadership, challenge, a focus on outcomes and accountability increases organizational appetite for strategic working. We examine the value of strategy units, their role and how they are best structured. We look at the uses and abuses of 'strategy toolkits' and conclude by re-emphasizing the importance of creating strategic appetite.

Chapter 7 considers the importance of vision and defined desired outcomes, and the role of the organizational mission statement and the effect it has on aligning the organization to strategic intent. We look at the importance of understanding the distinctive roles of outcomes, indicators and performance measures. We examine ways to define organizational activities in outcome terms, which both helps to enable 'co-production' (the achievement of outcomes by citizens and government working together) and can make it easier to measure outcomes themselves. We look at the importance of aligning the organization so that it supports achievement of strategy and offers 'line of sight' to all those who work in it, who deal with it or are affected by it. We consider the uses and abuses of targets and conclude with a short examination of the power of language in converting intent into reality.

Chapter 8 looks at how we think, and how our thinking converts into judgement and decision-making. What does neuroscience tell us about decision-making? What are the personal qualities that result in the right decisions on the strategic journey? What is the role of imagination and 'sensemaking' in strategy? In a world that bombards the brain with 'facts' and information, the final chapter makes the case for openness, curiosity and imagination.

The *Conclusion* is a summary of the book's main themes and arguments, and some strategic questions for the reader to consider.

Acknowledgements

The origin of this book rests with the former UK National School of Government. Very many colleagues at the NSG gave their advice and support to the research and writing of the book, above all the members of the strategy team including Peter Tebby, Tracy Roberts, James Mackie, Harleen Thati, Jim Scopes, Melissa Sorrell, Jan Polley, Cat Tully, Pam Hurley and also our colleague Sue Richards, who first uttered the fateful words: 'you really should write a book about public strategy'. Ann Maton made an enormous contribution through her extraordinary organizational skills, as did Della Chappell and her colleagues in the NSG library who supported the research process. Jonathan Marshall and Adam Steinhouse read early drafts and helped to reshape the book. More recently two colleagues at the Valuation Office Agency have been great supporters – Dyfed Alsop and Phil Bower. Rosie Ford gave space to think and to write.

More than a hundred colleagues from the worlds of civil service, parliament, academia and think tanks generously found time to be interviewed for the book or to give valuable advice on it, including Stephen Aldridge, John Benington, Michael Bichard, Faith Boardman, Chris Bones, Jonathan Brearley, John Bryson, Chris Carr, Jake Chapman, Rod Clark, Claire Craig, Andrew Curry, John Eldridge, Alex Evans, Janet Grauberg, John Greenaway, Ravi Gurumurthy, Catherine Haddon, David Halpern, Jean Hartley, Bernard Jenkin, Gerry Johnson, Paul Joyce, Neil Kenward, Rannia Leontaridi, Rupert Lewis, Joyce Liddle, Paul Lusk, Alistair Mant, Andrew Massey, Julian McCrae, Mark Moore, Geoff Mulgan, Una O'Brien, Carey Oppenheim, Tim Render, Alun Rhydderch, Gill Ringland, Jill Rutter, Jon Shortridge, James Smith, David Stevens, Matthew Taylor, Sam Tennakoon, Mike Thomas, Andrea Westall, Oliver Will, Ngaire Woods and Tony Wright.

The book would simply not have been possible without the patient guiding hand of our wonderful publisher Steven Kennedy at Palgrave Macmillan and the clear and wise advice of series editor Paul 't Hart.

Ipsos-Mori for the use of their long-term research on 'the most important issues facing Britain today', from which we drew material in order to create Figure 4.1 ('The lens of now'). This Ipsos-Mori monthly survey can be accessed on http://www.ipsos-mori.com/researchpublications/researcharchive/2905/Issues-Index-2012-onwards.aspx?view=wide.

We should make clear that all errors and omissions in the book are entirely the authors' own – our very many colleagues bear no responsibility for our mistakes.

Finally, the authors would like to acknowledge the considerable contribution made by family and friends, including, for Sean, his wife Sally and for Nick those who have over the years given him his head, the space and encouragement to understand public sector strategy.

SEAN LUSK
NICK BIRKS

Chapter 1

Introduction: Strategy – Everywhere and Nowhere

Strategy is, it seems, everywhere. Politicians, business leaders, work colleagues, teachers, sports coaches and bloggers talk about 'strategic choices', of making 'strategic plans' and 'acting strategically'. But what do they mean – what do any of us mean – when we use the word? Is 'strategy' one of those words that, through overuse and misuse, has become meaningless or, worse, irritating and pointless?

This book shows strategy really does matter. It is a distinctive approach to organizing a place, a people or institution that gives a sense of purpose and an understanding of the future. Strategy carries within it a grasp of the story – its beginning, its middle, and its many potential ends. A good strategy can mean that a crisis is averted, that a community avoids hunger or war or disease. Really successful strategies create prosperity, build strong cities and nations; they help people to live longer and to expect and achieve more from the lives they lead. Bad strategies are quite capable of doing the opposite – causing conflict, destroying communities and crushing hope. Strategy is a powerful instrument for change for good but poorly formulated, or with malicious intent at its heart, strategy can also be a force for ill.

Strategy is an overused word, often used to convey power, status or seniority. Yet the appetite for being strategic rises and falls cyclically. As we approach the peak of a cycle, we see ambitious visions being set by governments for 20 years hence, plans being published and energy building to a crescendo. An inspiring programme of space exploration is developed; speeches are made and budgets set. An agenda to make a region or bloc the most competitive economy on the planet is agreed; intentions are sincere and profound, treaties are signed, laws passed. A new doctrine is established to prevent persecution and genocide; resolutions are passed at the United Nations and foreign policies and military forces are given new aims. For a time everybody talks of going to Mars, of the Lisbon Agenda, of the responsibility to protect threatened peoples. And then the cycle breaks. Scepticism builds, people's horizons shorten to the immediate – to coping with the coming month, to the financial out-turn, to the electoral cycle. Money runs out, unemployment rates soar, military interventions go wrong. Problems press in from every angle and survival seems to depend on picking them off, one by one. The

1

world is uncertain and unpredictable and confidence plummets. Strategy is nowhere: the same leaders who were talking about strategy only a few months earlier now make a virtue of quick wins, of immediate results, of showing resilience in the face of all that uncertainty. Strategy becomes a dirty word – an airy-fairy intellectual exercise for the policy wonks and blue-sky thinkers on the one hand or for out-of-touch authoritarian state planners on the other.

Yet it is at times of crisis and stress that strategy is most important – for a well-conceived and well-executed strategy can make all the difference between recovery and collapse. The newly independent Singapore faced a crisis in the early 1960s on almost every front. Yet through strategic thinking, planning and action the republic was able to forge a distinctive and strong position in the global economy.

Strategy is in part having the confidence and appetite to frame the world in terms of ambitions instead of only in terms of problems. The Singapore example doesn't mean strategy can ignore 'real world' constraints or problems – quite the contrary. Nor does it suggest strategy will be an article of perfection. For all its success, some may see Singapore, a parliamentary republic with a constitution establishing representative democracy, as less tolerant of diversity of opinion than is usual in a multiparty democracy.

One of the triumphs of the human race is the extension of lifespans in the 20th century through advances in diet, medicine, housing, education, the nature of work and reductions in infant mortality. Average life expectancy at birth in the USA, UK, France and Germany in 1901 was around 49 years. By 2011 it was around 80–81 years. In less economically developed parts of the world progress is also being made: in India in 1960 average life expectancy at birth was around 41 years; by 2011 it had increased to around 65 years. In Egypt life expectancy at birth was around 46 years in 1960 and 73 years in 2011 (World Health Organization figures). Yet the political discourse in the early part of the 21st century about older populations is of a 'problem', even a crisis. Instead of developing a strategy to take the opportunity given to each human of a longer lifespan, instead of developing ambitions for our societies to exploit these billions of extra years of human life, we can all too easily be thrown back into the distinctly unstrategic mindset of wondering how on earth we will cope. Strategy in the public domain must articulate ambition or, in the jargon, 'desired outcomes' for the future.

At its heart public strategy carries choice about future society. In the private domain strategy is the means by which the business makes choices about its future. While corporate strategy has an impact on wider society in terms of the wealth the business creates, the services or goods it provides, the labour and other resources it consumes and the competitive position it occupies, private sector strategy is fundamentally an organizational preoccupation. Public strategy is often about organizational

BOX 1.1 Singapore: from mud bank to global economic power through strategy

Singapore, a city state on the southern tip of the Malay Peninsula comprising 63 islands with a population in 2013 of around 5 million people, became self-governing in 1959. In 1961 it established the Economic Development Board (EDB) to develop a plan for the future Singapore economy. In 1963 Singapore joined the Federation of Malaysia but, after a series of major policy conflicts with the Federation Government, Singapore became an independent republic in 1965. At that time Singapore's population was 1.9 million and its GDP was US$917m – a per capita income of around $450 a year. It had no natural resources – even water supplies had to be bought from Malaysia. The break from Malaysia brought with it loss of access to raw materials and to a large domestic market. The Singapore government understood that its only asset was its people – a mix of Chinese, Malay and Indian origin. It needed to find ways to ensure that its population had the skills they needed to prosper in a highly competitive and vulnerable situation – and make itself sufficiently attractive to prevent its population leaving for Malaysia or other countries.

Singapore had little choice but to export – and it decided to take a strategic view of which goods it manufactured for a global market (see Schein 1996). In the 1960s it encouraged major companies to invest in capital-intensive plant, like Shell Eastern Petroleum. It also increased production of garments, textiles, toys and niche products like hair wigs. By the 1970s successful marketing by the EDB and pragmatic policies by the Singapore government had made it an attractive location for start-ups. Singapore made sure it supported industries of the future – it shifted into computer chips, software and computer peripherals. In the 1980s Singapore became a leading manufacturer of silicon chips and disc drives; in the 90s, while continuing to manufacture computer hardware and software, Singapore made itself a leading centre in biosciences and pharmaceuticals. In the first decade of the 21st century Singapore focused its economy on R&D and intellectual property. In 2006 the Singapore government established the National Research Foundation to coordinate research and innovation strategies (Economic Development Board of Singapore 2013).

From 1965 onwards the Singapore economy grew at an average rate of 8 per cent.

resilience, too, but it also aims to change one or many aspects of society for the better. Public strategy is a matter of politics as well as of administration; it concerns citizens as well as employees; voters and bystanders as well as leaders and managers; society, neighbourhoods and families as well as customers and markets.

Almost all debate about strategy has been based on experience drawn from either the corporate or the military spheres. While there is much to learn from those fields, public strategy is distinct in important respects, and applying corporate or military lessons without adaptation leads to problems for governments and other public organizations, whether at national, regional or local level (we look at some examples of these problems in Chapter 3). Context is everything. If we blow on a candle we extinguish it. If we blow on a fire we help it burn. This book focuses on the context for public and governmental strategy. It examines what it is, why it matters, what makes it difficult and gives some practical guidance about how to make public strategy successfully.

Rethinking public strategy

The purpose of public strategy is to make lives better for people, so they can lead what Aristotle called 'flourishing lives'. Public strategy is strategy for the common good. It is strategy in the public or not-for-profit sectors, in social enterprises or in commercial organizations commissioned to deliver public value, and is distinct from the public relations strategy a corporation may have that seeks to engage or build trust with citizens or voters.

In the late 19th and a large part of the 20th centuries in industrializing economies, government commanded resources and was able to direct their use to social ends. The hierarchical organization came to prominence as an efficient means of coordinating and directing activity. In the public sector, centralization of resources and power made sense.

The 1980s saw most industrial economies deregulate markets and privatize state-owned industries to expose them to competition. In other attempts to reform the public sector, political leaders instigated initiatives to improve financial management. The UK and the US advocated market-oriented reforms collectively known as 'new public management' (Hood 1991) intended to make government more cost-effective. This spread to other developed nations (Australia, Austria, Canada, Denmark, France, Germany, Italy, Japan, the Netherlands, New Zealand, Norway, Portugal, Spain, Sweden). It was also embraced by developing countries in Asia, Africa and Latin America, transitional societies in Eastern Europe and African countries like Uganda, Zimbabwe, Tanzania, Malawi, Ghana and Zambia, and assumed the status of a global model (Haque 2009). An example from the US is President Clinton's *National Performance Review* in 1993 (renamed *The National Partnership for Reinventing Government* in 1998).

Osborne and Gaebler set out the case for such reforms in their 1993 book *Reinventing Government* arguing that the public sector need not deliver services; it should instead specify and commission them with a particular emphasis on funding outcomes rather than inputs – in their phrase 'steering not rowing'. The Mayor of St Paul's, Minnesota talked about government as a catalyst and facilitator: 'City government will have to become even more willing to interweave scarce public and private resources in order to achieve our community's goals' (Osborne and Gaebler 1992: 27).

There is an emphasis in 'new public management' on government as a commissioner and deliverer of services, rather than a shaper of the future, which we shall argue is the area where public strategy makes its most significant contribution, and where we see much strategic thinking outsourced to think tanks, many of which are aligned to a particular political party or ideology.

The effect of the new public management reforms, coupled with the growth of international markets, called into question whether national governments could continue to control and regulate as they had in the past when they do not command the resources. Peters explores arguments for whether they are still major actors in public policy, able to influence the economy and society through their actions, when the state's capacity for direct control has been replaced with a capacity for influence (Peters and Pierre 1998: 223, 226).

In addition to issues of governance, Verity points out (Verity 2012) that in the industrialized era, economics was the traditional background for strategy academics, yet in real life people didn't conform to the behaviours predicted by microeconomic models whose rules have little tolerance for the behaviour of human beings. 'Books written about strategy plus what is taught in classrooms are strongly weighted to the economist's view' (Verity 2012: 1–2). In the post-industrial era the discipline of microeconomics has developed, informed by learning from behavioural psychology, meaning that the 'rules' view of strategy derived from economics has begun to converge with the anthropological view that takes account of the observable behaviour of people.

Merchant (Merchant 2012) shows that traditional strategy, which played a significant and meaningful role in how organizations organized to win in the industrial era, is obsolete in the social era. 'If the industrial era was about building things the social era is about connecting things, people and ideas. Networks of connected people with shared interests and goals create ways that can produce returns for any company that serves their needs' (Merchant 2012: 6).

Another analysis (used by David Cameron, who subsequently became UK Prime Minister) combines these developments 'The 20th century was the "bureaucratic age" because advances in communications and travel made it possible to concentrate power in the central state. Whitehall [the UK's centre of national government] had a monopoly of information and capability: it knew the most and had the most resources to make things change. The national culture emphasised conformity and knowing your place. Top-down control was practical and efficient, fair and moral. In the 21st Century the state cannot control society, which no longer emphasises conformity and knowing your place' (Cameron 2007). Connected people have more resources than government.

Strategy in hierarchies is different from strategy in connected, networked, integrated, interdependent economies and societies. Sophisticated global business and employment market places, cost-free communications, and new public management have led to distributed government, interdependent and interconnected, whose populations are empowered by technology to communicate peer to peer, working with the voluntary and private sectors to deliver objectives. 'Connectedness makes it possible to bypass things, to "disintermediate" or cut out the intermediaries. The guerrillas can bypass their own government and speak direct to the world's media' (Mulgan 1997: 23). Add to this connectedness governments' ambitions for smaller, more efficient public sectors and we see a premium on clarity of objectives and desired outcomes as ways of aligning activity. How does government govern in networked societies? Certainly there's a need to test, learn and adapt, but this is not an environment where we can rely on muddling through, if we ever could. Scenarios expert Adam Kahane puts it this way: 'We often tell ourselves that we can succeed in transforming the future through forceful action. Increasingly often, however, we cannot. As the world becomes more complex, with more interdependency and more unpredictability and more actors with power and voice, it becomes more difficult to effect transformation unilaterally. We need new stories' (Kahane 2012: 91).

The benefits of strategy

One of the reasons why strategy has a bad name in some places is because it has become linked with the 'five-year plan' – the reductionist, hyper-rational notion that a master plan, a logic model, an organizational chart, a spreadsheet can solve all our existing problems, anticipate future ones and lead us to a golden future where child poverty is eliminated, there is affordable housing for all, climate change is solved and everyone lives healthy and happy lives. History tells us that plans like that rarely work. They are associated with totalitarian regimes or with early 20th century managerialism with its belief that rigorous process and clear targets can run society like a perfect machine, its cogs spinning ever faster to deliver efficient, productive lives. For others strategy is visioning and scenarios and narratives that lead to glossy brochures and not much else. This book shows that good public strategy is neither fluffy 'blue-skies thinking' nor neo-Stalinist authoritarianism, but a helpful way of understanding the world and an effective way of influencing the future.

FIGURE 1.1   *Six benefits of effective public strategy*

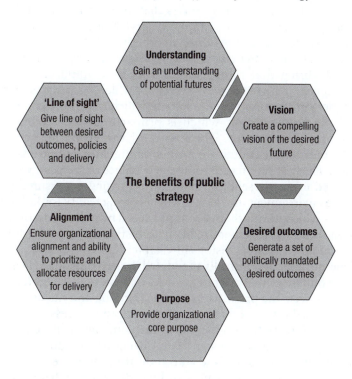

1. **Gain an understanding of potential futures**. Strategic organizations and leaders develop an understanding of the future. The future can never be fully known, but a range of potential futures can be identified, explored and prepared for. Its features can be defined, for instance using scenario-building techniques (see Chapter 5), and the strengths and weaknesses of existing organizations and policies can be projected into a range of futures and tested in them. The act of preparing for the future brings many advantages for governments, government departments, regional bodies and agencies as well as in preparing policy for a sector like food security, climate change, energy security, taxation and so on. Developing an understanding of a range of futures makes it possible to create and then monitor a set of indicators to give 'early warning' of which future appears to be coming about, and this can help to improve the resilience of government and agencies. Later in this book we will consider some of the techniques that are used to help build plausible potential futures.
2. **Create a compelling vision of the desired future**. Having a clearer understanding of likely futures helps governments and public organizations (and, indeed, private sector organizations) to be more resilient in whichever future comes about. In other words they are more likely

to cope, to survive, to get by. But is this enough? The job of governments and of the public agencies that are part of the framework of wider government is not simply to survive in different futures – it is also to try to *change the future*, in other words to describe a vision of a desired future and through a set of aligned policies and robust plans to help bring that future about. This is an important distinction between strategy in the private sector – which, broadly, is about optimal performance and profitability in whichever future comes about – and the public sector, which is primarily about achieving better outcomes for citizens. The nature of the vision and the desired outcomes that it contains are often matters for politicians to determine. The best visions are rooted in evidence of the past, well contextualized in the present and built with a strong understanding of the future environment in which it will become a reality (or fail to be realized) – which means that visions produced by politicians, officials and public working together are likely to be the ones that work best. We look in more detail at visions in Chapter 7.

3. **Generate a set of politically mandated desired outcomes**. Defining the set of outcomes that a strategy seeks to achieve is the 'golden buckle' that connects the process of strategic thinking and the understanding of potential futures on the one hand with the process of making and implementing policy on the other. Each outcome will sit at the 'head' of a policy process; it is capable of being broken down into sets of intermediate outcomes and into indicators. Agencies can set themselves performance measures to help determine whether the work that they do is contributing towards achievement of the outcome or not. The identification of outcomes becomes the catalyst that makes strategic thinking into strategy-making. It is easier to hold governments or agencies to account for achieving outcomes than for whether a whole strategy is being realized. Outcomes are the foundation for accountability between governments and government agencies on the one hand and the citizens to whom they are accountable on the other – though to some extent this depends on the relationships between politicians and officials being good enough to allow that to happen. We discuss outcomes in more detail in the next chapter. *It is worth noting that, particularly in North America, the term 'results' is often used instead of 'outcomes'. 'Results Based Accountability' and 'Outcomes Based Accountability' usually refer to the same thing and are used interchangeably in this book.*

4. **Give the organization its core purpose**. Some governments set a common vision and set of outcomes across all parts of government, for instance when coalitions publish a 'programme of government' after an election, or when governments set a five- or 10-year strategy for a particular sector, whether for economic growth, education or transport. Sometimes the landscape is less well-defined and public

agencies need to work out the vision and desired outcomes for themselves. In either case the vision and outcomes should inform the core purpose that the organization or range of organizations exist to achieve. We look in more detail at core purpose (sometimes called 'mission') in Chapter 7.

5. **Align, allocate and prioritize resources.** Once an organization has a core purpose that helps it to achieve a vision, and a set of outcomes that sit beyond the organization itself, it needs to look at its own design, staff, finances and capabilities. Is its design such that all its activities help to achieve its core purpose? Can it monitor how well outcomes are being achieved? Does it understand the extent to which its own activities are contributing towards the achievement of outcomes, for instance through effective performance measurement? Is it using strategy to change its processes, to develop its people, to change the way it deals with the public? Is it spending more in some areas and less in others to achieve a new set of outcomes? The degree of organizational alignment to the strategy it exists to bring about is a good way of measuring whether a strategy is in the process of being implemented or ignored. There is more on organizational alignment in Chapter 7.

6. **Ensure 'line of sight'.** The most successful strategies are engaging and offer clear leadership; they give leaders the narrative they need to connect the present to the desired future, to carry staff, stakeholders and public with them; they enable the people who work in public-facing roles to make the connection between what they do and why they do it, whether that is issuing benefit payments, collecting taxes, arresting law breakers, preventing crime, teaching five-year-olds or conducting social research. People should be able to make connections from their own working practices to the purpose of their organization and to the broader outcomes that their work contributes to achieving. We call this relationship between vision, outcomes, purpose and activities 'line of sight'. A good strategy will always offer line of sight, and we look at examples in Chapter 7.

Not all strategies will deliver all of these benefits. But the most effective strategies are systemic and holistic – that is, they understand the wider system in which they must be developed and applied, and they offer a complete response with a set of mutually reinforcing benefits.

Public strategy almost always needs the active support of politicians – and politicians can sometimes feel threatened by the strategic capability of officials if they feel strategy developed without their involvement using the bureaucratic and technocratic power of unelected officials limits their legitimate control of the agenda. This is one reason why strategic capability in government tends to ebb and flow. One set of politicians, concerned about lack of strategic capability, will invest in building the skills and institutions to deliver strong strategy. But if that strategic thinking seems to constrain politicians' 'room for manoeuvre', they – or their successors – are likely to dismantle the institutions they have created before they become 'too powerful'. The electoral cycle – typically four or five years, though sometimes shorter than that – is also a factor that can 'switch off' the appetite for strategic thinking. Politicians often need their officials to deliver within the electoral cycle. The popular perception is that delivering an objective in ten years' time does not win elections, though publics can be persuaded to support longer-term goals where this is done in the context of a coherent strategy. This presents a conundrum that we examine when we look at the problem of short-termism in Chapter 4, and at strategic institution-building in Chapter 6.

The pace of change

Concern about the pace of change is not new. The world changes faster than we notice because we adapt to the changes day-to-day. This has always been the case. The life of someone born in Europe in the early part of the 19th century is likely to have changed dramatically with the coming of railways, with urbanization and industrialization; the pace of change must have seemed remorseless to the new city-dweller of the 1830s or 40s. Someone born late in the 19th century would be almost certain to be touched by war, by political upheaval, by sweeping techno-logical advances including motor travel, telegrams and telephones, elec-trification and, later in their lives, air travel and television. It is not that the world changes ever faster, but that it always changes faster than we can conceive. Some say that what's different today is the degree of inter-connectedness and access to information. At a guess, Aristotle's students would have been saying similar things in 330BCE: faster ships, better harbours, faster tracks to ride faster horses with better messages. The pace of change *seems* to be increasing exponentially, but much depends on the human brain's capacity to *make sense* of the pace of change. Costless communication and increased access to information is just another change we have to adapt to.

Take the world of 1987, a world without mobile telephony (except for a privileged few), without text messaging and the worldwide internet. What were the issues facing governments of that time? In the UK the continuing transfer of state-owned industry to the private sector remained a preoccupation. This was the decade that saw governments in many developed industrialized countries move from being major manu-facturers and producers (of goods from cars to coal) and providers of services (from telephones to electricity) to regulators of services and the manufacturer of little at all. Western foreign relations were still domi-nated by the stand-off between the Soviet Union and NATO. Soviet forces were about to leave Afghanistan, and the West continued to back the mujahedeen. Spain and Portugal had only emerged from dictatorships in the preceding decade. They had just joined the European Economic Community. The economies of China and India were heavily regulated and opportunities for foreign investment, joint ventures and innovation were limited. In Africa conflict between the 'frontline states' of southern Africa (Angola, Botswana, Mozambique, Tanzania, Zambia and Zimbabwe) and an increasingly isolated apartheid regime in South Africa continued. The world was a different place, and governments made the choices to fit with that world.

Most of us would not have foreseen in 1987 that only a decade or so later a pensioner in Manchester would call a toll-free number to get an insurance quote from a young woman sitting in a call centre in Bengaluru, nor that a few years after that the same call centre service would have been returned to the UK, in part because customers of insurance companies wanted a more 'local' service and in part because the wage differential between the UK and India had begun to narrow. In 1987 people would have been much more likely to cite ozone depletion as a major environmental concern rather than greenhouse gas. Almost no one would have heard of avian flu, nor imagined that the US and global economy would be heavily dependent on capital from the People's Republic of China.

What sort of world will 2040 be? We might feel confident in some predictions: that there will be more electronic surveillance, more genetic engineering; less commuting to work, reduced use of fossil fuels; more drought and flooding. Yet even these predictions will probably be wrong. Why? Because we make them looking through the 'lens of now'; we assume that the world will change, but that it will change in the way that it is already changing. Experience tells us that it won't. One way to minimize the effect of the 'lens of now' is to identify a range of potential futures, avoiding the temptation to forecast by likelihood. We examine the effect of the lens of now, and how to overcome it, in Chapters 4 and 5.

By 2040 we might see a return to the countryside, or a flight to megacities. We might see locally-produced food, or a more global market than ever before. We might see a devastating new disease, or gene therapies for every ill. The world might be dominated by India as the new superpower, or by a resurgent European Union. We cannot know what will happen, but we can look for signals. Focusing only on the problems of today will not give us the answers we need for tomorrow.

Strategy where it matters

Strategy converts activity into action by developing an understanding of how the future state might evolve and by defining a vision of a future

BOX 1.2 South Africa's National Development Plan 2030: Our Future, Make it Work

In 2013 the South African government began the implementation of its National Development Plan 2030. This comprehensive plan offered a diagnostic of the problems facing South Africa as a nation, and a range of measures to improve almost every aspect of South African life.

South Africa can become the country we want it to become. It is possible to get rid of poverty and to reduce inequality in 20 years. We have the people, the goodwill, the skills, the resources – and now, a plan (South Africa National Development Plan – 2030: South African National Planning Commision 2012).

An important element of the plan had been the establishment of the National Planning Commission in 2009 which encouraged a robust national debate about the creation of the National Development Plan, with tens of thousands of submissions from individuals and groups representing South Africans from all communities and sectors. Following the publication of a draft National Plan in November 2011, the Commission consulted parliament, judiciary, provincial governments, financial institutions, trade unions, business and religious leaders.

The plan was criticized by some. COSATU (the Congress of South African Trade Unions) criticized the complexity and length of the national plan (484 pages), questioned the underpinning diagnosis, and argued that in too many places the plan is deliberately ambiguous, sidestepping controversy (COSATU 2013).

state, a set of desired outcomes meaningful to those who are expected to bring that future state about. Effective public strategy outlines the steps needed to achieve those outcomes, while being flexible enough to deliver or influence the emergence of a variety of futures. The people who devise and implement a strategy may be a small team, a group of employees, the residents of a town or city, the citizens of a nation or of many nations. However big or small the group, they are more likely to act effectively if they agree with the vision or, better still, if they had a hand in creating it.

One way of ensuring that a strategic process is meaningful is to ensure that it is *purposeful* – not simply a collection of ideas or lofty aspirations, but a set of desired outcomes that can be purposed. In other words, a series of organized actions can be undertaken to achieve the vision. Guatemala, a country that suffered a long civil war in the second half of the 20th century, underwent a national reconciliation process as part of building a post-civil war national strategy. Part of the process was a report which began with a line from the sacred book of the K'iche people (one of the Mayan ethnic groups). 'We did not put our ideas together. We put our purposes together. And we agreed, and then we decided' (Diez Pinto 2004: 79).

Checkland defined purposeful in the following way: 'Purposeful: Willed; thus "activity" which is purposeful becomes action' (Checkland 1981: 316). This notion of 'willed' – of the *desire* that underpins strategy – is one of the most easily overlooked aspects of public strategy. Nobel laureate Herbert Simon saw the importance of purpose in the administrative sphere. 'A great deal of behaviour, and particularly the behaviour of individuals within administrative organizations, is purposive – oriented towards goals or objectives. This purposiveness brings about an integration in the pattern of behaviour, in the absence of which administration would be meaningless; for, if administration consists in "getting things done by groups of people", purpose provides a principal criterion in determining what things are to be done' (Simon 1997: 3).

Strategy is the process that helps us to understand not simply how we will do a thing, but why we should do it in the first place. It is possible to argue endlessly over the best solution to a problem, to trade in alternatives, to argue over the evidence that supports one course of action over another. In *Gulliver's Travels* (Swift 1726) Lilliput was riven by disputes lasting generations between the Big-Endians and the Little-Endians, who took contrary positions on which was the proper end from which to eat a boiled egg. Swift satirized the religious and political disputes of the early 18th century world. It would be hard to find a strategic solution to the dilemma of which end of an egg to crack, but plenty of policy issues require a purposeful or goal-oriented approach rather than a comparative and non-strategic approach. Yet we often seem stuck in an endless trade of arguments about options without a sense of purpose, without an agreed vision of the desired future state.

Policy disputes rage on a series of apparently binary choices: social cohesion or social mobility? Mutualization or privatization? Collectivism or individualism? Strong citizens or informed customers? The state as commissioner of services or as provider? Free markets or regulated monopolies? Competition or cooperation? Localization or centralization? Deficit elimination or public investment? Economic growth or sustainability? We argue over the location of a hospital, the governance of a school, the regulation of the internet, the benefits and risks of nuclear power, the role of government in promoting healthy food, the levels of overseas aid to other countries, more or fewer airports, the age at which pensions should be payable. These are major issues for our own lives, our towns, our nations – yet our governments often attempt to make decisions without articulating the purpose or rationale behind these decisions beyond narrow criteria like cost or feasibility or popularity. To support an idea, we need to understand what it is we expect it to achieve and what a successful outcome will look like.

Sometimes it is hard for governments to articulate a clear vision of the future, either because of lack of agreement or because they value adaptability and responsiveness over achievement of desired outcomes. But

> **BOX 1.3 National interests and national security: the approaches of the USA, the UK and France**
>
> The USA, the UK and France have each published National Security Strategies that aim to assess the future strategic environment, identify the threats to each country and set out national interests and explain how these will be achieved. All identify broadly similar national security threats and interests, but the varying approaches make some a more effective statement of strategic intent than others.
>
> Historically, the USA has set out and pursued its priorities and national interest more overtly than many other Western powers. In its 2010 strategy '*The World as It Is, A Strategy for the World We Seek*' the USA identifies four enduring interests:
>
> - The security of the United States, its citizens and U.S. allies and partners.
> - A strong, innovative, and growing U.S. economy in an open international system that promotes opportunity and prosperity.
> - Respect for universal values at home and around the world.
> - An international order advanced by U.S. leadership that promotes peace, security, and opportunity through stronger cooperation to meet global challenges.
>
> (US National Security Strategy 2010)
>
> As with the UK and France, the USA also identifies the security threats it faces and its response. But the US is more specific and provides a clearer vision of its national interest and the world it seeks to create, with
>
> →

what we call 'leadership' aligns closely to a sense of identifying, committing to and achieving desired outcomes: it is almost impossible to lead without a sense of purpose. But sometimes it's more convenient for the vision to remain vague, and in some circumstances it will be right that the vision doesn't constrain the exercise of imagination by being overly narrow and excluding things not thought of. Three countries with a strong sense of projection of national interest in the wider world are the USA, France and the UK. Yet each adopts varying degrees of vagueness in articulating its national interest in a published national security strategy.

Conclusion: purpose

Being clear about the purpose of an activity changes it to an action capable of achieving a meaningful result. Having a goal to work towards motivates people. If they believe in it and have had a hand in shaping it

→

American values and history referenced throughout. This influences the way the USA implements its strategy, for example enabling a rebalance of effort towards the Pacific as part of a clear pursuit of defined national interest.

The UK strategy identifies many of the same threats as the USA, but is less clear on what its national interests are, in part because of a long-standing policy of successive governments not to define national security in law.

Our enlightened national interest: Our security, prosperity and freedom are interconnected and mutually supportive. They constitute our national interest (UK National Security Strategy 2010).

Although the UK National Security Council agreed two overarching objectives which are similar to the US interests, it is less clear what makes these interests specific to the UK rather than any other Western democracy.

The 2013 French White Paper on Defence and National Security takes an even wider view, aligning French interests with wider European and global interests:

- protect the national territory and French nationals abroad, and guarantee the continuity of the Nation's essential functions
- guarantee the security of Europe and the North Atlantic space, with our partners and allies
- stabilize Europe's near environment, with our partners and allies
- contribute to the stability of the Middle East and the Persian Gulf
- contribute to peace in the world.
            (French White Paper on Defence and National Security 2013)

they are capable of being ingenious as well as industrious in finding ways to achieve it. Strategy that sets a direction without explaining why anyone should follow it is likely to be poorly conceived in the first place, implemented half-heartedly and have a range of unintended consequences as public-facing staff create their own reasons for pursuing the strategy. Antoine de Saint-Exupéry captured the liberating quality of this sense of purpose in his book, published posthumously in 1948 as *Citadelle*, and republished in English in 1950 as *Wisdom of the Sands*: 'If you want to build a ship, don't drum up people to collect wood and don't assign them tasks and work, but rather teach them to long for the endless immensity of the sea' (Saint-Exupéry 1950).

Chapter 2

Public Strategy

Strategy is a word used since at least the Greek era; the English word is derived from the ancient Greek *stratēgos*, meaning a general (*stratos*: army; *ago*: leading). American academic and management consultant Michael E. Porter defined strategy as 'developing a broad formula for how an industry is going to compete, what its goals should be, and what policies will be needed to carry out those goals' (Porter 1980: vxi). But governments and other public organizations do not always compete with each other. Often they need to collaborate in order to secure desired outcomes not for themselves as organizations – whether those organizations are states, governments, municipal authorities, public agencies or charities – but for those they serve. We explore these distinctions between corporate strategy and public strategy in Chapter 3.

Canadian academic Henry Mintzberg was sceptical of attempts to define strategy: 'Ask someone to define a strategy and you will likely be told that "strategy is a plan", or something equivalent, a direction, a guide or course of action into the future, a path to get from here to there. Then ask the person to describe the strategy that his or her organization or that of a competitor actually pursued over the past five years – not what they intended to do but what they really did. You will find that most people are perfectly happy to answer that question, oblivious to the fact that doing so differs from their very own definition of the term. It turns out that strategy is one of those words that we inevitably define in one way yet often also use in another. Strategy is a pattern, consistency in behaviour over time' (Mintzberg *et al.* 1998: 9).

The notion of strategy as a pattern, a process or a system is helpful. Those who attempt to sell plans to organizations without requiring them to think, or who push an agency into action without engaging its people in a process of planning, rarely leave any lasting success for the organization or for the people that organization serves.

A good strategy understands what it is trying to achieve or the system it is trying to improve – it is clear about its purpose. In our impatience to decide on a course of action we don't always think through why we are undertaking it at all. It may be a knee-jerk response or it may be that the course of action we are pursuing may seem so like common sense we don't pause to consider the evidence. In *Everything is Obvious* Duncan Watts (Watts 2011) shows common sense misleads us into thinking that we understand more than we do, affecting our ability to predict, manage, or manipulate social and economic systems. He suggests that by under-standing why common sense fails we can improve how we plan for the future. It is this process of thinking through why something should be done, what should be done and how it should be done that is of real value. US President Eisenhower summarized this in a speech to the National Executive Reserve by saying: 'Plans are worthless, but planning is everything. There is a very great distinction because when you are planning for an emergency you must start with this one thing: the very definition of "emergency" is that it is unexpected, therefore it is not going to happen the way you are planning. So, the first thing you do is to take all the plans off the top shelf and throw them out the window and start once more. But if you haven't been planning you can't start to work, intelligently at least. That is the reason it is so important to plan, to keep yourselves steeped in the character of the problem that you may one day be called upon to solve – or to help to solve' (Eisenhower 1957).

What strategy is not

Because the word strategy is overused, sometimes to make a particular project or job seem important by prefixing it with the adjective 'strategic', it is easy to believe that something is a strategy when it is not. Here are ten things that strategy is not:

1. **An amalgamation of current policies into a single initiative.** Strategy requires choices. It involves an understanding of the current context and of potential futures, and it entails decisions about which of those futures is most desirable and how to bring that desired future about, as well as building preparedness and resilience for less desirable futures. A simple bolting together of everything that an organization is currently doing is not a strategy: it will fail and it will make future efforts to act strategically more difficult, because it will build scepticism about the meaning and effectiveness of strategic working.
2. **A document ('a noun instead of a verb').** Strategies can and do produce documents. But it is worth thinking of strategy primarily as a verb rather than as a noun. It is the process of making the strategy and of making it a reality that is of most importance. The published document is often relevant only to account for the process. What matters is the degree of engagement leading to its publication and the purposefulness of the activity that follows it. The longer a strategy document, the less effective it tends to be (consider the criticisms of South Africa's National Development Plan in Box 1.2). A single page of text or a meaningful image can often be much more effective than a hundred-page glossy strategy document that will be read neither by staff nor citizens.

3. **All-embracing**. Strategy requires scope and choice. A strategic vision that is at such a high level, that is so 'motherhood and apple pie' that no one can disagree with it is also likely to be one that no one cares about. Worse still, a strategy that ducks important questions about where to spend money and where to stop spending money, about which staff to keep and which to let go, about what skills and capabilities to increase and what to reduce is no strategy at all.

4. **To be left to consultants**. Consultant-made strategy can look convincing, partly, in the words of the saying, because 'an expert is the man from the next village' and often the outside perspective is particularly valuable to the organization paying for it. Consultants will bring experience of what's been successful in similar organizations in the same industry or part of the public sector. But if it hasn't fully engaged the organization or government that must implement the strategy in formulating it, and if it is not truly 'owned' then it is useless, because however sound its analysis and however rational its recommendations, it will not be implemented. Additionally, contexts vary from organization to organization, even those within the same sector. Huge amounts of tacit knowledge are held by the people working in the organization, and even the most assiduous consultant is likely to find it hard to tap into that knowledge fully. Snowden's seven rules of knowledge management (Snowden and Kurtz 2006) include 'people know more than they can say, and they can say more than they can write down'. But because strategy consultancy advice has been 'bought' it can feel permissible to the new 'owners' to put it on a shelf, admire it for a while and then forget about it. The organization has bought the noun, not the verb. There's also the problem identified by Pfeffer and Sutton in *The Knowing–Doing Gap* (Pfeffer and Sutton 1999) that 'best practice' is known to everyone, yet only certain organizations are capable of implementing it.

5. **To be left (entirely) to politicians**. It is essential that politicians are involved in the formulation of strategic intent at governmental and municipal level, and their equivalents (typically non-executive board members and trustees) are involved in strategic decisions taken by public bodies and charities. If they are not, not only will the strategy lack a mandate but, as mentioned in Chapter 1, politicians may come to feel threatened by the strategy and shut down strategic processes. But administrators must play a central role in the formulation of strategy, because they have a duty to develop the strategic capability of the organization in which they work; they are the people to bring continuity to strategic implementation and politicians need to be supported and encouraged to act strategically, just as they need to be supported in their work in seeing legislation through a legislature. Not all politicians are able to act strategically,

but non-elected officials in positions of senior leadership in public organizations must be strategic – and they have a duty (some might argue a moral duty) to encourage political leaders to take a long-term view, as well as to support politicians in achieving their shorter-term goals.

6. **Justifying (or condemning) past actions**. Good strategy acknowledges past actions and past mistakes, but it is primarily concerned with the future. It's often important to 'honour the past', in part because we can't know everything people were facing at the time. But the worst strategies simply justify decisions that have already been made, or indulge the natural human tendency to chase sunk costs, or attack decisions made by past management or governments just voted out of office. Those activities are the job of the propagandist, not the strategist.

7. **Certain about the future**. Good strategy instils confidence in a course of action to achieve a purpose. It does not ignore unexpected developments, or suppress challenge and questioning. Good strategy does not try to exclude uncertainty – it acknowledges it and continually seeks out signs to confirm or call into question its original analysis.

8. **A project**. Projects have a clear timeline, milestones and produce defined and measurable outputs. A strategy might be managed using project techniques, and a strategy will often be implemented using a series of projects. Strategy is a process that combines intent, policy choice and implementation. It is adaptable, and will often need to change course several times. The desired outcome of a strategy might itself need to be reviewed and changed. Projects should be seen as instruments of strategy rather than strategy the instrument of the project manager.

9. **About the organization alone**. Organizations have strategies, but the strategy should always be about the 'world out there'. In the public domain organizations are subordinate to their social mission, and the strategy must advance a broader mission rather than be preoccupied with the continuing viability of the organization. It should pay attention to the organization only to the extent it needs to continue to exist to enable the achievement of desired outcomes, whether improved public health, primary education, national security, tax collection, welfare support, environmental protection, improved infrastructure or something else.

10. **Devoid of public value**. The social mission of a public organization will define the public value that it exists to create. The most important measures of business success – profitability and future profitability, often expressed as shareholder value – are not relevant in the public domain, although financial viability is. Public value shows what it is that public organizations and the people who work

in them create that is worthwhile. This value is often easy to under-stand instinctively (the value of being able to read and write; the value of clean rivers; the value of treating everyone with respect) but can often be hard to measure, and harder to express in monetary terms. We examine public value in Chapter 3. Public organizations that mimic the private sector, and express their mission as being 'World class' or 'Operating in surplus' are likely to miss the point of why they exist at all.

Potentially effective strategies go wrong in the ways shown above when strategic intent, policies and the actions to deliver the strategic intent are pulled out of alignment or, worse still, when they become inverted, so that the methods of delivery or policies determine the strategic intent in ways that fatally compromise it rather than informing it. Of course there will be compromises when policies come up against the sometimes chaotic reality of operational delivery but some form of governance of the line of sight from delivery, policies and strategic intent needs to assure strategic drift doesn't happen unintentionally.

Thinking and analysis cannot achieve a strategy without planning and action; plans made without proper strategic thinking remain plans – pieces of paper that take up space on a shelf; and action without planning is a stream of activities not aligned with each other or to defined goals, leading to unintended consequences, money wasted and hopes dashed. Eisenhower wasn't advocating an endless cycle of evidence gathering, discussion or musing on options. But he was recognizing that much of the value of strategy comes from the process of devising it. Implementing a strategy will change it – if results are different from those originally envisaged that does not (necessarily) mean the strategy has failed.

Another problem that can arise is 'ivory tower syndrome', where behaviour is disconnected from the everyday world, often noble but generally impractical. In these circumstances politicians, or the most senior officials or the management board, can be at risk of working in a closed loop, preoccupied with devising the strategic intent and looking towards the policies that will support it, paying too little attention to implementation. Sometimes in these cases the strategic intent will be expressed as legislation, sometimes as a series of commitments or aspira-tions announced in speeches, sometimes in the announcement of a new agency or budgetary instrument. The risk here is of 'over-promising and under-delivering'. More practically, it manifests itself in a lack of interest in measuring results and evaluating the real effects of policies, which means that over time you end up with government and public bodies with very low levels of accountability (see Chapter 7 for more on measurement and accountability).

The converse can also arise, where those at the top can see very clearly what the right thing is to do, but worry about the cost or difficulty of

TABLE 2.1 Glossary: a dozen main terms

Driver ('of' or 'for' change): external forces that can be identified as elements in a wider system creating change over time (for example 'size of families') (see Chapter 5 for more on drivers of change).

Functional strategy: strategy within an organization to deliver a particular service or function, for instance an Information Technology (IT) strategy, or an accommodation or people or wellbeing or investment strategy. These strategies should be aligned with an overarching strategy for the organization, so that they have 'line of sight' to the organization's overall purpose and the outcomes it seeks to achieve.

Grand strategy: national strategy, usually with a particular focus on power and influence in the global context and with an emphasis on national security, defence and diplomacy.

Horizon scanning: looking beyond the usual sources and the usual timescales. Horizon scanning exercises will identify 'weak signals' of trends that are barely discernible but may become important (for example a new disease in an animal species as a possible signal of a human pandemic), and will look at a wide variety of sources, including academic, journalistic, social media and 'oddball'. They will also look beyond existing conditions – for instance to a world no longer using oil.

Indicators: One of a range of ways of measuring the impact of strategy (see Chapter 7 for more on different types of measure, including inputs, outputs and activities). An indicator may measure something inside an organization (for instance, staff engagement) or it may measure something outside an organization (for instance, public confidence in service quality).

Outcome: The ultimate desired result of a strategic or policy intervention or activity. So 'providing healthy food' is not an outcome, but 'eating healthily' is; 'providing 20 per cent more places on drug treatment programmes' is not an outcome (and may be a sign of failure demand) but 'more people off drugs and stay off drugs' is an outcome.

Public value: A theory, associated with Mark Moore of Harvard's Kennedy School of Government, in which the value of public strategy interventions is measured by combining an understanding of their legitimacy, their achievability and the social worth of their outcomes (see Chapter 3 for more on this).

Scenarios: A tool commonly used in strategy formulation in which a set of contrasting futures are developed, using robust techniques so that each future is plausible (even if improbable), and so that decisions can be made about, for instance, policy direction or resource allocation to either help bring a particular future about or to avoid that future from coming about (see Chapter 5 for more on scenario building).

Stakeholder: An organization or individual with influence over – or a material interest in – a strategy or important aspects of it.

Target: A defined goal to be achieved (for example, 'land a human on Mars'), sometimes accompanied by metrics ('... by 2030'), which are more likely to achieve perverse consequences the more precision they are given (for instance, 'treat all emergency patients within an hour' may result in quick but fatally bad treatment). See Chapter 7 for more on targets.

Trend: An observed pattern over time that can be projected into the future (examples include antibiotic resistance; ageing population; globalized capital markets). Trend analysis requires both an analysis of the resilience of the trend (in other words, when and how will it break?) and consideration of existing or potential counter-trends.

Wicked Issue: A situation that cannot usefully be identified as 'a problem' amenable to 'a solution'. Complex issues like obesity, ageing populations, international development, global security and climate change are 'wicked'. See also Rittel and Webber's analysis of 'Wicked Problems' in 'Dilemmas in a General Theory of Planning' (Rittel and Webber 1973).

implementation results in inaction. Or they might choose an option that is relatively easy to implement but that no one believes will achieve the right outcomes – the epitome of the sub-optimal strategy.

The UK's Institute for Government found the effects of policies once implemented are often complex and unpredictable and that desired outcomes are changed by implementation. They are also changed as the political/public discourse and direction changes – a robust strategy can cope with changes to the definition of the outcomes that it was developed to achieve. 'Given the complexity and mutability of most policy systems, good decision making will need to adapt as new information becomes available – and much of that information will come from the process of decision-making itself. Therefore, the people realising a policy need the capacity and opportunity to adapt it to local or changing circumstances' (Hallsworth 2011: 28).

Words like strategy, policy, objective, output, goal, target, aim, result and outcome are often used interchangeably and with little sense of their relevant meaning. Using words without precision in this area constrains our understanding and practice of strategy. Jargon and 'management-speak' are constant hazards in the strategy world. The best that we can do is to be alert to them and to ensure that meaning is understood and shared by those working on the strategy.

What is strategy?

One way to understand strategy is to think of it as the process that joins together the '**what**', the '**why**' and the '**how**' of any strategic intent.

The 'what' is the desired outcome and the options that might be chosen to achieve that outcome; the 'why' takes that desired outcome as a hypothesis, and tests why it might be the right thing or the wrong thing to do, exploring the context and also exposing the principles, ideals, beliefs (and prejudices) that have led to the hypothesis being put at all; the 'how' is the means by which a particular option will be brought about, including the choices we will make about the allocation or reallocation of resources, and what we decide to stop doing as well as what we start to do or do differently – strategy is about changing things, otherwise it is simply a 'wish list' that makes no tangible difference to anything.

For something like 'more policing' it is easy to envisage a process to secure budgets, put recruitment procedures in place, deploy additional police to the right neighbourhoods, and monitor their effectiveness and so on. Each element in this process will and should be argued over, evidenced, shaped and reshaped. But without a clear statement of what more policing achieves and why it is being undertaken at all, the process will not be a strategic one.

FIGURE 2.1   *Strategy as an arrow*

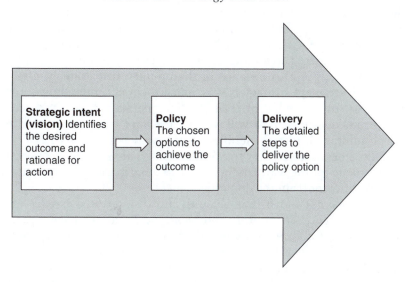

The strategy process can also be described in terms of **strategic intent**, which is the combination of identified outcome and the desire or belief that underpins that intended outcome; **policy**, which is the process of determining and choosing options; and **delivery**, which includes the securing of resources and the many activities that must be undertaken to achieve the policy. This sequence can be expressed as a 'strategy arrow'.

In the 'arrow' view of strategy, the strategy gives clear purpose and defines desired outcomes which in turn lead to informed choices about the options or policies to achieve that purpose and to effective means of delivering those options. In reality strategy rarely works this way: it is rare for clear strategic intent to flow perfectly into decisions about which policies will achieve the desired outcome. More often the process takes place in a series of iterations, backwards and forwards between strategic intent, policy and delivery. But clear outcomes hold the strategy together, enabling a series of policies and actions to bring about the desired end state, often sustained over a long period of time.

You'll see references to strategy being the means of delivering a policy, rather than policies being the way you deliver a strategy. This is because 'policy' is sometimes used as shorthand for the political intent – the vision. Added to this, an organization will have a set of 'policies' (sometimes called 'protocols') in various areas, by which it means the standard approaches it has decided on for things like the way it stores and classifies data.

In some languages there is no distinction (as in English) between 'policy' and 'politics'. In the military context it is more common to talk of strategy being the means to achieve policy, rather than policies being the instruments to achieve strategic intent. This is in part because in the military field the political goals are decided on by politicians and – except where the military are in control of the state – the division of responsibilities is considered an important one, and usually set out in the national constitution. It is also because in the military field (which, after all, 'invented' strategy) strategy is very much focused on the 'how', not on the 'what' or the 'why' of strategy. So generals will ask and seek to answer the question: 'how will we win this war?', and this is a debate in which military leaders generally do not wish politicians to intervene. Equally generals usually try to avoid entering publicly into discussion on the rationale for the war. Discussion of strategy in the military context is slightly different from the domestic context.

This does not mean that generals are disinterested parties in the 'what' and 'why' of military intervention. Events in recent years in Afghanistan, Iraq and elsewhere demonstrate that if the rationale or purpose is not established (or if it is not a credible and achievable desired outcome, but instead a 'wish list'), if the generals and their troops are insufficiently clear about what success looks like, then even the best-executed campaign will – indeed, must – ultimately fail. Lieutenant General Sir Robert Fry, a former Director of Operations at the UK Ministry of Defence, gave evidence on this to a UK parliamentary enquiry (House of Commons 2010: EV39)

> Sir Robert Fry: ... [Grand Strategy] has to start with a sense of national interest, it has to look at ends that are defined across a complete range of national interests and it then needs to be reconciled with the means that we have available to satisfy those ends. It is not fundamentally a complex affair.

The field of military strategy requires the long view. Recruiting and training the right number of pilots, of naval personnel, of ground troops requires an understanding of likely future threats and ambitions. Procuring the right weaponry, the right aircraft, ships and tanks all demand choices taken against a background of unavoidable uncertainty. In 1993 the United States began a series of post-cold war quadrennial defence reviews (US Department of Defense 1993–2010). The 1993 review predicted the rise of new regional power blocs following the breakup of the Soviet Union, and aligned its operational capability to respond to multiple threats. It did not prepare for the complex conflict in the Western Balkans and the demands of both offensive military operations and peacekeeping that the Balkans conflict entailed.

The 1997 review prepared for the dangers posed by Iraq and Iran, the threats generated by weak and failing states (in part driven by the

Western Balkans experience) and it also anticipated the possibility of unconventional attack from non-state actors on the US homeland – which became a dramatic reality most clearly in the attacks of 11 September 2001. The 1997 review also outlined the degree to which US assets themselves created an exposure to risk, particularly from unconventional threats from non-state actors.

The 2010 review took account of the continuing threat from terrorism, the potential threat from nuclear proliferation and the acquisition of nuclear weapons by fragile states and by non-state actors and the threat of cyber-attack on national interests, as well as the risks posed by climate change and rapid urbanization of coastal lands. But it did not – could not – foresee what threats would be relevant in 2020, from regional conflict in South Asia or West Africa, from conflagration in the Middle East, from water and energy disputes, or – more likely – something unpredictable.

This suggests that an outcomes-based approach to security and defence strategy is likely to be an important counterpart to a predominantly threat-based strategy. It is, in a sense, more helpful for states to describe the world they desire and to construct an international strategy that will help them to build that world than to attempt the impossible: to construct a strategy that will enable resilience to every threat. This approach has led the US and its main allies to anticipate and prepare for several simultaneous conflicts on several continents that are 'asymmetric' – in other words, to fight conflicts of different natures and against different types of enemy, both state and non-state, and to be clear that success in these conflicts is likely to depend on peacekeepers, on diplomacy and on international development aid as much as it will depend on raw military capability.

From grand strategy to functional strategy

The military will often seek, as in the example above, 'grand strategy' to help buckle together the 'how' of strategy with the 'what' and the 'why' of it in the context of national security and global ambition. 'Grand strategy' has a particular meaning and purpose, and is the subject of many other books. It is not specifically the subject of this one, although the role of high level (sometimes called 'overarching') strategy is our focus. Translated to commerce that high-level strategy might be called the corporate strategy; translated to the public realm that strategy might be at a national, regional, sectoral or agency level. These strategies will normally capture a strong sense of the wider political landscape and social mission.

Strategy can be made at levels other than at the national or high level. Providing there is alignment or 'line of sight' between a high-level strategy

BOX 2.1 The 'Safety Inspection Agency'

The strategy for the fictional 'Safety Inspection Agency' included the statement of purpose: 'We inspect industrial properties to ensure they comply with safety regulations'. This statement implied a strategic intent, and informed its policies and operational decisions.

The mission was narrow and focused on activities rather than on outcomes. The Agency set itself performance measures to inspect as many properties as possible. It disapproved of industrial properties that did not comply with safety regulations but measured its success not in terms of how safe properties were but in terms of how many properties it found that were unsafe. Finding lots of unsafe properties was a success. This drove behaviours that meant the agency invested little resource in getting information to industry to help it know whether properties were safe. It recruited staff for good inspection skills, not necessarily good communication skills. It had offices all over the country where its network of inspectors was based. It judged new policies in the field of industrial safety in terms of whether they strengthened inspection powers.

A series of explosions in chemical and petroleum plants meant a political spotlight fell on the Agency. It was able to show that it had conducted inspections of each of the plants where explosions had taken place and been critical of what it had found; and it had made lots of recommendations. The Agency regarded itself as 'in the clear'.

The Minister for Industry was a strategically-minded politician. She asked the Chief Executive what he was trying to achieve in his role. He explained the Agency's core purpose to the Minister and told her that it was not uncommon for the Agency to have to inspect the same property many times and make the same criticisms each time. She identified what

→

and the functional strategies (in this sense, the strategies of different business functions within an organization with a wider strategic intent) to support the high-level strategy, all should be well. Problems arise where functional strategies (for instance, an estates strategy, or an information technology strategy or a people strategy) are developed without reference to an overarching strategy. Sometimes this is simply unavoidable – for instance, because there is no high-level strategy for the government, department, city or agency. In these cases it is almost inevitable that the functional strategies consume ever more time and effort to achieve less and less. There is no 'line of sight' vertically, and they risk being uncoordinated horizontally, so that people might be recruited in the expectation of working in Frankfurt at the same time as the federal agency is acquiring a new headquarters in Berlin. The people strategy has been devised without reference to the estates strategy, and neither is informed by an overall sense of direction for the organization.

→

she described as a 'cycle of failure' and asked the Chief Executive about the rate of industrial explosions over the previous five years. He told her these were the result of things over which his Agency had no control. The Minister told him he was missing the point. A month later the Chief Executive resigned.

The new Chief Executive of the Safety Inspection Agency created a new strategy. The statement of purpose became one based on achieving desired outcomes: 'Industry is safer because industry knows how to keep its premises safe'. The Agency began to measure not how many properties it inspected, but safety incidents and how well industrial managers understood how to keep their properties and people safe. It monitored the effectiveness of its staff at communicating with industry and how receptive industry was to messages from the Agency.

The clarity of the new outcome/purpose identified the capabilities the SIA needed. It put more of its resources into communication, information and online services. It invested in training industrial managers, and reduced its workforce of inspectors. It relocated to offices where it could run training and internet programmes effectively, and saved money on its estates budget. It took a keen interest in helping to develop policies to make industrial properties safer. The number of industrial accidents and incidents didn't go down in the first year of the new strategy, but the Agency was monitoring the trends and, with 'leading indicators' to show, for instance, how safer practices were being introduced into industry and at what pace, it was confident that improvement would be seen within a year or two. The number of industrial accidents and other safety incidents began to fall annually by around 10 per cent from the second year of the new strategy.

Meanwhile those working on functional strategies can be busy recruiting staff or laying them off, outsourcing services or bringing them in house, relocating an operation from one region to another without any reference to the overall strategic direction. If those staff working in public-facing operations look 'up' only as far as the policy, without knowing the policy's intent or whether the policy is achieving its intended outcomes, there is a danger as great as in 'ivory tower syndrome' of lack of accountability. The activities of public-facing operations can be directed in ways that achieve poor results, because the desired outcome has been lost sight of. These, in turn, create adverse conditions for innovation (see the *Honda City* example later in this chapter) because people are disconnected from the source of their mandate and because they have too little understanding of the rationale or strategic intent that sits behind the organization's existence in the first place.

Where an organization is clear about its overall journey, say from a service that inspects factories to ensure that they comply with safety regulations to one that gives factories all the help they need to be safe, that strategic intent should inform every decision the organization takes, from who it recruits and how it trains its staff to what information it puts online to how it organizes its own information.

Core purpose

We said a good strategy will be clear about its core purpose. The fictional example in Box 2.1 shows how strategic intent flows into the purpose or mission of an agency charged with delivering it.

In both the earlier and later SIA strategies the purpose (or mission) reflects strategic intent. The first statement successfully aligns the Agency's policies and operations to deliver the strategy. The problem is that the purpose reflects a bad strategy, one that is too narrow and not focused on outcomes. The second strategy also drives alignment of the organization's policies and delivery approaches, but in this case, because it is based on outcomes, the purpose works to create the value envisaged by the strategic intent.

Richard Rumelt (Rumelt 2011) contrasts good and bad strategy: bad strategy isn't the absence of strategy; it's a company that thinks it has a strategy but has only a wish list of aspirations and goals. Bad strategy is a strategy which doesn't address an identified problem, or that misdiagnoses the issues. This happens because setting goals and aspirations is the more glamorous part of the process; identifying and analysing barriers to those goals is hard, detailed work. It might be that an enterprise will imagine someone else will be dealing with the detail, but without the detail of the barriers to delivering outcomes, there can be no strategy. Rumelt says strategy must be based on a thorough diagnosis aimed at fixing the disease, not treating the symptoms. He defines good strategy as a diagnosis of the challenge, a guiding policy for overcoming the obstacles identified by the diagnosis, and a set of coherent actions coordinated with one another to realize the guiding policy (Rumelt 2011: 77) – and he warns that, in the corporate world, financial goals are too narrow on their own to constitute good strategy.

The purpose or mission shapes what the organization does. It needs to be clear – but not so narrow that it constrains innovation. Let's look at an example – although from manufacturing, rather than the public realm, it illustrates the point.

Nonaka and Takeuchi explain that slogans like 'let's gamble' may seem cryptic or just plain silly to Western managers but (at least in Japanese companies) are highly effective in providing a sense of direction. Does the idea embody the company's vision? Is it an expression of top management's aspirations and ideals? As team leaders of the product development team, for example, middle managers are in a position to

BOX 2.2 Honda City ambition

In 1978, Honda inaugurated the development of a new-concept car with the slogan, 'Let's gamble'.

'This mission might sound vague, but in fact it provided the team with an extremely clear sense of direction. For instance, in the early days of the project, some team members proposed designing a smaller and cheaper version of the Honda Civic—a safe and technologically feasible option. But the team quickly decided this approach contradicted the entire rationale of its mission. The only alternative was to invent something totally new.' (Nonaka and Takeuchi 1995: 11–12)

The car Honda invented brought a new approach to design in the Japanese auto industry, leading to the new generation of 'tall and short' cars which were popular, especially in Japan, for the next two decades.

The Honda City example is one where the ambition not only urged the team forward to a goal, it gave them permission to tackle a critical issue in a new way, liberating them from the constraint of traditional views of what a car should look like.

remake reality according to the company's vision. Honda's vision of coming up with something completely new became a reality in the form of the 'tall and short' product concept.

This translates into the public sector context, where a high-level vision that isn't linked to the core purpose and supported by middle managers or those who deliver services won't be achieved. Gaining emotional commitment to the vision as well as ensuring that incentives and messages from senior managers and politicians consistently reinforce the importance of the vision are both important elements in turning strategic intent into strategy that is implemented. Lipsky identified the dangers of disconnect between strategic vision and the behaviour and actions of what he termed 'street level bureaucrats'. 'Lower level participants in organizations often do not share the perspectives and preferences of their superiors and hence in some respects cannot be thought to be working towards the agency's stated goals ... in such organizations policy may be carried out consistent with the interests of higher levels ... [but only through] ... the mutual adjustment of antagonistic perspectives ... [leading to] ... forms of non-cooperation that injure organizations' abilities to achieve their objectives because workers perform at less than full capacity' (Lipsky 1980: 16–17).

The UK's Institute for Government's System Stewardship report (Hallsworth 2011) found a policy is made and constantly *remade* by multiple players interacting in a system. Rather than just executing instructions, those who 'deliver' the policy are actually making decisions that change the purpose of the policy, underlining the value of governance and a clear overall aim or strategy.

BOX 2.3 The case of the national identity card that never was: getting purpose out of sequence

Shortly after the terrorist attack on New York on 11 September 2001, the then UK Home Secretary David Blunkett (the Cabinet Minister responsible for policing, immigration and homeland security) instructed his officials to prepare legislation for the introduction of a national identity card (Home Office 2002).

Throughout the succeeding eight years, which saw widespread public debate, divisions between government ministers, narrow majorities for the legislation in parliament and a complicated, costly – around £5bn ($8bn) – implementation project, what was never settled was the rationale or purpose for the national identity card (National Audit Office 2010a). At various times the following were given as reasons for its introduction:

- Combat crime
- Protect the UK from terrorism
- Reduce identity fraud
- Save public money by reducing benefit fraud
- Improve immigration controls
- Entitlement card to public services

Because no clear sense was developed at the beginning of the process of why the card was needed, what its purpose was and therefore what desired outcomes or benefits it would produce, even the best quality policy and implementation project work was doomed to fail. Government had jumped to the 'what' phase without testing the hypothesis against purpose and rationale – in other words without giving adequate consideration to why it should be done at all.

One of the first acts of a newly-elected government in 2010 was the abandonment of the national identity card programme. The minister responsible for identity and passport services personally participated in the destruction of the machine used to produce the cards.

The compass view of strategy

A compass is a helpful metaphor because it sets a destination and helps to guide the journey from the point of departure to arrival. It lets us project into the future (the destination) and plot our progress from the past (the point of departure). A compass is not a 'plan' – a fixed path or course of action from one point to another – it is, instead, an instrument that enables planning and guides the journey once it is under way. On a ship a compass allows a crew to set a new course to the chosen destination if their vessel (the policy, or chosen option in strategy terms) is blown off course, and it enables the crew to set a course to an entirely

FIGURE 2.2   *Strategy as a compass*

new destination while the journey is under way if it becomes clear that the original destination is unreachable (a revised desired outcome). Most importantly of all, the compass is not something that can be used only by the captain. If half the crew is washed overboard, every remaining member should be capable of reading the compass. Strategy should be an inclusive process – a tool for everyone.

The compass also represents the circularity of the strategy process. In this model we can see that strategic intent (or 'strategic direction') defines the desired outcomes for the strategy; these outcomes, in turn, help to shape the design of policies which, in their turn, frame the delivery process which should be designed to achieve the desired outcomes. The result – the degree of achievement of the desired outcomes – needs to be monitored, usually in the form of publicly accountable indicators, and learned from. At its heart the strategy is there to produce something, and in the case of public strategy that 'something' is public value – publicly valuable goods or products, which we'll explore in more detail in Chapter 3.

A compass is not the only tool one needs to navigate the future. A compass will not warn of rocks or whirlpools ahead, still less of an iceberg drifting towards the vessel. The crew need to scan the horizon for the unexpected. Tactics have their place. But tactics will not set direction or – alone – bring the crew and cargo safely into port.

Outcomes

If strategy is an approach to thinking, planning and action which establishes clarity about what is to be achieved, we need to define desired outcomes in the case of a specific organization or programme. What is it that government organizations typically exist to achieve? A typical national or regional road transport authority defines its purpose as 'to manage, maintain and improve trunk roads and motorways'; the US Army defines its purpose as 'to fight and win our Nation's wars by providing prompt, sustained land dominance across the full range of military operations and spectrum of conflict in support of combatant commanders', the UK National Health Service exists to treat illness and promote health; schools exist to educate young people and help them to realize their full potential. Yet in each case the value that these organizations creates needs to be more than what they themselves do, partly because, to take our first example, managing, maintaining and improving trunk roads may ultimately not be the most useful way to contribute to the public value of travel and partly because there may be other ways of managing, maintaining and improving trunk roads that have nothing to do with a road transport authority. The outcome, in other words, has a life independent from the organization, even though it may be highly dependent on the organization for its achievement.

When we express organizational aims in outcome terms we release far greater potential for the achievement of public value. For instance: 'People are able to travel by road safely and without delay'; 'People live in a safe and secure world, with strong international institutions that keep the peace and uphold human dignity'; 'People know how to stay healthy and receive effective treatment when they fall ill'; 'Young people are motivated to learn and are supported in their learning by able teachers who help them to develop the skills and knowledge they need to fulfil their potential.'

Outcomes must be co-produced. Schools cannot alone improve education. Children and parents and peer groups are crucial to learning; it's, not simply 'delivered' by schools. Highways alone cannot ensure that people travel speedily and safely; the number of drivers and their behaviour, the nature of the vehicles; the necessity to travel or the ability and inclination to work from home all contribute to the outcome. As the military know well, but others can forget, bringing peace and security to a city, region or state depends on the behaviour of the shopkeepers and farmers, plumbers and schoolchildren who live there as much as it depends on the actions of the security forces.

Peter Drucker identified confusion between planning for objects and planning for people (Drucker 1999: 2). Drucker saw strategy in terms of the decisions we make today about a future that is inherently uncertain, the realm of unpredictable people, not predictable objects.

The word 'outcome', like the word 'strategy', is much used but often ill-defined. The way we use the word makes a big difference to how it works. Theodore Poister defined it in this way: 'Outputs express what a program actually does, whereas outcomes are the results it produces' (Poister 2003: 38). Outcomes, when written clearly, are like a language that is understood by all those who live and work in a particular place. Targets tend to work more like a code, requiring a particular key to unlock and understand them and can be understood differently by those with the wrong key or no key at all – which is when (because misinterpreted) they tend to produce perverse outcomes (for more on targets and their effects see Chapter 7).

In a simple, linear, mechanistic model (the sort that rarely applies in government) an input is followed by an activity which leads in turn to an output. Achievement of that output might be shown by means of an indicator, but the most useful indicators look 'upwards' to the desired outcome, not 'backwards' to the output.

In the model (of our own invention) shown in Figure 2.3 achievement of the outcome depends on a set of activities, including that the money will be spent, that it will be spent on training school meal assistants, that the training is effective in encouraging healthier eating on the part of children and so on. Success in achieving the desired outcome will depend on a complex set of relationships between each element in the process, which in practice will behave in a systemic and at times unpredictable way, not a linear way.

A simpler policy process, and consequently the type governments often choose, would be to provide ten thousand more school meals each day (an input): relatively easy to achieve, even if not one additional meal

FIGURE 2.3   *Simple input to outcome chart – healthy school meals*

Input	Activity	Output	Indicator	Intermediate outcome	Desired outcome
£10m additional budget for healthy school meals	Training programme for school meal assistants	75% of school meal assistants complete training scheme	10% increase in children eating more healthy food	Children choose to eat healthy food at school and at home	Healthy children

is eaten. The outcome in Figure 2.3 is more meaningful, because it is what government is really trying to do: encourage healthier eating, measured not through whether more children are eating healthy food (as shown by the indicator) but whether they actually *choose* to eat healthier food (the intermediate outcome). Even achievement of this intermediate outcome is not the ultimate outcome or result that government seeks. The outcome is a description of the desired end state, in this case that children are themselves healthier. Choosing to eat more healthily at school and in their daily lives will be an important component in that desired end state, but it certainly will not be the only one. The desired end state is what is important; in one sense the degree to which government has or has not directly contributed to it is unimportant, because the end state will be achieved by many factors, including how family and friends behave, access to green space, ability to exercise and so on. What is important is whether the outcome has been achieved or not. Governments should be at least as interested in that as they are in measuring the efficiency of their own activities. We look more closely at these issues in Chapter 7.

Public strategy is more than solving problems

The problem-solving approach can be a reductionist process that skips over the rationale for intervention in the first place (in other words it misses out or doesn't explain strategic intent). A purely problem-solving approach can narrow the policy options too rapidly and in this way focus on implementing a solution, perfect or otherwise, to the 'wrong problem'. The narrow problem-solving approach carries the danger of limiting our ability to see the complexity in most situations and may mean that we miss the best courses of action available. Peter Checkland identified this in his 1960s research into systems methodology: 'Experience at the start of the research quickly showed that it was not possible to take for granted the concept of a "problem" and the activity of trying to solve it. This is obvious enough in retrospect but was a mild surprise at the time ... it became clear that [the research] was to be concerned not with problems as such but with *problem situations* in which there are felt to be *unstructured problems,* ones in which the designation of objectives is itself problematic ... They are conditions to be alleviated rather than problems to be solved' (Checkland 1981: 154–5).

The 'problem–solution' paradox explains a feature of public administration, whether from international bodies, national government reviews, the reports of think tanks or of parliamentarians. Papers identify sets of problems that need to be addressed by matching sets of solutions. On the face of it the sets of problems are identified accurately and the solutions seem sensible, and look as if they would work. Yet even when the recommendations of reports are implemented they don't work. This is because we ask 'What is wrong' and 'What would solve it?' instead of asking more strategic questions like 'Why haven't previous solutions worked?' and 'Why is it so difficult to implement change in this area?'

'Why not?' questions are often useful, and tend to be asked in two main ways.

Firstly, when considering the apparently unthinkable. Why not legalize all drugs? Why not remove all restrictions on euthanasia? Why not land humans on distant planets? Is it really not possible to travel at or beyond the speed of light? Free thinking and imagination are necessary if we are to have the genuine exploration of new purposes and the ability to set new directions vital to the strategic approach (we explore imagination and insight in Chapter 8).

Secondly, we ask 'why not' when seeking out the weaknesses in any idea. On the whole our critical-analytical capabilities are more strongly developed than our unfettered imaginative abilities, and we can be very keen to explain 'why not', in the sense of why something should not be done. Yet, despite our sense that many of our preferred solutions to problems and many of our new ideas are likely to be inadequate, we often pursue them anyway. This is because we tend to have a poor understanding of the obstacles that exist in the path of our desired outcomes. This is the 'problem–solution' paradox – our preoccupation with solutions causes us to see problems in a way that is amenable to the solutions we construct for them, instead of understanding problems in their wider context.

Most of the major strategic issues facing governments and other public bodies in the 21st century world can be understood more helpfully as 'sets of conditions to be alleviated' rather than as narrow 'problems to be solved': obesity, reliance on unsustainable economic growth, energy shortages, unaffordable pension funds, globalized finance, food scarcity, inequality within and between regions and nations, climate change – all of these are complex conditions which are tough to 'solve' but possible to alleviate. In a strategic mindset many of these can be seen as opportunities to develop new approaches to achieving desired outcomes.

Complexity is not confined to the public sphere. Corporations can also fall into the 'problem-solving trap'. These complex issues are sometimes called 'wicked issues' or 'wicked problems' because they have a large number of interdependencies, and have the features of the 'balloon problem' where an intervention in one area creates a problem in another. The label 'wicked' distinguishes them from 'tame problems' – the sort of soluble problems in maths or chess where there are clear limits or boundaries around the system. Almost by definition, government will have solved tame problems. The terms 'wicked' and 'tame' were formalized by Horst Rittel and Melvin M. Webber (Rittel and Webber 1973: 155–69).

Ashby's law (Ashby 1956) of requisite variety holds that a system must reflect the variety of its wider environment to function resiliently – which in social science will be impossible to do because of the number of permutations, underlining why some problems are 'wicked':

> Companies tend to ignore one complication along the way: They can't develop models of the increasingly complex environment in which they operate. As a result, contemporary strategic-planning processes don't help enterprises cope with the big problems they face ... many strategy issues aren't just tough or persistent – they're 'wicked.' Wickedness isn't a degree of difficulty. Wicked issues are because traditional processes can't resolve them ... A wicked problem has innumerable causes, is tough to describe, and doesn't have a right answer ... Environmental degradation, terrorism and poverty – these are classic examples of wicked problems. They're the opposite of hard but ordinary problems, which people can solve in a finite time period by applying standard techniques. Not only do conventional processes fail to tackle wicked problems, but they may exacerbate situations by generating undesirable consequences. (Camillus 2008: 100)

Grint (2008) discusses tame and wicked problems in terms of authority (that is, legitimate power) referencing Etzioni's definitions of compliance as coercive (an army or prison), calculative (an organization) or normative (institutions or clubs with shared values). Grint shows that management and leadership are two forms of authority rooted in distinctions between certainty and uncertainty. Management deals with familiar, linear problems that may be complicated but resolvable, for example having Standard Operating Procedures. These tame problems are puzzles to which there is a right answer. Leadership deals with novel problems that are complex, not complicated, and where there is no clear relationship between cause and effect. Wicked problems are partly defined by the absence of an answer on the part of the leader. Grint cites health as a wicked problem, because of infinite demand, yet finite economic resource (Grint 2008: 13).

This distinction between leadership and management, between the familiar and comprehensible and the novel and unfamiliar echoes the differences between the ways in which our left and right brain hemispheres process the world. The left hemisphere gives a narrow focused attention to something it already knows is important, the right hemisphere is vigilant more broadly for whatever might be. 'If it is the right hemisphere that is vigilant for whatever it is that exists "out there" it alone can bring us something other than what we already know. The left hemisphere deals with what it knows and therefore prioritizes the expected — its process is predictive. It positively prefers what it knows' (McGilchrist 2009: 40). We look at this again in Chapter 8.

A wicked problem needs a system view. In a hierarchical culture which uses rules, key performance indicators (KPIs) and targets, 'all concern for what the target is intended to achieve is sacrificed to the target itself. This is not because the target needs more regular updating, it is because the target is merely an element of the system but it is not the system, and target-setting tends to replace the ends with the means, the system with the element' (Grint 2008: 14–15).

Approaching climate change with linear point remedies treats it as a tame problem. In Grint's example reducing carbon fuels by switching to biofuels intensifies another problem – reducing the arable land available to grow food.

Because wicked problems are associated with uncertainty the leader's role with a wicked problem is to ask the right questions of the collective rather than provide the right answers. 'These three forms of authority – that is legitimate power – Command, Management and Leadership are, in turn, another way of suggesting that the role of those responsible for decision-making is to find the appropriate Answer, Process and Question to address the problem respectively' (Grint 2008: 14).

Why problem-solving is so prevalent

Governments are designed to solve problems. Election campaigns are often built around public undertakings to 'bust crime', to 'tackle unemployment', to 'give schools freedom', to 'eliminate the deficit', to 'protect the environment', to 'defeat terrorism'. Each of these issues is capable of being approached strategically, and there are good examples of such approaches that we explore in this book, but typically governments at both a political and administrative level attempt to crystallize the issues requiring attention into problems, because problems are seemingly amenable to a solution. In so doing large parts of the complex field are inevitably excluded and the chosen 'solutions' produce results that generate, in turn, a new set of problems to be 'solved'.

We are so used to the undesirable consequences of the well-intended but often short-termist and problem-oriented actions of governments that we have grown to accept such courses of action as inevitable: from the construction of high-rise housing projects in the 1960s that produced housing that few wanted to live in to the deregulation of the financial markets in the 1980s and 90s that resulted in the near collapse of the global banking sector in the following decade. This tension between problem-solving approaches and more strategic approaches is often manifested in tension between politics and strategy. The two can work harmoniously, but often they do not.

One of the attractions of the problem–solution cycle is that tackling problems is visible and heroic, whereas preventing problems means all

BOX 2.4 New South Wales, international evidence and dangerous dogs

The Government of New South Wales introduced a comprehensive piece of legislation to ensure that pets ('companion animals') were safe and did not cause a nuisance (the NSW Companion Animals Act of 1998). In compiling and in subsequently reviewing the legislation they examined international practice in Canada, the UK, the USA, Belgium and the Netherlands. Their review showed that legislation restricting particular breeds didn't work (Seksel 2002). More effective were programmes that encouraged and educated dog owners to manage their dogs in particular ways. In the Netherlands requirements to muzzle certain breeds of dogs, to keep them on a leash and to neuter them were more effective than outright bans, reducing attacks by around 40 per cent in three years. In the UK 1991 legislation that focused on specific breeds reduced dog attacks by less than 1 per cent over a similar period. In one study bite attacks by humans were more common than those by the most common breed of dog involved in attacks on humans – the German Shepherd Dog.

Following a number of high profile dog attacks in New South Wales in the decade following the introduction of the 1998 legislation, more restrictive breed-specific requirements were introduced in 2008 and 2010 and were planned for 2013, despite the evidence that such legislation was unlikely to be effective. The pressure on politicians to 'solve the problem' outweighed their experience that a broad strategy that focused primarily on the behaviour of owners would yield better results (New South Wales Government 2013).

the effort and good work is invisible – in the words of Paul Seabright in *The War of the Sexes*, an 'inconspicuous sacrifice' (Seabright 2012). It's also difficult to measure the value of preventing a problem occurring despite recognition that 'an ounce of prevention is worth a pound of cure'. Establishing cause and effect – that your action prevented the problem – is difficult, because it's hard to demonstrate counterfactuals. This makes strategic measurement (Chapter 7) in the field of national security agencies particularly tough. We cannot know what would have happened without the intervention, nor can we know if others might, without the action undertaken by the security agency, have acted to prevent the problem that we believe we prevented.

Another attraction of the problem–solution cycle is that it is reactive. We might think that a proactive government is preferable to a reactive one but it's easier to demonstrate competence by reacting confidently to events than to do the tough and often indiscernible work of developing and then implementing strategy. If 'casework' is what you are familiar with then it is quite probable that casework is what you will become good at and casework that you will seek out as your preference. This is, very often, what happens to governments.

Problems are rooted in the past and in the present. Our understanding, unless disciplined by the future-focused thinking that is a function of strategy, can all too easily fail to consider the trends and counter-trends of change that will bear our solution aloft in the future or drag it down to the depths. So even if we find a good 'solution', these solutions often do not last. We find that we have constructed a solution to something that has already changed. That is why the policies governments devise and implement so often miss the mark. It is like throwing a stone at a tin duck that is moving at 40 miles an hour without making any allowance for how far it will have travelled in the time between our throw and the impact.

Problem-solving reacts to the difficulties of now – too many hospital acquired infections, too few or too many mortgages being made available, the bonuses of bankers too high. These are legitimate concerns of a government, but they are not necessarily for governments to 'solve' – they are more likely to be for hospitals and for banks to tackle, or better still for the patients and families of those who use hospitals and the customers and the shareholders of banks. What governments can and should do is set an overall strategic direction to help those who are actually responsible for achieving better outcomes in hospitals or in the financial sector to do so; in this way governments create the conditions in which 'condition alleviation' can take place. Instead of trying to solve problems themselves, they enable others to do so.

The problem-solving approach can pull attention away from looming strategic challenges that are further off – for instance, too little energy, too little food, too much travel, not enough houses, until these challenges are manifesting themselves as urgent problems to be solved. At worst, problem-solving encourages governments and their agencies and partners to take actions that make the strategic challenges worse.

This phenomenon arises in part because governments are, understandably, interested in solutions, and a solution requires a problem to solve. Solutions can be pointed out to citizens, and they often appear to have changed the environment. The actions of government that make a lasting difference are almost always the result of strategic approaches where the context has been understood, where the 'why' has been articulated as well as the 'what' and the 'how' and where clear goals have been set and achieved, often over several years. When governments make these strategic transformations to their nations or regions or cities they are praised – but often only long after they have left office. It can take time for a strategy to bear fruit.

BOX 2.5 The Plano Real: Brazil's strategy for long-term economic growth

Brazil had been plagued for decades by high inflation. In 1989–90 the inflation rate reached 2,700 per cent. A series of measures was taken to stabilize the currency, from indexation to the launch of new currencies (four between 1986 and 1990), and the freezing of bank accounts and taxes on financial transactions, but the lack of a comprehensive strategy meant that each measure in turn failed. In 1994 then finance minister (and later president) Fernando Henrique Cardoso introduced the Real Plan (Clements, IMF 1997).

At the heart of the plan was a vision of consumer confidence in a stable domestic market that was attractive to foreign investors. A new currency, the Real, was launched at parity with the US dollar. The government set high interest rates which attracted foreign currency, allowing the Real to appreciate in value against other currencies and reducing the cost of imported goods. Reductions in public deficit spending further reduced inflationary pressure. Increasing consumer confidence meant that many poorer families opened bank accounts for the first time, less fearful that the value of their earnings would erode in weeks or months. This created a domestic consumer boom, leading to increased business investment and employment (Rohter 2010).

The broad and systemic intervention learned from the previous attempts to stabilize the Brazilian economy, and understood the domestic and international context in which the measures were to be deployed. It was successful and Brazil's economy fared more strongly than almost any other in the global recession of 2008–10.

Conclusion: touching the future

You can make strategy at different levels as long as you have clear alignment between the levels and are working to the same vision or overarching outcome. Informing strategic intent with the tacit knowledge held by people within the organization (the chaotic reality that your strategy will encounter when it's implemented by the staff who have to deliver the strategy) is an ingredient of successful strategy.

A sense of curiosity, open-mindedness, the belief that it is always possible for things to be better than they are: these are helpful qualities for anyone involved in working strategically. But this needs to be curiosity as a discipline. History is both the discipline of understanding the past and the past itself. Stanford explained this distinction as 'history1' (the past) and 'history2' (narration of the past) (Stanford 1986).

It can be helpful to think of the future in a similar way, with strategy acting in the same relationship to the future as the discipline of history acts in relation to history as the past. This is not to suggest that the future will be like the past. This is one of the fundamental hurdles that prevent or constrain strategic thinking, which we consider more closely in Chapter 4. Too often we underestimate the impact of the strategic shocks that make the future very different from the past. Strategy is both a discipline to help us shape future action and is itself changed by that future action – evolving, uncertain and never fully known. It is worth noting that history itself is never truly known. David Staley described this phenomenon in the following way: 'The future cannot be predicted. This should not prevent us, however, from creating useful representations of the future, and indeed, history is an excellent method for creating such useful representations. A future2 is very much like a history2: both are grounded in evidence, both are the product of inferences drawn from that evidence, both are representations, in that both are a substitute for something (either the past or the future) that is absent. As long as we are referring to scenarios and not to predictions, we soon learn that history and future are more analogous than we have previously considered' (Staley 2010: 17).

But strategy has yet another dimension, something history lacks. Because strategy should bring us to states that are yet to be, it is also a statement of purpose, purpose that encapsulates desire, belief and evidence, expressed as strategic intent, often through the medium of politics. We cannot change the past (though we can change our understanding of the past). The future, however, is amenable to change through the agency of intent and action: that is the point of strategy.

The best way to bring the future about is to imagine it, creating 'memories of the future' as Shell describes its scenario process. That is not simply a matter of 'dreaming'. Strategy is envisaging a future state and the means to bring it about. Arthur C. Clarke's forecast in 1945 (Clarke 1945) that satellites would one day encircle the earth acting as a net for communication became a reality. Clarke's prediction was made more likely by his own conception of the future – he was not merely stargazing, but expressing strategic intent, describing options and helping to make it possible for the scientific and commercial worlds to bring that future about.

> An 'artificial satellite' at the correct distance from the earth would make one revolution every 24 hours, i.e.: it would remain stationary above the same spot and would be within optical range of nearly half the earth's surface. Three repeater stations, 120 degrees apart in the correct orbit, could give television and microwave coverage to the entire planet. I'm afraid this isn't going to be of the slightest use to our post war planners, but I think it is the ultimate solution to the problem [of how to provide widespread television and microwave coverage]. (Clarke 1945)

In his 1979 work *Fountains of Paradise* (Clarke 2000) Clarke describes the construction of a space elevator in the form of a structure rising from the ground and linking with a satellite in geostationary orbit to raise payloads to orbit without having to use a rocket – something imagined that isn't yet a reality. We'll discuss the factors that favour the exercise of imagination and judgement in Chapter 8.

Intent is a projection into the future. Even our most simple human desires are such projections. When we feel hungry we project our hunger onto a construct of food and we make a plan for how we will find that food, whether by running through a forest and throwing a spear at a deer or walking to the corner shop and buying a loaf of bread and some cheese. More complex political desires, the desire to change a community, to improve its housing or educate its children are also projections into the future. Past events are 'real': a birth, a death, a house built, an education, an army assembled – all of these have happened, and some of them walk with us into the present. But ideas of the future exist; their potential is as tangible as events in the past, and they influence us in our action in the present as forcefully as past events influence us. These can become, to some extent, 'self-fulfilling prophecies' or what Barbara Adam (Adam 2004) calls 'colonising the future'. Their implications can shape our lives – hence 'panic buying' when a rumour circulates that a product currently in abundance will at some unspecified point in the future become scarce; hence a run on a bank when customer confidence is lost, very often because of an expected future development that may or may not come to pass. In underplaying the 'reality of the future' and particularly in giving too little weight to our capacity to shape that future we often condemn ourselves to a present that is less confident and more hopeless than it needs to be; we allow ourselves to be mired in problems rather than buoyed not simply by hope, but by plans to turn that hope into reality. That, in essence, is what strategy is all about.

Chapter 3

Corporate Strategy and Public Strategy

Much of the language and approach to strategy in the public sphere is imported from the commercial world – the world of corporate strategy. Many of the world's leading consulting firms offer advice on the effective development of both corporate strategy and public strategy. In the corporate world the value this advice adds will show in terms of the performance of businesses that bought advice and acted upon it. That advice might be reflected in short-term sales, profits, return on investment, share price and dividends. The public sphere has, broadly, used the same advice and the same consultants as the corporate sector because some of the experience of making strategy in the private sector is applicable to the public sector and because there is little guidance specific to the public sphere. This raises the question of applicability and efficacy: how can we know from the commercial domain what is or isn't applicable, and how can we know whether it works?

It's hard to evaluate the value of the spend on strategic consulting advice and, because governments are often poor at evaluating the performance of policies in terms of results achieved, it's difficult to attribute relative performance to particular strategic approaches. In the private sector the effects can be seen on the bottom line, and while it can be difficult to disaggregate the various contributing factors to an improved or worsened performance of a particular product line or service, the incentives to do so are strong. The viability of the business might depend on it.

Differences between corporate strategy and public strategy

American academic Wallace Stanley Sayre (1905–72) coined the phrase 'public and private management are fundamentally alike in all unimportant respects'. Many writers on public administration have since taken issue with Sayre's adage, noting the close parallels between public and private management and attempting to identify the most significant distinctions and what drives them. Graham Allison (1980) noted the similarities as well as the differences between the two spheres, while bemoaning the lack of useful comparative research. Allison recognized the importance of the political dimension to the process of setting strategy in the public sector, but did not explore how that relationship affected and distinguished public strategy from private strategy.

Some argue that corporate strategy in the world of business and public strategy in the world of government are essentially the same things, albeit operating in different contexts. Others argue that corporate strategy and public strategy are categorically different, with little if any room for mutual learning. Bozeman (1987) argues that all organizations are public to some degree, and that the distinctions, insofar as they can be drawn at all, tend to arise from the degree of political authority (for instance, manifested in the degree of regulation) versus the degree of economic authority over the organization (for instance, financial freedom and the ability to raise capital). Bozeman considered the 'publicness puzzle' at length, by which he meant the puzzle of determining what it was that made a company public or private. 'Perhaps the most important issue that could be clarified by further resolution of the publicness puzzle is the basic question of allocation of functions and responsibilities among sectors ... virtually any function is, at least potentially, amenable to "privatisation"' (Bozeman 1987: 4). Bozeman notes the slipperiness of defining public goods, and observes that public organizations can deliver private goods and private organizations can deliver public goods.

While Bozeman and Allison and the very many others who have pondered the similarities and distinctions between private and public organizations are undoubtedly right when they observe that many of the functions, cultures and processes of public organizations are similar to private organizations (and *vice versa*), there is a general tendency to overlook the significance of the distinctive *purposes* of public organizations on the one hand and private organizations on the other – though we need to recognize that purpose can change over time, and can even be lost over time. As an example, the Tennessee Valley Authority (established in 1933 and still a federally-owned corporation) is a public organization delivering a mixture of public and private goods. But it was the purpose or social mission of the Tennessee Valley Authority at its outset that made it distinctly public, for its aim was to achieve the economic development of a starkly economically depressed region of the USA at the height of the Great Depression.

To understand public strategy, we must take a keen interest in understanding the purposes (or desired outcomes) for which any public organization or programme is established. Strategy is, above all, the achievement of outcomes, often over the long term. This book takes the view that there are important (often overlooked) distinctions between the private and public spheres, which means that while lessons can be learned – in both directions – they also need careful interpretation if sometimes damaging misapplication of experience from one sphere to the other is to be avoided.

Corporate strategy typically tells the business which market it is in; business unit strategy helps it to define and develop its competitive advantage within that market. Gerry Johnson and Kevan Scholes made the following distinction: '[For corporate strategy] Strategic decisions are likely to be concerned with or affect the *long-term direction* of an organization ... Strategic decisions are likely to be concerned with the *scope of an organization's activities* ... Strategy can be seen as the *matching of the activities of an organization to the environment* in which it operates.' For business unit strategy, 'strategy is about how to compete successfully in a particular market: the concerns are therefore about how advantage over competitors can be achieved; what new opportunities can be identified or created in markets; which products or services should be developed in which markets; and the extent to which these meet customer needs in such a way as to achieve the objectives of the organization – perhaps long-term profitability, market growth or measures of efficiency' (Johnson and Scholes 1999: 7–12).

Neither definition is well suited to strategy-making in the public sphere. The emphasis in each is on how a business will adapt to perform successfully in a range of uncertain futures. This is what profitable companies do – they anticipate change and sell their goods and services into changing markets, outperforming competitors. In the corporate sector 'good' equates to profit and to the creation of shareholder value. 'Bad' equates to loss and, at worst, bankruptcy. There's no clear and direct equivalent of profit, shareholder value or bankruptcy in the public sphere. Governments that fail to balance the books occasionally run out of money and experience a fiscal crisis (as in the case of Argentina's default on its debts in 2002) – but the country carries on, albeit often in a volatile and socially and politically distressed state. What's 'good' in relative and absolute terms is debated, contested and evolves constantly. That is the essence of politics. A strategic approach is no substitute for that debate, but provides a means of helping to define 'good' – in other words, a way of reaching agreed political goals, the strategic intent – and which policies will achieve the intent.

Perhaps the best-known guru of corporate strategy is Michael Porter, whose *Competitive Strategy* (1980) is among the most-read text books on the subject. As the title suggests, Porter places great emphasis on how a commercial enterprise fares against its competitors, summarized in his five competitive forces: the threat of entry from potential rivals; the bargaining power of suppliers; the bargaining power of buyers; the threat of substitution of existing products or services by new ones and the intensity of competitive rivalry (Porter 1980: 4).

Porter's five forces are a helpful way of understanding the strategic context in which any private sector business operates. A business, whether a large corporation or a small owner-managed firm, needs to pay attention to its own survival: the greatest threats come from new competitors; from new products; from loss of customers; or from an inability to supply customers the right products or services at the right price. Strategic businesses keep a constant eye on their operational environment – on their competitors, on their markets and customers, on their products, on their suppliers – and they respond swiftly to any changes to ensure that they maintain cashflow, maximize profit and shareholder value. The most successful businesses foresee change and are able to capitalize on it. They stay ahead by understanding their operating environment better than their competitors. They launch new products into existing markets and they use new products to expand their markets, as well as finding new markets for existing products. They take risks and expect a certain amount of experimentation and thus allow for a certain amount of failure. Eric Beinhocker (Beinhocker 2007), in his analysis *The Origin of Wealth* showing the economy as an evolutionary system, points out that Microsoft, one of the world's most profitable companies, backed multiple strategies in the 1980s, not just investing in the new Windows user interface but also in rival platforms including MS-DOS, UNIX, and applications for the rival Apple platform. 'The effect was to create an adaptive strategy that was robust against the twists and turns of potential history' (Beinhocker 2007: 335–7). Contrast, too, the world of venture capital, where investors in a portfolio of ten projects will expect nine to fail – they just cannot predict which of the ten will succeed.

Governments, like businesses, have to foresee the need for change, to provide services that meet the needs of citizens. But successful governments do more than being resilient by responding to change; citizens expect them to shape the future itself. Global concerns like climate change, international development, world trade, a stable financial system, common security and human rights demand a strategic approach, with a vision of the desired future and a plan for how that vision will be achieved. Domestically, providing services that people use and value, for instance in health, education and policing, is an important element of governing well, but it is not enough, and can be costly. People need to know whether these services are actually achieving outcomes – real and desired changes for the better – and achieving such change depends on behaviours governments must influence and lead through the policies they choose.

Successful businesses encourage internal challenge as a means of increasing organizational robustness. They use market intelligence and analysis to identify the shifting demands of customers and suppliers before customers and suppliers themselves are fully aware of them, and shape demand by creating markets for new products and services. In this way strategic businesses become – and maintain their position as – market leaders. They shape and reshape their businesses so that they are configured in the best way to deliver products and services in a constantly changing business environment. The profits they make are an

BOX 3.1 Nokia: from galoshes to smartphones: vision and diversity

Nokia was founded in 1865 as a wood pulp manufacturer, with a small paper mill exploiting hydro power. A century later Nokia had grown to be a manufacturer of tyres and footwear as well as paper products and, crucially for its future development, of electronic cables and a range of hard goods linked to the electronics industry. Its primary market was domestic: Finland. During the economic downturn of the 1970s, Nokia's senior management developed a vision for the company's future growth, focusing on globalization and a move into high-tech products, while maintaining business diversity. The firm moved first into the manufacture of colour TVs, then into computer production (Johnson and Scholes 1999).

In the mid-1990s Nokia moved out of consumer electronics, recognizing that it could not compete with the Far East and also keen to look ahead to developing global high-tech markets. It divested itself of all businesses that were unaligned to mobile telecommunications.

In 2010 Nokia was the world's largest manufacturer of mobile phones. Yet by 2012 Nokia's market position had deteriorated significantly. In July 2010 the company announced a 40 per cent drop in profits and in 2011 it posted a loss on trading of 1 billion euros. In two years it fell from being the world's leading producer of smartphones to a position trailing both Apple and Samsung. The company reassessed its position, announcing a partnership with Microsoft in 2011. It cut around 4,000 jobs in Europe and transferred more of its manufacturing to the Far East (Nokia 2013).

For Nokia to regain sustained profitability it will need to develop a new strategy, and perhaps move into new products entirely. In September 2013 Nokia sold its mobile phone business to Microsoft, transferring 32,000 of its staff to the new owner. The remaining business's shares increased 34 per cent on the news. Nokia will continue to produce telecoms equipment and seek to innovate, though probably not with galoshes.

excellent indicator of success, though by no means the only one. A loss is an equally excellent indicator that things need to change.

The requirement for a healthy financial bottom line in the private sector (whether or not in conjunction with good social and environmental performance) gives visibility to the achievement of short-term outcomes: the sales promotion that sells more goods or the increased profit margin on those goods because of decreased unit costs or a more efficient delivery chain or a breakthrough into a higher-value market. These are easily measured and understood. For companies with long-term investments, perhaps in heavy capital plant; energy production; chemical processing or defence equipment, short- and medium-term financial indicators are less important than understanding whether the business can keep operating over 10, 20, 30 years until it sees the return on its investment. Relationships with its shareholders, its employees, its stakeholders, with governments and regulators become even more vital than for the manufacturer of, say, household goods. This means strategy-making by corporates operating in long-term industries like the energy sector or in defence equipment can resemble that in government or other public organizations.

Providing shareholders have faith in the long-term potential profitability of the company they will continue to invest with confidence in eventually seeing returns even in temporarily unprofitable companies. The notion of 'shareholder value' – the value to shareholders from the strategic decisions that grow earnings, dividends and share price – captures a sense of legitimacy and trust beyond the organization, how the business will operate over the longer term and whether it will become financially sustainable, and of the purpose of the business beyond short-term profit. That's not just whether those who own shares or stocks in the business get a good return on their investment, but takes account of the longer-term sustainability of the business, and its reputation with customers and stakeholders – whether it offers good employment opportunities and is a responsible 'corporate citizen'. Yet shareholder value won't give us a fundamental sense of what the business is there to achieve beyond its own continued existence; it doesn't define the mission or outcome for the business – all important in the field of public strategy, but of less (if any) relevance in the private sphere. The role of shareholders illustrates the difference. 'Total shareholder return (TSR) is the owners' ultimate method of evaluating management's value creation performance to date and into the future. It matters little that the company's market value has increased 20 per cent to date. Unless there is clear evidence that future TSR will do just as well or better, the owners will probably follow the path of their self-interest and look elsewhere. All capital has alternative uses. So a complete and objective performance assessment requires comparison of expected future returns from this corporation with the best of the alternatives' (Clark and Neill 2001: 5).

This shows a key similarity and a key difference between private and public strategy. The similarity is that private businesses have to be as concerned for the long term as governments and public organizations. The difference is that 'shareholders' of governments and public organizations are citizens, and they can't easily choose to place their investment elsewhere. Governments can use the market for social ends by commissioning services rather than delivering them, and letting citizens choose public services from a variety of private providers. That's in part offering citizens the choice of where to spend their money just as corporations in the market economy do, so that competition between providers will increase productivity. But citizens have (or should have) a far more committed level of interest than would a shareholder in the civic goods that governments provide. Defence, law and order, public health, education, energy security all require more than self-interested decisions about return on investment.

We often characterize governments as having the 'unique power to compel', for instance through conscription, through enforcing payment of taxes, through criminalizing certain acts and behaviours and punishing those who fail to obey. But compliance is rarely enforced; in the great majority of cases it is given willingly, or at least contingently – people pay their taxes, obey laws and participate in elections if they believe the system of which they are a part is fundamentally fair and functioning, and the government retains moral authority. Obeying the law is a social act, driven by recognition of the value of civic goods. Citizens are more than shareholders and the obligations of governments to their own citizens – and even to the citizens of other nations – go beyond the obligations of any private business to its shareholders and its employees.

Outcomes and public strategy

What, then, are the differences in the *purposes* of private and public ventures and do private businesses exist only in order to make profit? In other words, is their strategic intent, or purpose, to be profitable? If not, then what? John Kay offers an answer to this question:

> For years I struggled with the idea that if profit could not be the defining purpose of an organization, there must be something else that was its defining purpose. If business did not maximise profit, what did it maximise? I was making the same mistake as those victims of the teleological fallacy who struggled for centuries with questions like 'What is a tiger for?' ... Businesses do not maximise anything. The most successful business leaders like Marks or Walton or Gates pursued the unquantifiable, but entirely meaningful, objective of building a great business. A great business is very good at doing the things we expect a business to do – rewarding its investors, providing satisfying employment, offering goods and services of good quality at reasonable prices, fulfilling a role in the community – and to fail in any of these is, in the long run, to fail in all of them. (Kay 2010: 154)

The distinction between the public and private spheres lies in the purposive, or outcome-focused, nature of the activities and the institutions that carry them out. A public organization, whether a government, a non-profit social enterprise or a charity, must always try to achieve outcomes that sit beyond the success of the organization itself. Endeavours that are purposive in this way create a collective, or public, value at some point in the future – schools, universities, libraries and health services. The purposive nature of the activities makes it strategic.

A social enterprise is a business that trades for a social purpose. It will have a clear sense of its 'social mission': which means it will know what difference it is trying to make, who it aims to help, and how it plans to do it. It will bring in most or all of its income through selling goods or services. And it will have clear rules about what it does with its profits, reinvesting these to further the 'social mission'.

For example, a provider of social housing will wish to make a surplus on subsidized rents or affordable housing provision, which it will use to invest in its social purpose. Bringing a commercial discipline to a social mission is important because if it risks insolvency it won't be in a position to fulfil its purpose.

Public value

The private sector has 'shareholder value' as its measure of performance. In the public domain 'public value' is an equally useful concept. It makes explicit the role of the legitimating or authorizing environment and binds administrative capacity with political power. It places outcomes at the heart of public endeavour, and makes clear why a strategy that concerns itself exclusively with operational excellence can never be a sufficient strategy. It offers a public domain equivalent to 'profit' in the private domain. Profit describes the gain resulting from the employment of capital, the additional value created by the business; public value describes the public gain from the investment of money, time, collaboration and trust in the activity, the value created for society, the civic good.

Public value is the value that government co-creates with its citizens and citizens value. It's not just 'what does the public most value' but also 'what adds value to the public sphere?' (Benington and Moore 2011: 22). Public value is a relatively new and developing political and administrative theory. The concept was developed by Mark Moore of Harvard University's Kennedy School of Government, its best known exponent.

Some theorists characterize public value as a combination of three dimensions: services, outcome and trust. That makes understanding the theory of public value difficult because these are so closely interrelated as to be indivisible. In particular, while quality of services or achievement of outcomes are straightforward, 'trust' is hard to determine because it goes beyond public engagement or traditional political mandates, though both are important. Public value emphasizes the role of the collective, and suggests that the collective good is more than a simple amalgamation of individual goods. Public value emphasizes the importance of the accountability of both elected and unelected officials. It sees accountability in itself lending legitimacy to ventures creating public value, and describes the collective accountability environment as the 'authorizing environment', likening the importance of the authoriz-

FIGURE 3.1 *The 'public value triangle' (based on Mark Moore's 'strategic triangle of public value') (Benington and Moore 2011)*

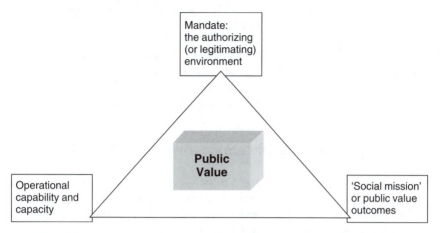

ing environment to the discipline of the market environment for private sector managers.

Public value theory offers an important refinement to public choice theory, the theory that portrays citizens as making self-interested choices and politicians and officials as similarly self-interested and committed to growing and maintaining their areas with no market to regulate their existence. 'Public choice theory can be defined as the economic study of nonmarket decision making, or simply the application of economics to political science...the basic behavioural postulate of public choice, as for economics, is that man is an egoistical, rational, utility maximiser' (Mueller 2003: 1–2).

The public value triangle offers a powerful insight into public strategy. Mark Moore poses public managers these questions: how will you build your legitimacy? How will you ensure you are able to deliver operationally? Have you worked out what your public value outcomes are? He points out that public organizations that have no mandate (or authorizing environment) cannot survive, however noble their mission, and however capable their operational abilities. Equally, no public organization can last long even with a strong mandate and a clear mission if they are not operationally capable. But – worryingly – public agencies can carry on for years (and perhaps indefinitely) producing no valuable results if they can maintain both a strong mandate and have the operational capability to deliver the goods that mandate demands, regardless of whether the goods they produce are publicly valuable. This is the public value challenge: to create public value, an organization must have all three corners of the triangle in place: mandate, capability and clear mission. It is not particularly hard to think of public organizations that are clearly mandated and operationally capable, but which seem to have lost a focus on creating publicly valuable outcomes – organizations which, smoothly and reassuringly, 'turn the handle', but to what end?

Moore also makes the point that the building of mandate is not a passive exercise. It is for public managers to work to create the mandate – and they should not assume that it will be handed to them by a minister or mayor. They may need to work directly with clients, lobby groups, a range of politicians and the public to help create their mandate – not substituting the role of elected politicians or subverting political will, but being prepared to engage creatively with the political process.

Authority, legitimacy, accountability and trust

Within government it can be hard to get agreement on desired outcomes and operational objectives. That's because it involves more than elected politicians; it's not only elected politicians who provide the necessary authorizing environment for strategies to be developed and implemented. Directors of services, members of boards and other senior people inside departments, municipal authorities and other public agencies need to approve not only the broad aims of strategies but often the fine detail of their operationalization. This can be time consuming and debilitating but, because working in the public domain is achieving outcomes for the public rather than for the organization, scope for autonomous action, whether by individuals, teams or agencies, can be constrained by lines of accountability to legislators. This constraint is, on the one hand, necessary, important and can work to the benefit of the achievement of outcomes, while on the other hand it can be stifling of innovation, responsibility and genuine accountability.

On the positive side of the account, public strategy is funded by taxpayers and developed for the benefit of the users of a service, for particular groups of residents or for citizens as a whole, and needs to be legitimated by those whom citizens democratically elect. Yet in many democratic countries voter turnout is often low – particularly for local elections. In practice the authority of elected officials is often delegated to officials, inevitably so given the size and complexity of government in a modern state. The legitimating authority of the democratic element may be so remote and have been delegated so many times that it's invisible. When the delivery of public services is outsourced either to the private sector or to the non-profit sector or to a combination of both, lines of accountability can become fractured between electors, shareholders and the supporters and donors of charities. This means legitimacy and accountability are 'networked', that is, they do not lie exclusively with a single individual or organization, whatever claims are made to the contrary.

The process of deliberative democracy offers the possibility of creating less self-interested and, at the same time, more collective exercise of

BOX 3.2 Deliberative democracy in China: accountability, authority and public power

In 2004 the municipal leaders of Zuguo township in Wenling City decided to use a deliberative democracy approach to make decisions on a series of public investment projects. This was not the first time deliberative democracy had been used in the city, but it was to be larger than previous exercises: the total value of the proposed projects, ranging from parks to roads to sewage facilities, came to $12 million; the total that could be spent as a result of the deliberative exercise was a little over $6 million.

A representative sample of 275 of Zuguo's approximately 120,000 residents was selected to participate in the one-day deliberative event. Opinions were sampled both before and after the event. These showed a shift away from supporting more local village-based projects and towards projects that would benefit the wider community, like sewage facilities, parks that the city as a whole would benefit from and a major connecting road (Fishkin *et al.* 2010).

The local Communist party leadership was surprised by some of the decisions taken by the deliberative democracy group, but the decisions were endorsed by the local People's congress and implemented.

Some question how democratic the increasing use of deliberative democracy in China really is. The Chinese constitution continues to forbid competition between political parties, and the issues that are put before residents for deliberation can be carefully selected. However, it is one approach to increasing participation in decision-making, in making officials directly accountable to their communities and thus in increasing legitimacy. As local Party Secretary Jiang Zhaohua observed: 'Although I gave up some final decision-making power, we gain more power back because the process has increased the legitimacy for the choice of priority projects and created public transparency in the public policy decision-making process. Public policy is therefore more easily implemented.'

Deliberative democracy is an approach used in many multiparty democracies, including the US, Denmark, Britain, Italy and Bulgaria. Its use in the Chinese context tells us something about the desirability of building public legitimacy for policy decisions, whatever the formal political frameworks (Zhou 2012).

power by individual citizens, and can provide new forms of legitimacy and authorization for public officials.

Those working inside a public organization need a sense of authority to be with them at all times – an 'enabling environment' – if they are to achieve outcomes. This authority depends on leadership and responsibility-taking for standards of service, as well as (ideally) achievement of outcome. The evidence of whether a particular agency or programme is achieving the goals it exists to achieve is often sparse. It's more common to measure whether a service is efficiently run or the satisfaction of its users. It's unusual to measure the value it's adding to the creation of outcomes or civic goods – that is, public value.

There's often frustration in government over the lack of innovation by public officials compared with those who work in the private sector. Lack of innovation is, in part, the product of the administrative cultures and forms of accountability that constrain it. It's also the result of a focus on adherence to process and too little focus on vision and, to a large degree, a sense that authority and responsibility rest elsewhere, somewhere 'above', not with the individual or team. Yet the individual or team may be the only people in a position to join purpose and operational capability with the authorizing environment.

Other considerations hamper the creation of outcomes implied by strategic intent. Some are to do with the nature of bureaucratic organization, as Michael Lipsky observed: 'To deliver street-level policy through bureaucracy is to embrace a contradiction. On the one hand, service is delivered by people to people, invoking a model of human interaction, caring and responsibility. On the other hand, service is delivered through a bureaucracy, invoking a model of detachment and equal treatment under conditions of resource limitations and constraints, making care and responsibility conditional' (Lipsky 1980 71).

The increasing use of digital channels to deliver public service – largely absent when Lipsky was writing in 1980 – casts bureaucratic detachment in a different light. Superficially, the impersonal nature of online services implies that bureaucratic detachment will increase. Yet successful digital services designed with the end user firmly in mind focus on the achievement of the desired outcome more than a traditionally-delivered service.

Those working in the public domain must be publicly accountable. In the private domain, employees are accountable to customers and managers, boards are accountable to shareholders and, to varying degrees, to their employees, and the company is held to account by the press and is often also accountable to regulators of one sort or another (Bozeman's 'publicness puzzle'). But accountability is different in the public sector. The sets of rules remind politicians and officials alike that they hold their offices in trust for the public, but they can have the effect of reducing the sense of responsibility for achievement of outcomes at lower levels of seniority. Accountability through politicians to the legislature or through elected local officials to city residents can, perversely, reinforce a sense of isolation from the public, instead of helping those working in the public domain to feel accountable to the public for what they achieve. Employees can see themselves as accountable up to the hierarchy rather than out to the public. 'The appetite of professionals for improvement in service quality is being undermined by a stream of topdown, sometimes conflicting, initiatives and changes in policy priority. The growth in arms length delivery bodies controlled by policies sent down a vertical departmental delivery chain (with financial flows to match) has also often made it harder for services to be coordinated and joined up at local level to meet the needs of the citizen. Policy making that is directed in this way can lead to outcomes that are impractical for the front-line to implement and ultimately futile for the service user. This issue, of course, is particularly salient in times of economic downturn, when achieving optimal value for resources spent is critical' (Sunningdale Institute 2008).

The public value model emphasizes outcomes and encourages those who work in the public domain to win legitimacy for those outcomes, not only through formal channels of authority (though those remain important) but also through those who will help to create the value of the outcome and through those who will benefit from the value created: the people and organizations in the delivery system and the citizens who not only consume services but co-produce the achievement of the outcome (for instance, the parents of school age children).

Accountability can build public trust and confidence in both the outcomes government seeks to achieve, and in its organizational capability. The internet lets governments make data available to the public. With the right encouragement the public can be helped to use these data not simply to hold government to account but to participate in the shaping of outcomes and services.

Accountability used in this way can

- build the legitimacy of the outcome
- give officials a direct role in generating trust and authority
- strengthen the formal authorizing environment by increasing its contact with the public.

Accountability can also help to change the behaviours of officials and make them more responsible and innovative in pursuit of the achievement of desired outcomes, and at the same time more connected to sources of both informal legitimacy (through building the support of stakeholders and clients) and to formal legitimacy – typically elected officials – by helping to mobilize public support and interest in civic life.

A good example of an effective accountability structure that has improved performance is from the US State of Virginia. Other US states with accessible and effective performance and accountability reporting include Maryland, Minnesota and Oregon.

Clarity of outcome or public value is vital to the success of any strategy process and the element most easily overlooked, because organizations in the public domain can become preoccupied with the services they provide and their authorizing environment without understanding and re-evaluating their social mission or outcomes. The wholesale adoption of corporate strategy processes can entrench rather than challenge this

56

BOX 3.3 The Council on Virginia's future: accountability for outcomes, not just for activity

The Council on Virginia's Future was established in 2003 to establish a 'roadmap for Virginia's future' (Virginia – Council on Virginia 2003). The enabling legislation said:

> 'Roadmap' or 'Roadmap for Virginia's Future' means a planning process that may include some or all of the following sequential steps: (i) developing a set of guiding principles that are reflective of public sentiment and relevant to critical decision-making; (ii) establishing a long-term vision for the Commonwealth; (iii) conducting situation analyses of core state service categories; (iv) setting long-term objectives for state services; (v) aligning state services to the long-term objectives; (vi) instituting a planning and performance management system consisting of strategic planning, performance measurement, program evaluation, and performance budgeting; and (vii) performing plan adjustments based on public input and evaluation of the results of the Roadmap.

The Council subsequently submitted to the Governor and the State legislature a vision and set of long-term goals:

Vision: Responsible Economic Growth;
Enviable Quality of Life; Best-managed State Government

Long term goals:

Be recognised as the best managed state in the nation
Be a national leader in the preservation and enhancement of our economy
Elevate the levels of educational preparedness and attainment of our citizens
Inspire and support Virginians toward healthy lives and strong and resilient families
Protect the public's safety and security, ensuring a fair and effective system of justice and providing a prepa\red response to emergencies and disasters of all kinds
Ensure that Virginia has a transportation system that is safe, enables easy movement of people and goods, enhances the economy, and improves our quality of life

This vision and set of goals became the core of the Virginia Performs accountability system (Virginia Performs, 2013). According to the *Pew Center on the States* rankings of government management Virginia has in recent years consistently outperformed most other states in the US (Pew Center on the States 2008).

tendency, because such approaches focus on existential threats – the resilience and competitive advantage of the organization not on what the organization exists to achieve. The concept of public value provides a useful corrective. It ensures that outcomes – or mission – are always in the minds of politicians, managers, employees and public as services are developed and outcomes are shaped.

Kay puts the same issue in a slightly different way. 'An old story tells of a visitor who encounters three stonemasons working on a medieval cathedral, and asks each what he is doing: "I am cutting this stone to shape", says the first, describing his basic action. "I am building a cathedral", says the second, describing his intermediate goal. "And I am working for the glory of God" says the third, describing his high level objective' (Kay 2010: 40).

One of the reasons public value is a strategic concept is because clarity of mission – and constant re-evaluation of mission – can have the effect of building rather than diminishing organizational and social resilience. For instance, library services around the world are threatened as home internet access in many countries reaches 80 per cent or more of the population, diminishing the value of libraries as sources of information. Traditional book borrowing rates are in decline and access to books through smart phones and other devices is increasing. It is right for governments, local authorities and communities to question whether they need libraries at all in these circumstances. Despite any vigorous emotional and intellectual attachment we might have for libraries, if they aren't being used their value must be diminished and their purpose must be called into question.

Municipal libraries became widespread only in the 1850s onwards, and libraries played an important role in extending literacy. But that does not mean that libraries continue to be the right means of achieving the desired outcome. Yet what is the desired outcome? It may be that other organizations are better placed to achieve such missions. That is a strategic choice. But it is very helpful for libraries – and for all other public organizations – to express their mission in outcome terms or as a 'social mission' because this also allows them to modify their organizational purpose to create maximum public value. In this way organizations can help to secure their own existence in contributing to building civic goods. Too often organizations build a vision of the future and describe outcomes solely in terms of the role the organization plays in *responding* to that future instead of how it will try to *shape* that future. This responsiveness is tempting to an organization that feels vulnerable but it ultimately diminishes rather than increases their resilience as organizations, precisely because they are defining the world in their own terms instead of defining themselves in terms of the world.

BOX 3.4 New Zealand National Library: in a global context

The New Zealand National Library had been thinking hard about how the world was changing. The demands of digitization helped set the pace of change, but many other factors also drove the library's visionary and strategic approach to transformation. These included a new building, a clear understanding of the library's place in promoting an information society and a sharp focus on its role in promoting and gathering the knowledge and culture of New Zealand and the Pacific (New Zealand National Library Annual Report 2011):

> In essence, this strategy describes how one of New Zealand's great national cultural institutions will transform its operations to unleash the potential of the digital environment. It is a strategy that will use national and global broadband networks to connect New Zealanders to information important to their lives in a more equitable and useful way. It is about the democratisation of information and the fostering of public digital space so that significantly more of the stories and intellectual endeavours of New Zealanders will be accessible online. This includes New Zealand digital content from businesses, communities, marae, researchers, and young New Zealanders. New Zealand will be online and available to the world. Global networks will bring the world's knowledge-banks to New Zealand.
>
> This is a strategy that will realise Toffler's Future Shock prediction of a 'high tech high touch' world. The National Library will continue to take care of the nation's rich tangible documentary heritage in the collections of the Alexander Turnbull Library, as well as using technology to unleash new content online and create greater access to these collections. Importantly this is not only a strategy about content creation, but about how we will preserve New Zealand's memory in perpetuity so that New Zealanders can always explore and understand the journey that is New Zealand and the Pacific.

Public outcomes and the 'profit-equivalent'

Government is a non-profit business. This does not mean that government, whether at national or local level, whether a central department or an agency, need not care about its financial bottom line. Clearly it must, in the same way that a social enterprise is only able to deliver its social mission if it is financially viable. If an agency or local authority is incapable of operating within its budget it may need to cut costs, for instance by closing offices or programmes and reducing staff numbers, or it may seek additional funds from its primary funder (usually central government) or find new sources of funding – perhaps through charging those who use the services it provides. Local governments may be able to raise more money locally by increasing the tax or levy they charge residents and businesses if they are able to. Often cost-cutting and revenue-raising will be necessary at the same time. If a central government department is overspending it may need to cut costs in the same way, and it may seek additional money from the Treasury, often requiring legislative approval. A national government may need to reduce costs and raise additional revenue through taxation or through borrowing. Public confidence will be a factor in the extent to which increasing taxes will be politically feasible and international confidence will be a factor in determining the ability of a government to raise funds through borrowing. Managing financial viability is an operational issue and without operational capability – of which financial management is a crucial component – then government can achieve nothing else.

But governments do not exist simply to have 'operational capability' or only to deliver important public goods like defence and the rule of law. Nor do they exist primarily to provide other goods and services like transport networks, education and health services, pensions or housing, although often they are one of the providers of such goods and services. Governments exist to achieve better outcomes for their people whether the debate is about providing them directly or commissioning the services from others.

Mark Moore's 'strategic triangle' places organizational capability alongside legitimacy and social mission as the main components in a non-profit organization's 'balanced scorecard' – he suggests that non-profits must always understand their social mission – a mission that lies beyond the services that the non-profit itself provides. 'The important difference between for-profit and non-profit managers' use of financial and non-financial measures can be described in the following simple aphorism: For-profit managers need non-financial measures to help them find the means to achieve the end of remaining profitable. Non-profit managers, on the other hand, need non-financial measures to tell them whether they have used their financial resources as effective means for creating publicly valuable results (Moore 2003: 5).

Moore equates this understanding of the value that non-profit organizations create to that of sustainable profit or shareholder value in private companies. This is a helpful comparator for government as well as for non-governmental non-profit organizations; the role of profit in the private sector is of such importance since it is firstly *a necessary goal* for businesses to achieve with reasonable regularity if they are to continue to exist, and secondly the crucial measure or symbol of *whether their product is of value*. The work of Kaplan and Norton (Kaplan and Norton 1996) in developing the balanced scorecard was not to deny the importance of profit but to ensure that companies did not overlook non-financial factors like customer service, operational excellence and staff engagement that enable companies to sustain their profitability and competitiveness over the long term. Companies are essentially the services or products they sell, coupled with brand, and profit is the ultimate measure of the value of those services or products. By contrast, the ultimate measure of government is the value it creates in terms of outcomes like 'safe communities' or 'healthy people' or 'children who fulfil their potential'. Because these outcomes are only partly the product of the services that government provides (and only partly the result of anything government itself does), we need some way of measuring the value that government adds in particular fields of activity, some equivalent of profit. Public value offers us an important step towards finding that conceptual equivalence.

Finding the exact equivalent of profit in the world of public strategy may elude us. One of the difficulties is that profit is measured in monetary terms, whereas monetizing the value of desired outcomes like 'longer lives' or 'unpolluted air' or 'children who fulfil their potential' distorts the outcome. Monetization doesn't count the second meaning of profit, which is profit as a symbol of value. We can monetize the benefits and disbenefits of, for instance, longer lives, measuring additional years of economic productivity on the one hand and the additional cost of pension payments and use of health services on the other, together with many other measures. Actuaries have sophisticated means of measuring these costs and benefits, and are important to governments in calculating their future liabilities in terms of pensions and death benefits as well as savings resulting from mortality. At its most extreme monetization can land governments and businesses in difficulty, as in the case of a report on behalf of tobacco company Philip Morris (in Box 3.5).

On one level the argument attributed by the press to Philip Morris that early deaths (essentially voluntary in nature) could save the Czech Government money may have been factually sound and evidentially reasonable (although subsequent academic assessment has found significant flaws in the original calculations made for the company). But the normal public response to such apparently evidentially sound and rational measures is nervousness because desired outcomes in the public domain – the safety of our communities, the fulfilment of our children's potential, the cleanliness of the air we breathe, life itself – are more than commodities. Many would argue they are rights.

The world's two most profitable companies (excluding energy producers, banks and the ubiquitous Wal-Mart) are Apple and General Electric at \$41.7bn and \$13.6bn respectively (Fortune 500, August 2013). Their profitability is a result both of the businesses producing goods that people want to buy at a unit cost that is sufficiently low and at a price that is sufficiently high, and a symbol of the value of the products they produce.

BOX 3.5 The Czech Government and Philip Morris: monetizing the value of life?

In 2001 an international affiliate of US tobacco company Philip Morris commissioned a report from consultants for the Czech Government showing that the government made a net gain of $147m from tobacco-related taxation and savings in 1999. The report added up the costs of tobacco use for things such as medical care for smokers who are sick or who set themselves on fire and the loss of taxes they would otherwise pay while they are recovering. It subtracted this from gains such as the tax charged for tobacco and the lower level of state benefits drawn by smokers because they die early.

When the report came to light, it sparked protest, with some US newspapers carrying advertisements from anti-smoking groups which showed a picture of a corpse with a toe tag reading: '$1,277. That's how much a study by Philip Morris said the Czech Republic saves on health care, pensions and housing every time a smoker dies' (Shirane *et al*. 2012).

Philip Morris said the work had been commissioned without its knowledge and released a statement, saying the study 'exhibited terrible judgment as well as a complete and unacceptable disregard of basic human values'.

Governments, public agencies and non-profit social enterprises can produce services and achieve outcomes at low cost and with high levels of success. If they do, they are well on the way to being 'socially profitable'. But the symbol of value, which in a private company is represented by profit, is incapable of monetization in the public domain. Even where a profit may not be made for many years, private companies are still able to raise money and to create shareholder value, but only in the expectation of future profits. The 'social profitability' of outcomes is a yield which may not show for many years. The relatively new field of 'Social Impact Bonds' serves to emphasize the distinction: Social Impact Bonds invite private capital to invest in the achievement of outcomes, for instance the reduction of reoffending by ex-prisoners. Investors will receive their money back with a small profit if the outcomes are achieved. The Social Impact Bond is particularly attractive in a model where government has outsourced the delivery of services to charities and other non-profit organizations, which often struggle to gain investment funding and cannot always afford to carry the financial risk of delivering a service over several years. But a key feature of Social Impact Bonds is that the risk of failure continues to be underwritten substantially by government itself (Mulgan *et al*. 2010).

'Social profitability' is a product of the political value placed upon the public product (the outcome or result) as well as of public support and a recognition of long-term impacts well beyond the cycle of annual measurability and often beyond a typical electoral or economic cycle, producing tensions between shorter-term political imperatives and longer-term strategic goals that we consider in the next chapter. How are we to measure the true value of the education system except over a cycle of thirty or more years? How are we to measure the value of the choices we make about how to organize national defence except over a cycle of ten to 20 years, given the time it takes to procure the right weapons, to train people to use them and, more relevantly, for threats to materialize or, most importantly of all, to be prevented from materializing (something that is notoriously difficult to measure)? And how are we to value the intergenerational obligations, which bear on education, infrastructure, natural resources and the planet itself?

Senator Robert F. Kennedy (1968) put it this way: 'Our Gross National Product, now, is over $800 billion dollars a year, but that Gross National Product – if we judge the United States of America by that – that Gross National Product counts air pollution and cigarette advertising, and ambulances to clear our highways of carnage. It counts special locks for our doors and the jails for the people who break them. It counts the destruction of the redwood and the loss of our natural wonder in chaotic sprawl. It counts napalm and counts nuclear warheads and armored cars for the police to fight the riots in our cities. It counts Whitman's rifle and Speck's knife, and the television programs which glorify violence in order to sell toys to our children. Yet the gross national product does not allow for the health of our children, the quality of their education or the joy of their play. It does not include the beauty of our poetry or the strength of our marriages, the intelligence of our public debate or the integrity of our public officials. It measures neither our wit nor our courage, neither our wisdom nor our learning, neither our compassion nor our devotion to our country, it measures everything in short, except that which makes life worthwhile.'

There has been much interest in issues of intergenerational justice, and some countries have established offices of an 'ombudsman for future generations' or 'commissions for intergenerational equity', either accountable to governments or to legislatures. These roles have tended to focus particularly – but not exclusively – on issues relating to sustainable development and environmental protection. The best-known example is probably Hungary's ombudsman for future generations ('Office of the Parliamentary Commissioner for Future Generations'), but others include Finland, Canada, New Zealand and Israel. The political mandate for such roles is still far from secure. Although Hungary's commissioner's role was guaranteed by the Hungarian constitution, it has recently been modified following a constitutional amendment and subsumed into a broader role protecting a range of fundamental rights.

There's no magic solution to the conundrum of how we value the outcomes produced in the public sphere; no neat equivalent to profit. But we must strive to value these outcomes, or at least not fail to value 'socially profitable' outcomes, even though we might always struggle to place a numerical figure on them.

Organizational resilience

The achievement of 'socially profitable' outcomes depends to a greater or lesser extent on strong public institutions as well as the successful co-production of those outcomes with citizens (we examine co-production in the next section). Successful firms are resilient. Their understanding of the context in which they operate, their anticipation of future competition in products, services, customers and suppliers, their ability to reshape their businesses to operate profitably in those different futures are among the things that make them resilient.

Public organizations need to be resilient, too. Government departments and agencies need to anticipate change, to ensure their workforce has the right capabilities to deliver the goals they aim to achieve, to ensure they are able to change their policies and their relationships to cope with different futures. Nations must also seek to develop resilience, enabling them to compete economically as export markets change, as access to resources changes; to ensure they have the energy, food and water they need for basic security, to predict and respond to demographic change.

Governments have an important role in ensuring national resilience. In some countries government has a bigger role, in others a smaller one. A bigger variable than size of role is capability. The government of Canada is more capable of building national resilience than, for instance, the government of Somalia (see Chapter 6 on the building of organizational capability). Below the level of national governments, states, regional and sub-regional bodies and local authorities all perform roles that equate to those of strategic corporations in gathering analysis that helps them to understand potential futures and build resilience. Departments, agencies and other public bodies, similarly, will perform an important role in building the resilience of a community in times of change. An effective Fire & Rescue Service will, for instance, ensure that it is as good at preventing fires as putting fires out. It will use intelligence so that it understands where and why fires most often occur and take action to make fires less likely. In many countries this has resulted in much higher levels of community engagement by Fire & Rescue Services, particularly in places where fires are more likely to occur, for example in deprived neighbourhoods. It understands that community engagement and education programmes are different skills from those of putting fires out. In order to become a more *publicly resilient* organization, the service has had to change and understands it must continue to expect change.

This is a different question from that of how the Fire & Rescue Service should organize itself to maintain its *corporate resilience*, as if it were a business in the private sector. Imagine a Fire & Rescue Service was so successful in achieving its mission of preventing fires that the number of fires in one area fell from 1,200 a year to 120. It would have used its inputs (public money, its employees, citizen engagement) in a series of activities (education, installation of smoke alarms) leading to outputs (safer kitchens, educated householders, safer factories and shops) that led to the desired outcome or civic good of safe homes and workplaces and fires prevented. This successful creation of public value would rightly lead government to wonder whether it was still necessary to have a Fire & Rescue Service at all. It would certainly consider reducing the funding for the organization by, perhaps, 90 per cent. How should the Fire & Rescue Service act strategically in this case? Let us first consider how a private business would act.

The difference between corporate organizational resilience and public organizational resilience

Let's imagine the board of fictional private sector company the 'Smoke Alarm Company PLC' ('Smarmco'). For the past three years Smarmco has been the market leader in the manufacture and sales of smoke alarms in San Serriffe. They have 70 per cent market share and sales have been on an upward trend until this year when they have been stable. Profits are good, and dividends to shareholders high. Smarmco products are price competitive and their smoke alarms are known to have exceptional life and reliability. Indeed, they are the preferred supplier of smoke alarms to the public sector San Serriffe Fire & Rescue Service (SSFRS). The board realizes that they are nearing market saturation. Business intelligence shows them that new housing, retail refits and so on will provide a continuing market, but at much lower levels of sales than in the current year. What should they do? The board considers several options:

- seek to increase market share further
- bear down on production costs to increase margins
- increase product price to maximize short-term profit
- change their product to build in obsolescence
- diversify into new products, for instance smart meters and car alarms
- seek new markets overseas, for instance in nearby Lindorland
- seek to gain shareholder agreement to sell the company to one of their competitors (that is before the share price starts to fall)
- seek to acquire another business in another sector.

It may be that Smarmco decides to do one or several of these. Clearly they need to act if they are to continue to maintain profitability and to create shareholder value. The board is rightly concerned to maintain the resilience of the business, and their market intelligence has helped them to anticipate their changing operating environment and to prepare accordingly.

Is the position the same for the public sector SSFRS, which can expect a 90 per cent drop in demand for their services and the possibility that their continued existence is called into question? What is the board of the SSFRS to do? The organization could consider adopting a course of action similar to Smarmco. They could seek to ensure that they find new ways of operating successfully.

For instance they might (A):

- move into the community safety business in new ways, perhaps by offering training schemes for young offenders
- train all their operational staff as paramedics and move into emergency medical care
- offer their facilities for private hire and entertainment
- seek alternative funding streams for their organization, for instance by launching a lottery or a subscription service
- seek new markets for their services, perhaps by competing to provide Fire & Rescue Services with the Lindorland Fire Service.

Alternatively SSFRS might (B) try to stimulate renewed demand for their services by setting small fires which they need to attend.

Or (C) the board of SSFRS might suggest to their funders that there is no reason for their organization to continue to exist in its current form, and to advise that it is wound up and the residual service required is transferred to the Cosmopolitan Police Service (CPS), with an additional funding stream given to the CPS met from part of the savings found from closing the Fire & Rescue Service.

Let's examine each of these three courses of action open to public sector SSFRS. To take our first example (A), here we can see that the board of the SSFRS is concerned to find new ways of creating public value. One or more of the options they are exploring might do so. They would need to persuade their funders – politicians, both in local and central government – that it is sensible for the SSFRS to perform these tasks, in much the same way that the board of Smarmco would need to seek the approval of their shareholders for their plans. But for a public organization the need for legitimation goes far wider than for a private corporation. The SSFRS would have to persuade local residents that it should perform new or wider roles. It would need to work closely with the Cosmopolitan Police Service to satisfy them that its role with young offenders supported the outcomes that the CPS was trying to achieve, and the San Serriffe Ambulance Service would need to be persuaded that additional paramedics were of value. Depending on how the SSFRS was constituted in law, it is likely that it would require special permission and perhaps legislation to be able to raise additional funds directly – and the San Serriffe Treasury would no doubt wish to ensure it reduced its funding through national or local taxes commensurately. Seeking to compete with neighbouring Lindorland's Fire Service to provide fire services there would be subject to the agreement of the Lindorland authorities, who would need to be clear that having two or more fire services would benefit their population. And the SSFRS would need to know that they would have some access to funding to support these new services.

Considering this attempt to build organizational resilience should make us realize two things: one, a public service is *not straightforwardly in competition* with other providers. There is usually a good reason for this. In London, England until the 1830s fire services were provided by competing insurance companies who would attend fires only in the homes of those who paid premiums to their own company. This produced problems, not least of which was that fires spread from the homes of the uninsured to the homes of the insured, by which time the fire was much more difficult to extinguish and lives in the community were lost. The matter of whether those who had perished were 'free riding' on a service for which they had not paid was of less concern than the moral imperative of a community being able to prevent its members perishing unnecessarily in fires. Putting out fires came to be regarded as a public good, in much the same way as the maintenance of law and order came to be seen as a public good. This is not to say the position could not shift again, nor is it to say that public organizations are never in competition with other providers whether in the public domain or the private. State-run health providers are, to an extent, in competition with private health providers; state schools are, to some extent, in competition with private schools; public transport providers are in competition, sometimes with each other and almost always with private cars and alternative forms of transport. The point is not that there is no place for competition in the public domain, but that *public organizations cannot define themselves in terms of their competitive position* in the way that private firms must, because to do so is likely to be unhelpful – it may lead them to make the wrong decisions for the wrong reasons.

In examining the position at (B) we may be tempted to dismiss this easily. Setting fires only to put them out would almost certainly be a criminal act. It would certainly be a form of corruption for the Fire & Rescue Service to do so simply in order to secure their future position. But to take a slightly more plausible example, let us examine the use of speed cameras on roads. Let us imagine police forces were able to retain the fines levied on motorists. This money would be available to the force not only to spend on reducing speeding, but to spend on other services.

A number of police forces might find the additional income useful. They might develop an interest in maintaining the level of income from fines. But what are speeding penalties for? The police forces may even become keen to maintain a certain level of speeding. This could be in their organizational interest, but it would not be in the public interest, which would like to see no speeding (except – acting selfishly – individually, when in a hurry) and thus greater safety for motorists and pedestrians alike. If the provision of speeding cameras and supervision of the detection and fining system were given to a private company, it would be in that company's interest to maintain the level of fines and thus income at a certain level unless its contract had some form of provision to reduce speeding.

Private companies will seek to secure their organizational future through profit and shareholder value. Public organizations exist to achieve *socially profitable* outcomes – civic goods. Public organizations which become preoccupied with their own futures instead of aiming to create public value are not wholly unlike the San Serriffe Fire & Rescue Service deciding to light fires only to be able to put them out. *Public value and shareholder value are different.*

To examine our final example, in (C) the board of the SSFRS recommends that the organization is wound up. This, one might think (absent public choice theory, which holds that there is no market to constrain the vested interests of politicians and officials in growing their areas), should be commonplace in the public sphere. What is important is the degree to which the SSFRS can add value through its activities to achieving the outcome of safe homes and workplaces and the prevention of fires. It has not failed in this activity. Indeed, it has been so successful in adding value, so socially profitable, that the desired outcome has been largely achieved. Naturally it will take some continued effort and vigilance to ensure that homes and workplaces remain safe and that fires are prevented, but the board has taken the view that there are other organizations better placed to do this, and that the resources used by the organization could be used more efficiently and effectively elsewhere. In other words, it has assessed where value-adding activities lie in the future and determined that they lie outside the organization.

In practice public organizations rarely wind up of their own volition. But their legitimators and funders – politicians – do close down organizations, merge organizations, reshape organizations constantly. Why aren't public organizations keener to do this themselves? Because many public organizations identify the future with their own survival. They adopt the lessons of corporate strategy too directly and find new roles and new ways of legitimating their work. This is sometimes justifiable – but not always.

Organizational self-perpetuation is not a legitimate goal in the public sphere. 'What, then, is the university's purpose? Harvard is not Wal-Mart

– or even Bloomingdale's. Its purpose is not to maximize revenue but to serve the common good through teaching and research. It is true that teaching and research are expensive, and universities devote much effort to fund-raising. But when the goal of money-making predominates to the point of governing admission, the university has strayed far from the scholarly and civic goods that are its primary purpose for being' (Sandel 2009: 183).

In the public sphere the desired outcome always needs to be bigger and more important than the organization; in the private sphere the organization must find products and services that are – in effect – no bigger than it is. In the public sphere success is achievement of the desired outcome, whether through the activities of the organization or by others. In the private sphere success is indivisible from organizational success.

Public organizations can learn from the private sector. But they can get it wrong. The key is understanding the different context and knowing 'when to stop'; when to look beyond the organization to what the organization is trying to achieve. It's just as important for public organizations to build resilience to contribute to the achievement of desired outcomes as it is for private organizations, but the resilience they need to build is that of a wider system that will achieve the desired outcomes. Often, when there's a new government following an election or a change of leadership, there's a reorganization. New ministries and agencies are formed; others are merged. The new organizations create their own organizational brand. Logos are created, corporate strategies and visions are published; premises are altered; new business cards are printed. This isn't simply costly it is also a misinterpretation of how to act strategically, driven by the private sector paradigm of the importance of corporate resilience and the value of brand. One audit of government reorganizations in the UK over a period of just four years 2005–9 estimated the gross cost of reorganization and rebranding at £780 million ($1.26bn) (National Audit Office 2010b: 5).

Those who work in the public sector are likely to be motivated by what outcomes they work to achieve rather than by the relative success of their organization, yet departments and agencies focus huge effort on corporate branding and identity, encouraging the very 'silo' behaviour (where different parts of the organization operate without reference to what other parts are seeking to achieve) which governments usually say they deplore. Doing away with corporate branding within central government not only saves money, it assists collaboration. The Government of the Netherlands has done away with corporate branding and also ensured that all of its civil servants based in The Hague have access to each other's offices, instead of requiring separate business passes for every building as is the case in many other national capitals. A number of ministers in the Netherlands government are 'programme ministers' instead of departmental ministers, for instance a minister for youth and families, focusing on achieving outcomes in this area, with a budget but without a formal department. These modest reforms have saved money and improved performance. They have helped government to focus on outcomes, not on itself.

Collaboration and competition in the public sphere

In the last part of the 20th century many governments encouraged the creation of competition in the provision of public services to raise productivity. In some cases this applied to services which stayed in the public sector. The UK National Health Service used several approaches to create something akin to a market: it separated 'commissioners' of health services from 'providers' of those services; those using the NHS were allowed to choose who treated them to create competition between hospitals and the primary services provided by general practitioners (family doctors) who remain outside the NHS, although funded by it. Several different political motivations were at work in the introduction of these measures: a belief in choice as a means of improving standards; a belief that monopoly provision increases costs and reduces standards; and faith in the efficiency of markets in allocating resources.

Much of this thinking seems instinctively right. Breaking up monopolies and creating competition should bring efficiency, improved quality of service and innovation. As state ownership of public transport provision, of telecommunications, of energy production was, to a greater or lesser extent, phased out across Europe in the 1980s and 1990s, costs fell and quality of service increased. This brought benefits to consumers in terms of price, levels of service and access. But these same changes also brought significant problems for governments in a period of growing insecurity of supply, when the market may struggle to provide. If governments regard access to heat, light and telecommunication as essential civic goods (if not, strictly, public goods in economic terms), it is hard not to take a keen interest in their continued supply. Because carbon-based energy resources are finite, are in increasing demand and may present serious risks to the world's climate, the chosen model of competitive provision seemed less adequate in 2013 than 1993, even though in 1993 state-owned provision seemed, in the main, anachronistic and inefficient. Private sector suppliers must contend not only with known uncertainties of supply, infrastructure, competition including new types of energy supply, they must also contend with an unstable regulatory environment and with the competing ambitions of rival suppliers and governments and nations. A strategic and collaborative approach – a 'blueprint' to use Shell's terminology (*Scramble* or *Blueprint*? at www.shell.com) – seems more desirable than simple competition.

This is not an argument for Soviet-era state monopolies in the provision of boiled sweets, tractors and rubber boots. But, at times, goods like health provision, education, transport, heating, lighting and food may all be regarded as essential civic goods. When these goods are in short supply it becomes difficult for governments to stand aside when the market fails: 'just as the market failure model interprets collective choice in terms of the aggregation of individual choices, so it interprets collective actions as the aggregation of individual actions. But armies, production lines, hospitals, railways and schools function because people work as teams. And in appraising the performance of teams, issues of incentives are relevant, but only part of the story. There is a large middle ground between the excessively utopian belief that everyone will do the right thing once they perceive what it is, and the excessively cynical assumption that everyone is principally driven by the prospect of personal financial gain. It is in that middle ground that both the public and private sectors of modern economies function' (Kay 2007).

What do these issues tell us about the differences between corporate strategy and public strategy? Once again we can see that the lessons of corporate strategy, with the emphasis on the success of the organization or business and its performance relative to its competitors is of only limited relevance to the field of public strategy, where the only success that counts is the degree to which desired outcomes have been achieved; this success is more likely where different organizations – and different types of organization – collaborate than when they compete. Moreover, our very conception of what is public and what is private is likely to shift significantly over quite short periods of time. As was seen globally in 2008, banking is an essential public service; a civic good. We would have been unlikely to see it in that way in 2005, and are unlikely to see it that way in the future – but, for a time, nationalization of banks and huge bailouts by governments to keep banks solvent seemed quite acceptable. The nature of private and public goods, and the dividing lines between them, is not immutable; it is subject to social-political context. As Bozeman suggested, they are hard to define as purely public or private (Bozeman 1987: 50).

Are the public customers of services or co-producers of outcomes?

In the public sphere the public may, incidentally, be customers of services provided by government, public authorities and non-profit enterprises. That is usually only one aspect of their relationship with the provider of the service. The customer of social housing is a tenant, a user of a service, a citizen, but is also part of the wider expression of a community that has declared an interest in a desired outcome of affordable housing, of ensuring that families are housed decently, that homelessness is eliminated.

For government and its agencies, their interest in the public is – or should – only ever partly be that of service provider to customers. It would be entirely appropriate for the desired outcomes in housing to be achieved through for-profit businesses – as is often the case, both through private landlords and home ownership. But that would not alter the role of the public authority in looking beyond the profitable transaction of housing provision to the bigger outcomes. That is why the users of services in the public sphere are never 'just' consumers.

The trend over the past two decades has been to refer to the public as 'customers' of public institutions and this approach, while carrying certain advantages, also carries risks. As customers in a restaurant, as the purchasers of a car from a dealer, as the users of banking services, we make demands in the knowledge that we are paying for a service. If we are served an inedible meal we will ask for it to be replaced or for our money back. If the car's brakes fail the day after we had them serviced, we expect the dealer to pay for their repair. If the bank charges us too much for their services or pays us too little on our deposits we will – or, are able to – move our account to another bank. We won't feel any responsibility for making the restaurant, the car dealer or the bank a better business in future. If anything we will avoid using their services again. We may even tell our friends about how poor their services are, and damage their reputations. We may think that is deserved. But as citizens, as members of the public who are also users of public services, we have a role in ensuring that the service is improved. Beyond that, we also have a role in 'co-producing' the outcomes that a health service or a policing service or a street cleaning service delivers.

The concept of 'co-production' involves the citizen helping to create the desired outcome, for instance improved public health. A citizen who uses a cardiac health service will not simply be a consumer of, say, medication for angina. She will also have shared responsibility for ensuring that she takes her medication regularly, that she does not smoke, that she eats healthily, maintains a healthy weight and takes the right amount of exercise. The outcome of a healthy person cannot be achieved without the person participating actively in achieving it. The point is made well in the following extract from a New Economics Foundation report: 'William Beveridge's 1942 Report which founded Britain's post-war welfare state was cautiously hopeful, though it warned of the consequences of undermining people's sense of personal responsibility for tackling common problems. What seems strangest, reading it 60 years on, is that it assumes that spending on health and welfare will make people healthier and more self-reliant. Beveridge calculated that the cost of the NHS, for example, would fall' (New Economics Foundation 2008: 9).

To what extent are the public the 'customers' of public services and to what extent the 'co-producers' of outcomes? The answer to this question varies. Let us consider some examples:

- A national public broadcasting network, for instance, Germany's ARD, is a public organization, funded by a licence. Its product is consumed by viewers, listeners and internet users; it is in competition with many other providers. Its position is close to that of a corporation in the private sector, and the users of its service can properly be regarded as customers.
- City transport authorities are often run as companies but with the city council as its primary or sole shareholder. But these authorities, even where they provide trains, subways, trams, ferries and buses and when they licence taxi operators, are almost always in competition with other transport providers, including private car owners. Those who use its services are primarily customers, although they will often take an interest in the wider goals of improving transportation generally across the city, and regard the city-owned or regulated transport providers as having a role beyond that of being a profitable operator.
- Municipal authorities are often the providers of social housing, usually at low cost to tenants, sometimes as a direct service and more commonly through non-profit organizations. While those who seek to use these services could go elsewhere, the degree of competition with other providers is low. It is still appropriate to see those who use its services as customers.
- A national revenue and tax collecting authority offers a service to taxpayers, but is also an enforcer of tax collection. Notwithstanding the element of compulsion inherent in tax collection, modern tax collecting agencies usually regard those who use its services as customers because the relationship has a similar feel to that between, for instance, an insurance firm and its customers, with high volume transactions taking place largely on an annualized basis. But those who use its services are unlikely to see themselves as its customers. For tax collectors in an era when deference to authority is in sharp decline, it becomes even more tempting to treat those who must pay taxes as if they were customers who could choose not to pay. It is at least questionable whether seeing taxpayers as 'customers' is helpful either to the public or to the tax collection authority other than for reminding its workforce that they serve the citizens who pay their wages, and the moral responsibility to provide good service when customers can't walk away. Citizens also tend to take a keen interest in whether others also pay their taxes. In this sense they are co-producers of a taxation system that is fair and consistent in overall terms. They pay their taxes in part because they expect others do.
- Agencies that aim to get the unemployed into jobs often provide state benefits to those seeking work as well as trying to find jobs for those who are out of work. Their relationship with those who use its services is that of a service provider to a customer, although users have relatively little choice about whether or not they use the services provided.

While the user of the service is, in some respects, a customer, the outcome (finding and keeping a job) has to be co-produced with the job-seeker, and will depend on the job-seeker's ability to keep appointments, perform well at interviews, keep healthy and many other factors.

- Schools provide education to children. Children and their parents have some choice about which school they attend. Schools could call school students customers but few do, because the relationship is not that of customer to service provider. Neither children nor parents see themselves as the 'customer' of the school. Educational outcomes are an obvious area of 'co-production'. Even the best teachers will struggle to help their students to learn if the student is undernourished, poorly housed, a member of a street gang or physically abused at home.

- Family clinicians provide primary health services to their patients. This is clearly a form of customer service. In some places this is a private transaction, in others it is paid for by the state. Most patients are also able to exercise some choice in which doctor they see. But is someone who seeks a medical diagnosis from a professional their customer, or their patient? Does the word 'patient' carry with it duties of care that go beyond the duty of care an insurance company has towards one of its customers? And can health treatments only work in co-production with the patient? The answer to these questions is surely 'yes'.

- The police deal with crime and work to prevent crime. They are providing a service to the communities in which they work and they could – and sometimes do – refer to those who use their services as customers. But is someone who has been arrested a customer? Given the often conflicting demands of a police service's 'customers' – from wishing to see offenders detected (the public) to wishing to see offenders punished (victims) to wishing to see the police service run at the lowest cost (police authorities) to wishing to avoid detection (criminals) – is it at all helpful for a police service to see those with whom it deals as customers? Aren't safe communities, successful convictions, a law-abiding citizen all a matter of co-production?

- Prisons provide a service both to the wider community in terms of ensuring those who receive custodial sentences remain in custody and to those in custody, ensuring that they are kept in decent conditions. In what sense are prisoners customers other than being protected and treated fairly and respectfully? While a prison that successfully detains its prisoners is not necessarily an example of co-production, a prison that successfully reduces reoffending, for instance through education programmes and through effective work with offenders up to and following their release probably is. Prisons that help ensure offenders have new skills, are drug-free, and on release can find employment, housing and build good relationships with loved ones are engaged in co-producing, with offenders and many others, the outcome of reduced reoffending.

Is it simply the context of the particular public service that determines whether it is appropriate to regard the public as customers or something else? Is the notion of the customer problematic in the public sphere because of the public's role as legitimators of the service that is on offer and as co-producers of the outcome the service seeks to help achieve? If we accept that the work of all public services is to achieve desired outcomes beyond the scope of the organization itself, then are those who use public services *ever* only customers, or are they *always*, in addition, acting as citizens, as part of the wider community, even in the apparently straightforward cases of the German broadcaster ARD or of the passengers who use the services of the Cairo Transport Authority?

In the private sphere customers are important not simply as the purchasers of goods and the users of services but as the *raison d'être* of the business. 'It is the customers' continued willingness to buy a company's products that allows a company to survive and succeed. It is the customer's decision to buy a product or service that sustains the claim that the organization is creating something valuable for society' (Moore 2003: 6).

Are the same behaviours appropriate in the public domain? Those who promote the creation of competition, choice and markets within public services might argue that they are. These are the behaviours that ultimately improve the quality of service, that ensure that the bank offers rates that compete favourably with other banks, that ensure the garage ensures its cars are roadworthy. In the same way a hospital needs to be as clean as other hospitals or better, a town council needs to offer garbage services that are as reliable and efficient as other town councils or better and so on. But the difference is this: part of the responsibility for ensuring the improvement of public services rests with us as citizens. We 'own the business' of government. If we owned the restaurant, the motor dealership, the bank, then we would almost certainly act not just as a customer, but also with a sense of responsibility for its improvement. For government and other public agencies to think of the public purely as consumers of services, and for the public to think of themselves in this way is to limit significantly the creation of value in the public domain. It is to misunderstand the purposes of government.

A further paradox: while it is often, on the face of it, useful for public organizations to encourage their employees to think of those who use the services it provides as customers as a way of improving the quality of service to the individuals who use the service, it is almost always unhelpful for those who use those same services to think of themselves as customers, because they are less likely to act with an interest in co-producing the desired outcomes the organization exists to achieve, and more likely to act in their narrow self-interest, which is how customers should act for a free and competitive market to work efficiently. To close the paradox we can see that it is not helpful for the organization to encourage its own staff to think of those who use its services solely as customers either. It should, instead, encourage them to think of them as a combination of *stakeholder, trustee* and *customer*: both customer of services and co-producer of outcomes.

Conclusion: creating new futures

The job of government is not simply to provide services or, indeed, civic goods or to create resilience in the face of change. The strategic challenge facing governments is greater even than those confronting global corporations of the scale of Microsoft or Siemens, Coca-Cola or GlaxoSmithKline, ExxonMobil or SinoPec. While the biggest challenges – climate change, energy insecurity, obesity, HIV-AIDS, demographic change, water shortages, terrorism, poverty – face corporations as they face governments, for corporations these challenges make up the operating environment in which they must find a way to thrive. It is not – fundamentally – the job of corporations to tackle these challenges, to make a better world, even though many will seek and will have a vital role to play in making it so. It is the job of governments not only to find ways of 'operating' in such futures, of building resilience for their nations, communities and sectors, but to have, and to achieve, ambitions to change the prevailing conditions for the better.

One aspect of strategic work is to understand how, for instance, a city will continue to thrive socially and economically in circumstances where water supplies are reduced to 20 per cent of current levels, or where more than 40 per cent of the working population is morbidly obese. This is the part of strategy work that equates to some extent to corporate strategy, which understands how the business will thrive in adverse futures where competitors, customers, suppliers and products have changed significantly. But another part of the work of strategy in the public domain is to understand how, in this case, the city can have abundant water, or how the city can have a population which is of a healthy weight, eating sensibly and taking exercise. In other words, it is the job of governments to choose a different future and the job of public strategy to realize a different future.

There are, of course, innumerable examples of private business and corporations, as well as of non-profit enterprises and charities that have changed the world and there are also plenty of examples of such businesses that set out to do so. Many of the 15th- and 16th-century European explorers were businessmen confident that the world would be changed by the products they would find and sell. The great railway expansion of the mid-19th century was fuelled by shareholder money and the remarkable vision that railways would change the world. Henry Dunant founded the Red Cross in 1863 and in doing so he, and the movement he founded, not only transformed the care and safety of victims of war, but also the provision of relief to those who suffer in peacetime disasters. Steve Jobs was the archetype of the visionary business leader, whose Apple corporation set out not simply to do computing differently, not only to change its organizational fortunes (which have not always fared well against Microsoft), but to change the way people listen to music, the way people communicate with each other and the way people use computing in their daily lives.

But not all businesses can or should work in the way that Apple works. Many simply need to make good shoes, and to compete effectively with other shoe manufacturers, or to make a breakfast cereal that no one needs to eat, and that is high in sugar and salt, but to make a good profit in doing so and to outsell its competitors. But governments and public organizations and social enterprises *all* need to work rather like Apple works and beyond that – to operate outside and beyond themselves, less concerned with their own organizational survival than with the difference – the public value – they create, and the way they change the world.

Consider the case of the European Union. This was conceived by Jean Monnet, Robert Schumann (respectively, the official in charge of France's national economic plan and the French foreign minister in the immediate post-war period) and others in the aftermath of the Second World War as a means of creating a supranational form of government that would so bind together the economic interests of European nations that war between them would become unthinkable. The scale of this ambition was so great that Monnet and Schumann and their successors adopted the approach of the Sun Tzu, the 5th-century BCE Chinese general (Sun Tzu 2006) seeking to extend the political project through a series of subtle steps, each one broadly acceptable, though if seen altogether likely to cause alarm among the publics of the larger European nations.

The public sphere can learn a great deal about organizational resilience and renewal, about the creation of value and about customer service from the private sphere. But because the business of public organizations is fundamentally different from the business of private firms it can be profoundly unhelpful if those leading public organizations lose sight of the greater public purposes that their organizations were called into existence to realize.

BOX 3.6 Building a new future for Europe – the Messina declaration

In 1951 the leaders of six European countries established, with the signing of the Treaty of Paris, the European Coal and Steel Community (ECSC). The Treaty, which established supranational authority over coal, coke, steel, iron ore and scrap and a court to settle disputes between member states, was explicitly a political endeavour to be achieved through economic means. After the wars of 1870–71, 1914–18 and 1939–45, there was a determination to build a European peace centred on Franco-German reconciliation. In 1954 measures to establish a European Defence Force stalled and, in June 1955, the foreign ministers of the six ECSC states met in Messina, Sicily to discuss how to proceed with the agenda of European integration: this resulted in the Messina declaration (Nugent 2006):

> The governments of the Federal Republic of Germany, Belgium, France, Italy, Luxembourg and the Netherlands believe the time has come to take a new step on the road of European construction. They are of the opinion that these objectives should be achieved first of all in the economic sphere. They believe that the establishment of a united Europe must be achieved through the development of common institutions, the progressive fusion of national economies, the creation of a common market, and the gradual harmonization of their social policies. Such an agenda seems indispensable to them if Europe is to preserve the standing which she has in the world, to restore her influence and her prestige, and to improve steadily the living standards of her population.

The declaration led to the Treaties of Rome, establishing in 1957 the European Economic Community and the Atomic Energy Community. A series of enlargements followed, beginning in 1973 with Denmark, the UK and Ireland, followed by the Maastricht Treaty in 1992 setting the foundations for monetary union and for a common foreign and security policy (Fontaine 2000). By 2013 the European Union had 28 member states.

The project has not been one of simply building the resilience of the European economies, though it has undoubtedly helped to do so; it has been a conscious if not always explicit strategy to create a new kind of jurisdictional entity, neither empire nor nation state, neither multilateral organization nor alliance, based upon a clear strategic vision.

The European Union relies for its survival on a continuing drive towards the achievement of strategic goals. When that momentum dissipates the EU tends to find itself in trouble. This was characterized (in a quote attributed to him) by Walter Hallstein, the European Commission's first President, as Europe being 'like a bicycle, it has to keep pedalling forwards, or it falls over'.

Chapter Four

Barriers to Strategic Thinking

Embracing uncertainty is central to strategic thinking, but is an unfamiliar skill for many. Uncertainty is often something we feel we need to resolve and remove. We make assumptions that narrow the range of uncertainty to something we can identify as risk, because we can, or believe we can, judge risk – we can identify and quantify it and put mitigations in place to help us to control it. Assumptions we make are helpful when we identify and state them, so they can be open to challenge, but strategy built on unstated assumptions that were once valid, but over time have become outdated is not a good basis for future strategy. In these cases our assumptions become so-called 'toxic' assumptions. The discipline of risk management has its own set of tools and techniques, yet those for uncertainty management are less familiar and, unlike risk which, rightly or wrongly, we tend to see as objective (Douglas Hubbard exposes our fallibilities in *The Failure of Risk Management* 2009), uncertainty involves judgement about the future – about yet-to-be-identified states.

The nature of government and public organizations conspires against acting strategically but at the same time rejects uncertainty. Voters expect elected officials to be authoritative and politicians find it hard to admit not knowing. Lines of accountability, up to politicians and senior officials and out to the public, users of services and private and non-profit sectors, can act as a brake on the innovation that creates public value. The relationship between officials and politicians can mean that alignment of outcomes with strategic intent isn't clear, and the political process can mean desired outcomes aren't identified or get lost in implementation. Applying principles of corporate strategy without adaption adds confusion too.

A particular obstacle is the difficulty in getting people to take enough interest in the future. Urgency is the enemy of importance and there is always an abundance of problems needing attention. This draws minds of politicians and officials away from the longer term. Playing in the human bias for the present (see pp. 101–2) creates a reinforcing loop that resists strategic thinking. In this chapter we examine this phenomenon, and the institutional arrangements that reinforce it.

Knowing what we don't know

In 1998 US Secretary for Defense William Cohen commissioned a bipartisan group chaired by Senators Gary Hart and Warren B. Rudman to look ahead to the issues that would shape US national security in the coming century, and make recommendations. The US Commission on National Security in the 21st Century, known as the Hart–Rudman Commission, made its final report in January 2001 – 12 days after President George W. Bush's administration had taken office. The Commission foresaw the possibility of attacks by non-state actors on US soil of the kind that took place on 11 September of that year on New York City and Washington, DC. Senators Hart and Rudman spent the period from January to June 2001 urging the Bush administration to accept its recommendations, and had meetings with Secretary for Defense Donald Rumsfeld, Secretary of State Colin Powell and National Security Advisor Condoleezza Rice. Recommendation number one in its final report (US Commission on National Security in the 21st Century, 1998–2001) read: 'The President should develop a comprehensive strategy to heighten America's ability to prevent and protect against all form of attacks on the homeland, and to respond to such attacks if prevention and protection fail.'

Any strategy process must make choices, which means privileging some evidence. The recommendation could have been discounted for a variety of legitimate reasons. Peter Schwartz, who advised the Commission, covered some of these in his book *Inevitable Surprises* (Schwartz 2004). Speaking to the London *Financial Times* newspaper in 2003 he said the Bush administration chose in its early months to focus not on terrorism, as the Commission recommended, but on ballistic missile defence and China. By definition, most of the possible futures developed will prove to be wrong, the fact that one turned out to be right was not surprising. 'The Commission's work ... did not prevent the attacks but they did contribute to the decisive speed and competence with which the US responded.'

A year later, in February 2002, Secretary for Defense Donald Rumsfeld made the following statement (restating the Johari self-awareness model from the 1950s) (Luft and Ingham 1955) at a press briefing: '[T]here are known knowns; there are things we know we know. We also know there are known unknowns; that is to say we know there are some things we do not know. But there are also unknown unknowns – the ones we don't know we don't know.'

Although the statement attracted derision at the time it's clear that understanding what we know and being aware of the limits of our knowledge is crucial to the ability to learn, to plan, to look out for the unexpected. The future is a known unknown that is itself filled with unknown unknowns. We cannot predict the future. Let's be thankful we can't. If we could predict the future, we could not change it, and changing the future is what public strategy it is all about.

People find it difficult to conjecture the idea of the unexpected side effects of sweeping change. We don't dismiss the idea of change but can't conceive of the changes in human behaviour that flow from the idea. Think of just one, refrigeration, which has changed eating habits, world trade, shopping, farming, work patterns, domestic life and threatened the ozone layer. It is these changes that have most significance for governments – behavioural change that policies aim to initiate, encourage or impede.

Why is it that we are able as individuals and as businesses and organizations and governments to embrace the concept of new technology, but at the same time struggle with the social and economic changes that flow from such technology? Why is it that even where we see change coming, we are so poor at seeing the *effects* of change? The problem isn't ignorance, it's the way human psychology deals with knowledge and our inability to understand the second order effects of system change. For now we'll look at five manifestations of this phenomenon:

- seeing problems through the 'lens of now'
- groupthink
- expert bias and the problem of prediction
- muddling through
- short termism.

These aren't wholly separate problems – each is mutually reinforcing. Recognition of them is the first step to being strategic.

The lens of now

As Bill Gates puts it, 'people often overestimate what will happen in the next two years and underestimate what will happen in ten' (Gates 1995: 316).

What will the world be like in 2030? We looked briefly in Chapter 1 at some of the typical forecasts of the future: more electronic surveillance, more genetic engineering; less commuting, reduced use of fossil fuels; more drought and flooding. Yet because such predictions look through the 'lens of now', we assume that the world will change in ways it is already changing. The one safe prediction is that it won't. History tells us that change happens in unpredictable ways, though too often what we understand as 'History' has been stripped of its contingency and presented as a settled panorama of events. Philip Roth in his novel The *Plot Against America* (Roth 2004: 113) refers to history as 'the relentless unforeseen': 'Turned wrong way round, the relentless unforeseen was what we schoolchildren studied as "History", harmless history where everything unexpected in its own time is chronicled on the page as inevitable. The terror of the unforeseen is what the science of history hides, turning a disaster into an epic.'

FIGURE 4.1   *The 'lens of now'*

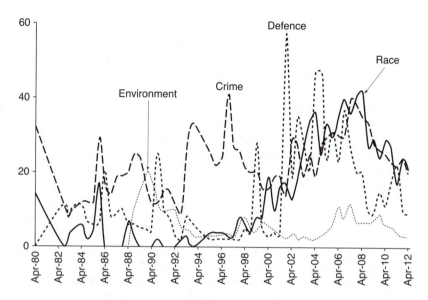

Source: Ipsos-Mori, *The Most Important Issues Facing Britain Today* (Ipsos-Mori 2013).

Research company Ipsos-Mori has been running a survey of public opinion on 'The Most Important Issues Facing Britain Today' since 1974, producing a monthly issues index from interviewing a representative sample of around a thousand adults aged 18 and over across Great Britain. In the above figure the vertical axis shows the percentage of the sample who have spontaneously raised the issue without prompting. We have omitted some of the dominating trends, like the economy, unemployment and inflation, as well as health and education. The figure shows the significant fluctuations in public concern about four issues: defence (which includes foreign affairs and international terrorism); race (which includes immigration); crime (which includes law and order, violence and vandalism); and the environment (which includes pollution). In each case it is relatively easy to identify 'triggers' which drove public concern – for instance, the first Gulf war increasing concern about defence issues in the early 1990s, and the terrorist attacks on New York in September 2001 again stimulating public concern which was then sustained for much of the following decade as the Iraq war and the Afghan war continued.

Without attempting here a detailed analysis of what prompted these or other spikes in public concern, the point is that the salience of events understandably influences public opinion. If we were to 'cut a slice' through Figure 4.1 in, say, April 1990, it would give a very different 'lens' on public concerns than the same lens in April 1991, or April 1997.

Politicians are required to respond to events, and to respond to public opinion. But politicians who focused only on issues of public concern would tend to always see issues through 'the lens of now'. Politicians – and others working in the public sphere – need to be able to see beyond the lens of now. They need to be able to think strategically, otherwise they risk making the assumption that issues of dominating concern in one year (whether that is acid rain or a Gulf war or a terrorist threat) will be of equal concern next year, or in five years' time. At the same time they need to continue working on issues that are no longer of public concern but that will re-remerge in five or ten years' time.

The tendency to identify the concerns of today as of abiding concern and to project them forward isn't 'wrong', but can be a trap because it limits our ability to think, plan and act in a way that helps us to respond to future change, let alone shape that change. Adding to our 'lens of now' problem is the way we look back and convince ourselves that we did, after all, foresee developments (or at least, that they were foreseeable): that banking crisis, that spike/slump in oil prices, that food shortage/food glut, the disruptive strength of those warlords we armed. Persuading ourselves that we foresaw concerns that emerged later can shut off the learning essential to adaptation. Nobel laureate Daniel Kahneman sums it up in this way: 'The idea that the future is unpredictable is undermined every day by the ease with which the past is explained' (Kahneman 2011: 218). The human mind creates plausible (and sometimes, implausible) narratives to connect point events and, because we can do that in retrospect, we acquire false confidence that we can also do it in prospect. After 9/11 it was considered that if one piece of information held by government had been passed to another person it could have been prevented. This is known as 'joining up the dots', yet four dots have 64 patterns and ten have 3.4 trillion (Lazaroff and Snowden 2006: 71). It is impossible until after the event to be certain of making the appropriate linkage of information.

Strategic governments do more than simply respond to the concerns of the day: they learn from what has happened in the past and what has happened elsewhere and adapt policies as a result. In this way they develop the capability to expect potential change in the future, and then spend time thinking, analysing, planning and, where necessary, acting to adopt the change. That is one important component of good government. As members of the public, we all are entitled to see things through the 'lens of now' and we are entitled to delude ourselves that we knew what was going to happen all along – but we are also entitled to expect our governments to do better.

Strategic thinking gives individuals, businesses, organizations and governments humility about the future that mitigates against seeing everything always and only through the lens of now. It sensitizes us to the signals the future gives us today.

Change takes place in ways that can be obvious or hidden. Much social and attitudinal change is gradual and it's only when looking back you can identify profound shifts in behaviour that seem to have happened overnight. What was normal suddenly seems abnormal. Driving under the influence of alcohol has been illegal in most countries for many years, yet until the mid-1980s people would 'take the chance' of a few drinks and hope not to be caught. Then, as if overnight, drinking and driving became socially unacceptable. Similarly, attitudes to speeding in some parts of the world are changing – at one time people would boast about how fast they drove, yet such bragging today is tantamount to threatening behaviour. And attitudes in some countries to smoking in offices or on public transport have changed to the extent that it no longer seems normal, as it once was. All these are examples of behaviour change policies, to denormalize tobacco use or raise awareness of the perception of risk to others from speeding. Other forms of change are seismic in their effect. The impact of the coordinated attacks on New York and Washington in 2001 (9/11) was obvious, immediate and profound, although the longer-term effects in terms of attitudes towards terrorism and towards the United States remain unclear.

Groupthink

Strategic thinking thrives on cognitive diversity – people who think differently from each other – but like any organization, the public sector is likely to be staffed by 'people who think like us'. The value organizations place on consistency, conformity, corporacy, the standardization of work or even strategic alignment itself, together with the need for people to achieve consensus and make decisions in groups, can predispose them to thinking similarly and being intolerant of those who don't.

The mental shortcuts we use to take the load off our effortful, conscious reasoning (Kahneman 2011: 24) extend to taking cues from wider collective intelligence by 'reading' what others like us are doing. This works well most of the time, where we are operating within and sharing the same context. We don't have to make the effort to remember what day to put the refuse out for collection, we see when others have; in countries or states that have alternate side parking (a traffic law that varies the side of a street people can park their cars) we don't have to know the day of the week or whether it's an odd or even date (depending on local regulations). We are prompted by what others do. If we see someone running to a bus stop we assume they have more information about the time of the next bus than we do. This is usually reliable, at least often enough to trump the effort of conscious reasoning, even taking into account the times it doesn't work, for example when our neighbours' habits don't take account of a change to the refuse collection day after a public holiday. In an individuated society we seek to find comfort in our actions by copying others around us.

Our social brains, optimized for social relations, are copying machines. We are wired to copy as an 'adaptive strategy' and we avoid the effort of reinventing what someone has already done. Copying strategies include copying the majority and copying successful individuals (Bentley *et al.* 2011: 29–31). Copying depends on visibility of the choices of others and number of choices (Bentley *et al.* 2011: 114). In situations where we can see the choices of only a few people and there are few options, we make effortful rational choices by weighing costs and benefits; where the choices are those many people are making and the options are limited our copying is 'directed' by friends; with many options and few people we make random guesses, but when we can see the choices of many people and there are multiple options we use 'undirected' copying. Popularity lists (rankings) that let us follow others are an example. These 'agents of conformity' mean popular songs become more popular and unpopular songs more unpopular when rankings are given than when people make choices independently (Salganik *et al.* 2006).

'Fitting in' is part and parcel of who we are and makes daily life easier but the 'Abilene Paradox' (Harvey 1974) shows that agreement can be a problem. Harvey uses an anecdote to illustrate our bias to fitting in with other people who are fitting in with us. A married couple hosting a visit by the wife's parents on a hot July afternoon in Texas travel fifty miles to a cafeteria in Abilene. The meal was poor and the journey hot, tiring and dusty. Reviewing the trip when they returned revealed that everyone would have preferred to carry on sitting on the back porch relaxing in front of the fan with cold lemonade playing dominoes, yet all had put aside their own views and preferences to be agreeable to a suggestion from the husband, who feared people might otherwise grow bored. The paradox is why everyone agreed to something none of them wanted to do. Harvey shows how this can happen in organizations when we do things we think are expected of us that no one wants. He states the paradox as 'organizations frequently take actions in contradiction to the data they have for dealing with problems and, as a result, compound their problems rather than solve them' (Harvey 1974: 69).

Harvey says that what Irving Janis (see later in this section) describes as examples of the conformity pressures known as groupthink are not the coercive effect of group pressures (group tyranny), but should be conceptualized as mismanaged agreement. Harvey opens up the possibility that individuals feel they are experiencing coercive conformity pressures when they are responding to the dynamics of mismanaged agreement. On this view it's the inability to manage agreement, not the inability to manage conflict, that's a major source of organization dysfunction. Individuals put aside private views perhaps to be seen as corporate or from fear of questioning a project the group is committed to. He cites the Watergate burglary in the United States in the 1970s (the administration's attempted cover-up of its involvement in breaking in to the national headquarters of its political rivals at the Watergate office complex in Washington, DC) where a wide assortment of people went along with something they knew was stupid and illegal. He identifies the anxiety people suffer when they think about acting in accordance with their beliefs, which he calls the Hamlet syndrome, because they cannot make up their mind whether to suffer in silence or to oppose. Do people go along with what they think of as nonsense or make a report the president may not like to hear? This 'action anxiety' is reinforced by negative fantasies about what will happen if they act sensibly. Existential risk, separation, alienation and 'loneliness ostracism' are powerful disincentives when people have a fundamental need to be connected, engaged and to relate. They do not want to be denounced as disloyal, or be seen as not a team player. Much behaviour within an organization thought of as reflecting the tyranny of conformity pressures is really an expression of collective anxiety inhibiting individual action.

Coupled with this psychological drive to fit in there's a wider social pressure to conform. In some circumstances this can be so powerful that we will even deny the evidence of our own eyes in favour of the view of the group. Asch looked at how social forces constrain people's opinions (Asch 1955) and the extent to which the views of authority figures or peers would change opinion even when no arguments were provided. In Asch's study, groups of seven to nine people included one experimental subject; the rest of the group in turn identified lines of clearly different lengths as the same length before the subject gave their opinion. The subject could act independently, repudiating the majority or go along with the majority but repudiate their own senses. In ordinary circumstances individuals would make mistakes less than 1 per cent of the time but under group pressure accepted the wrong judgements of the group in 36.8 per cent of cases. Varying the size of the group showed the influence of group pressure grew markedly up to a group size of three, but increasing the group size to fifteen added little to the overall effect. Asch concluded that consensus is an indispensable condition for life in society but that when produced by conformity it pollutes the social process.

Turning this learning in on ourselves, the authors and readers of this book risk being unrepresentative members of a small, untypical group. Research by a team from the University of British Colombia (Henrich *et al.* 2010) suggests behavioural experimenters assume their findings are of universal application, though the subjects of their experiments are often educated students in rich, Western, industrialized countries. They found 96 per cent of psychological experiments take place in countries with only 12 per cent of the world's population, who could be outliers.

Research has assumed aspects of behaviour are hardwired functions of the human brain common to everyone, without testing how strong an influence culture might be.

Groupthink is associated with the work of Irving Janis who studied the tendency of small decision-making groups to try to minimize conflict and reach consensus without sufficiently testing, analysing, and evaluating their ideas. His work (Janis 1972, 1982) suggested that pressures for consensus restrict the thinking of the group, bias its analysis, promote simplistic and stereotyped thinking, and stifle individual creative and independent thought. He looked at case studies of the Bay of Pigs invasion, Pearl Harbor, and the Korean War, counterpointing these with examples which avoided groupthink (the Cuban Missile Crisis and the Marshall Plan).

William Safire points out (Safire 2004) that it was William H. Whyte who originally coined the term groupthink in 1952 (Whyte 1952) and that it now means 'the result of successful pressure to conform', more pejorative than 'conventional wisdom', a 1958 coinage of the economist John Kenneth Galbraith, based on 'received wisdom', in turn rooted in 'received custom', a 1382 church term for the teaching of tradition. Whyte identified the difference between instinctive and rationalized conformity. He later wrote, in *The Organization Man* (Whyte 1956) of the role of large corporations in subordinating the individuality of employees to conform to the demands of corporations in return for loyalty, security and belonging.

Whyte offers his working definition of groupthink as *rationalized* conformity which holds that group values are not only expedient but right and good as well, differentiating it from *instinctive* conformity ('a perennial failing of mankind'). He argued against what he saw as the deification of group harmony and social engineering that manipulated the individual into the group role in a country where 'individualism' – independence and self-reliance – had been the watchword for three centuries. He recognized that we have had to learn how to get along in groups but feared the view that the individual himself had no meaning – except as a member of a group. Black and white was no longer determined by fixed precepts but by what the group thinks.

Whyte was writing following the Second World War, perhaps trying to make sense of the way society was developing in peacetime, where large corporates were taking the place of the armed forces in which individualism was subservient to clear goals, and he refers to society at that time as 'bewildering'.

Janis applies the term groupthink to a small, cohesive group striving for consensus in specific, narrow, circumstances. On this definition there's little evidence that groupthink played a role in the decision to invade Iraq (Hutter 2009) even though it may have been present in the intelligence community looking for evidence of WMD.

BOX 4.1 Weapons of mass destruction: groupthink in action?

One way of justifying the decision to invade Iraq in 2003 was that deci-sion-makers in the US and UK governments convinced themselves of the existence of an Iraqi programme to develop chemical, biological and nuclear weapons. The results of the post-invasion search conducted by the Iraq Survey Group largely discredited this. Leaving aside whether Saddam Hussein had sent misleading signals about concealing weapons of mass destruction to confuse his opponents, two 2004 inquiries identified group-think as a factor in believing there was a programme to develop and deploy weapons of mass destruction, one in the US, the *Report of the Select Committee on Intelligence on the U.S. Intelligence Community's Prewar Intelligence Assessments on Iraq* (United States Senate 2004) and another in the UK, the *Review of Intelligence on Weapons of Mass Destruction* (House of Commons 2004). The UK review said:

> There is also the risk of 'group think' – the development of a 'prevail-ing wisdom'. Well-developed imagination at all stages of the intelli-gence process is required to overcome preconceptions. There is a case for encouraging it by providing for structured challenge, with estab-lished methods and procedures, often described as a 'Devil's advocate' or a 'red-teaming' approach. This may also assist in countering another danger: when problems are many and diverse, on any one of them the number of experts can be dangerously small, and individual, possibly idiosyncratic, views may pass unchallenged.

Announcing the findings of the US Senate inquiry Senator Pat Roberts, chairman of Senate Intelligence, told the Washington press corps 'that the intelligence community was suffering from what we call a collective groupthink ... [T]his groupthink also extended to our allies and to the United Nations.'

In ordinary language people use the term groupthink more indiscrim-inately than Janis, to cover any circumstances where there's been no process for taking account of diverse opinion whether through struc-tured challenge or expecting all members of the group to perform a role as 'critical evaluators' (Janis 1982: 172) though not necessarily diverse, or appointing a couple of group members as devil's advocates (Janis 1982: 267). McQueen (2005) questions whether a small cohesive group must be present in order for pressures of concurrence to arise. In her study of the application of the groupthink model to the case of US deci-sion-making leading up to the invasion of Iraq, McQueen highlights several elements of Janis's theory that require further analysis and perhaps even re-evaluation (McQueen 2005: 72). McQueen also identi-fies worst-case thinking as a contributor. 'Entertaining worst-case scenarios and planning for the worst can be a useful exercise in any decision-making setting. Indeed, considering all alternatives is a central means of preventing the occurrence of groupthink. However, the dangers of acting upon worst-case thinking – a prospect that the United States is uniquely able to contemplate due to its unparalleled status on the world stage – are extremely serious' (McQueen 2005: 73). 't Hart (1994) identifies three group processes that many of Janis's preconditions for groupthink trigger and proposes adding to these by looking beyond the small group making the decision and adding the broader group context in which the decision groups operate: 'it is crucial to understand groupthink as a contextual phenomenon i.e. viewing group decision making in its wider intergroup, organizational and political context' ('t Hart 1994: 277).

An early example of groupthink in a wider group than those analysed by Janis appears in Han Christian Andersen's classic story of 'The Emperor's New Clothes', where the emperor, his advisors and his subjects convinced themselves that the emperor wore splendid clothes when he was, in fact, naked. In Andersen's story 'groupthink' was exacerbated by the fear of being branded naïve or ignorant if one saw his suit for what it was, and it was encouraged by the reward of being regarded as wise for failing to see (or pretending) that it did not exist. It took a 'naïve' child to challenge the perceived wisdom. The child was able to offer challenge and surface and expose the assumptions that the crowd at the emperor's parade shared.

Asch's experiments revealing strong pressures for conformity took place in the 1950s. If today we are more inclined to celebrate individuality (when social media fulfil, in new forms, innate needs for connectedness) we might wonder whether we would see the same today. But our look at 'directed' copying (in the world of music, with social feedback from download rankings influencing choice) suggests our disposition for taking cues from social norms (collective intelligence) is still prevalent. In *The Blunders of our Governments* (King and Crewe 2013) the authors tip their hats to many transforming successes of government strategy but identify contemporary examples of groupthink ('inner circles') and the role of groupthink's near neighbour 'cultural disconnect' in policy disasters, resulting not just in soaring costs but unquantifiable human misery.

Wishful thinking strategy, where the larger group, and perhaps the whole organization, hopes a particular course will deliver change (for example, that if government provides its services online, people will use them and it can make savings by closing its traditional channels to its users), may also happen because the small 'in group', working within the dynamics of a much wider group, as 't Hart envisages, avoids structured challenge and doesn't explore and understand the views of opponents, and is predisposed to stereotyping them.

This is likely if wishful thinking leads to laziness or complacency so that a planned intervention doesn't take account of people's preferences. Think of those encouraged or pressured to use digital services. If they are doubtful – or fearful – about the need for this at the outset then the intervention and even offers of free devices might leave them not just unmoved but actually angry or repelled. 'I meet my friends while queuing at the post office for my pension' or 'How can they waste all this money'. Initiatives designed to offer convenience and save money by designing online government services sometimes took this 'build it and they will come' approach, yet making services available online didn't mean people would use them. Preferences behind current behaviour need to be understood before designing interventions that rely on changed behaviour. Identifying user preferences and barriers brings the technique of consumer insight and behavioural science to strategy. For example an initial assumption might be to improve the quality of the food to increase take-up of school meals (in pursuit of a wider outcome), but insight might show that children seek companionship in their break times, and that it is the inability to sit with friends that's the barrier to take-up. That would make the initial assumption a toxic one, because you might spend money on implementing a strategy that would not contribute to the desired outcome.

An issue related to groupthink is 'wilful blindness' discussed by Margaret Heffernan in her book of the same name (Heffernan 2011). In the 2006 case of the US Government vs Enron, the presiding judge instructed the jurors to take account of the concept of wilful blindness as they reached their verdict about whether the chief executives of the disgraced energy corporation were guilty. If they failed to observe the corruption which was unfolding before their very eyes – 'not knowing' was no defence. Heffernan shows human nature makes us prone to wilful blindness. Taught from infancy to obey authority, and absorbing the importance of selective vision as a key social skill, humans exacerbate their tendency to become institutionalized by joining organizations run by like-minded people.

Ackoff makes the same point in his introduction to the Hopper brothers' *The Puritan Gift* (2009). 'We learn by identifying mistakes and correcting them. It is not sinful to be wrong but it is sinful to fail to learn from it. There are two kinds of error: those of commission, doing something that should not be done, and those of omission, not doing something that should be done. The latter are much more serious than the former. Most corporate failures are due to errors of omission. A firm that records only mistakes of commission (as almost all do) and punishes them (as most do) creates an environment in which the best way to retain one's job is to do as little as possible, preferably nothing … But progress is not possible without change' (Hopper and Hopper 2009: xii).

How do we reduce the risk of groupthink? Few of us are potential geniuses, mavericks willing to risk sustained ridicule by vested interests. Individualism courts ambiguity – it can be pejorative: 'he was a loner' (someone who didn't fit in) or the heroic 'whistleblower', but most people like consensus even in societies that value individualism and the frontier spirit. Whyte says (Whyte 1952) the answer is not a return to a 'rugged individualism' that never was. One mitigation is self-awareness of our predisposition for the company of like-minded people to agree with each other (because they work in the same or partnering organizations). Janis suggests that awareness of the shared illusions, rationalizations and other symptoms fostered by the interaction of small groups may curtail the influence of groupthink in policy-making groups (Janis 1982: 276). This extends to questioning our satisfaction with consensus and making an effort to introduce diversity into our thinking, recognizing that working with strangers is effortful and demands skills. Whyte recommends a conscious, deliberate effort by the organization not only to accommodate dissent but to encourage it. Harvey recommends confrontation in a group setting, gathering organization members who are key figures in the problem and its solution into a group setting. Formalizing and legitimizing the role of challenge (Butler, Whyte, Janis) becomes important as does exposing the thinking beyond a small group – possibly to strangers or diverse crowds as Surowiecki recommends (Surowiecki 2005). In the particular circumstances of small-group decision-making, Janis also recommends the holding of a second-chance meeting after a preliminary consensus has been reached. 'To encourage members to reveal vague forebodings, it might not be a bad idea for the "second-chance" meeting to take place in a more relaxed atmosphere far from the executive suite' (Janis 1982: 271). Scenarios (Chapter 5) also provide a safe harbour for thinking the unthinkable in an organization.

Lack of challenge and unquestioned assumptions can cause particular problems in a world of experts.

Expert bias and the problem of prediction

One reason the Bush administration may have de-prioritized the Hart–Rudman Commission's recommendation to prepare for asymmetric threats on the homeland might have been that the administration decided to focus on security threats from states, because that favoured its particular expertise-set. We, perhaps unconsciously, filter or favour solutions that fit our expertise. 'Experts will always disagree with generalisations as experts should. Fine grained analysis is the expert's prerogative. However, the more fine-grained the expert analysis, the more difficult it may be to see an overall pattern: it cannot be other than the view from close up. This will inevitably lead some to the conclusion that no pattern exists, but I believe this to be a mistake. One has to stand back in order to see patterns at all: there is a "necessary distance" for such pattern recognition to work' (McGilchrist 2009: 241). Because we are 'pattern-matchers', finding a match with our expertise is 'good enough' – we stop pattern-matching as soon as we see a match, rather than continuing to search for other, more optimal, matches. Simon (Simon 1997) showed that human beings lack the cognitive resources to optimize.

All of us make what prove, with the benefit of hindsight, to be misjudgements. What may be less forgivable is if there is insufficient open-mindedness to the new and unexpected.

Surowiecki (Surowiecki 2005) finds that a diverse collection of independent people are likely to make some decisions and predictions better than individuals or experts. For reasons we've shown, diversity is hard to find in organizations that self-select for particular staff and have an emphasis on conformity and a bias for action (a corporate bias in tension with the individual's fear of action as we saw in the Abilene Paradox). Richard Sennett (Sennett 2012) identifies that living with people who differ racially, religiously or economically is the most urgent challenge facing civil society today, and it may involve working with people you don't understand and don't like. These essential forms of cooperation with strangers represent a skill or craft that Sennett says we must learn.

Expert opinion is helpful if it is relevant. If we are concerned about a leaky radiator we seek the advice of a plumber, not a heart surgeon; if the brakes don't work properly on our car we take it to a garage mechanic, not to a psychiatrist. But even relevant analytical expertise comes with its own problems. Philip Tetlock showed that the political and economic predictions of experts were only slightly more accurate than chance, and worse than algorithms. He observed: 'Researchers have shown that experts, from diverse professions, can talk themselves into believing they can do things they manifestly cannot. Experts frequently seem unaware of how quickly they reach the point of diminishing marginal returns for knowledge when they try to predict outcomes with large stochastic components: from recidivism among criminals to the performance of financial markets. Beyond a stark minimum, subject matter expertise in world politics translates less into forecasting accuracy than it does into overconfidence (and the ability to spin elaborate tapestries of reasons for expecting "favourite" outcomes)' (Tetlock 2005: 161). Tetlock found that experts are led astray by how they think, not what they believe. He likened them to the 'hedgehogs' (from philosopher Isaiah Berlin's essay *The Hedgehog and The Fox* 1953) who know one big thing and see the world in terms of a single idea and interpret all events through this framework. As the saying goes 'to a man with a hammer, everything is a nail' (variously attributed, including Maslow 1966).

Let's take the example of oil market experts. The increase in the price of a barrel of oil from \$23 in early 2000 to \$56 by early 2007 suggested a peak of around $80 in the period 2008–12; few if any experts thought the price would rise beyond $100 a barrel. Indeed, the US Department of Energy's own independent expert panel made the following forecast in mid-2003: 'From anticipated high levels throughout 2003, oil prices are projected to decline significantly to $23.27 in 2005, before rising by about 0.7 per cent per year to $26.57 in 2025' (Energy Information Administration 2003).

The precision here ('26 dollars *and 57 cents* in 2025') adds spurious authority to an inaccurate forecast. By July 2008 the price of a barrel of oil stood at $147 a barrel and global inflation soared as the price of nitrates for food production as well as energy costs for production and transportation of raw materials and finished goods spiralled. Just six months after the forecast the price fell, and since 2008 prices have fluctuated.

Charles Manski (Manski 2003) calls this phenomenon *The Law of Decreasing Credibility*: 'The credibility of inference decreases with the strength of the assumptions maintained.'

Understandably, oil companies will need a planning assumption to use in business cases to test for returns of investment and how to prioritize the allocation of capital. But which expert should a government ask for a forecast of the price of a barrel of oil in 2020, let alone 2025? Oil experts? Economists? Political scientists? Russia-watchers or Gulf-watchers? Arctic experts or wind turbine manufacturers? A long-distance lorry driver or a greengrocer?

The answer, of course, is all of them.

Broad and diverse judgement counters expert bias, groupthink and lens of now thinking. The problem with professional expertise is less the 'lens of now' – many experts are comfortable making long-range forecasts in their field, and while their forecasts are often influenced by the patterns of evidence with which they are intimately familiar, this can sometimes constrain imagination and reject what doesn't fit that worldview. Similarly, the need for focus can exclude peripheral vision necessary for situational awareness.

There's a range of expert prophecies notorious for being wrong (even if some of the best known prove to be anecdotal), including: the view in the 1950s that the UK would never need more than half a dozen computers to take care of all the calculations the UK would ever need; that heavier than air flying machines were impossible; that France had no need of the telephone because it had plenty of messenger boys. Far from helping judgement, the *professional lens* or professional bias can distort the analysis and judgement of highly intelligent and successful people: microeconomists tend to see the world through a microeconomic lens, lawyers through a legal lens, IT experts through an IT lens and so on: 'Individual differences in styles of reasoning among experts parallel those documented in other populations of human beings. Whatever label we place on these individual differences … a pattern emerges. Across several samples and tasks, people who value closure and simplicity are less accurate in complex social perception tasks and more susceptible to over-confidence, hindsight and belief perseverance effects' (Tetlock 2005: 162).

Increasing specialism is a response to greater complication but can lead to trend-based knowledge and a familiarity with historical patterns being coupled with lack of challenge, groupthink, and professional rein-forcement. This is one reason why hospital managers might say 'the neurosurgeons will oppose this, but the anaesthetists will be up for it', or the Defence Department can be confident that the Navy will favour a particular proposal while the Air Force will bitterly oppose it, even where the proposal is apparently neutral in its effect on the two services. Different professions see things in different ways. Within government departments this tendency can be reinforced by the way 'in-house' analytical advice is organized. Problems may arise when particular professions (natural scientists versus social researchers, for instance, or lawyers versus marketing experts) feel no need of evidence and analysis from other disciplines, even though combining a range of evidence and techniques gives a more robust basis for decisions. Politicians, typically from a different professional background and exposed to a wide range of evidence beyond that of their ministries, agencies and city authorities, can usually see that the world doesn't fit one particular model.

Often breakthroughs come from interdisciplinarity, or 'mashing up' disciplines where an expert applies the techniques or findings from one discipline to another. Transferring from one discipline to another can be uncomfortable for the expert because they will be seen as 'alien' – not 'real'. The biologist may be doubtful of the academic qualifications of the psychologist, however impressive they are. We're back to Tetlock again, but this time we are seeking his (Berlin's) 'foxes', who know lots of little things. The UK's Foresight Programme, whose role is to help government think systematically about the future, synthesizes evidence from as many as 80 scientists from narrow specialisms, all speaking different expert languages (and perhaps different languages) to inform governments on future strategies for things like obesity, flooding or the future of identity. Retailers use innovation in developing their products – for instance, 'cook–chill meals' or machine washable wool suits. One major UK retailer regularly exposes its staff working in one area to other areas: as a result people working in the food division, who were wrestling with consistency in hand buttered bread for its new range of ready-made sand-wiches (itself an innovation), realized on a visit to a clothing factory that the silk screen printing machines could be used to butter bread.

The field of behavioural economics offers the prospect of bringing together several different professional lenses in a way that should be help-ful to those developing strategy. 'Standard economics adopted a set of assumptions about our economic instincts for, primarily, mathematical convenience. The truth is that orthodox economics assumes that people are independent, rational, selfish materialists because it makes it easier to do the sums when you try to add all the people and firms together to get a complete picture of the economy ... In recent times, however, some researchers, including psychologists, sociologists and economists, have begun to examine our economic instincts scientifically ... What distinguishes behavioural economists from traditional economists is not expertise or technical sophistication, but their scientific approach' (Lunn 2008: 22–3).

Experts, whether economists or from other professional backgrounds, matter. But we need to challenge the orthodoxy of expert advice and ensure that expert advice itself challenges received orthodoxies. At its best, expertise offers

- challenge
- understanding of patterns of evidence
- understanding of the range of evidence
- understanding of potential future trends
- understanding of potential future counter-trends
- diversity of professional opinion.

Muddling through

Some politicians and some countries adopt a political process that is consciously non-strategic, where decision-making relies on a process of identifying existing problems and seeking consensus as to their solution – or 'muddling through'. Germany and Japan, for instance, tend to adopt a consensual, problem-solving approach to government, and broadly reject strategic, visionary approaches. They have a strong understanding of the 'wickedness' of problems. This inevitably raises questions about the real value of strategy. If strategy does not correlate with success, is it worth doing at all?

Fifty years ago Charles Lindblom (Lindblom 1959) observed that incrementalism was dominant in policy-making, and concluded there must be a reason it was prevalent and gave this 'muddling through' approach the status of a science which he argued was more effective than the scientific rational approach. He described the two different forms of policy-making as the Rational-Comprehensive (or 'Root') method, and the Successive Limited Comparisons (or 'Branch') method.

In Lindblom's *The Science of Muddling Through* (1959) he described and compared the strategic method (which he called 'root'), which he considered unachievable, with the pragmatic 'muddling through' approach (which he called 'branch') which he said was what governments tended to adopt in practice, whether they wanted to or not.

Rational-comprehensive (Root) [entails]....
Clarification of values or objectives distinct from and usually prereq-
uisite to empirical analysis of alternative policies ... Policy-formula-
tion is therefore approached through means–end analysis: First the
ends are isolated, then the means to achieve them are sought ... The
test of a 'good' policy is that it can be shown to be the most appropriate means to desired ends ... Analysis is comprehensive; every
important relevant factor is taken into account ... Theory is often
heavily relied upon
... [whereas in] ...
Successive Limited Comparisons (Branch)
Selection of value goals and empirical analysis of the needed action
are not distinct from one another but are closely intertwined ... Since
means and ends are not distinct, means–end analysis is often inappropriate or limited ... The test of a 'good' policy is typically that
various analysts find themselves directly agreeing on a policy (without their agreeing that it is the most appropriate means to an agreed
objective) ... Analysis is drastically limited:

- Important possible outcomes are neglected
- Important possible alternative potential policies are neglected
- Important affected values are neglected ...

A succession of comparisons greatly reduces or eliminates reliance on
theory. (Lindblom 1959: 81)

Lindblom's analysis was influential. He questioned the way policy-
makers tried to use a linear, rational approach to produce policy solutions to complex problems. 'For complex problems, the first of these two
approaches is of course impossible. Although such an approach can be
described, it cannot be practiced except for relatively simple problems
and even then only in a somewhat modified form. It assumes intellectual
capacities and sources of information that men simply do not possess,
and it is even more absurd as an approach to policy when the time and
money that can be allocated to a policy problem is limited, as is always
the case' (Lindblom 1959: 80).

In many ways Lindblom was identifying that policy-makers were dealing with complex adaptive systems where, as Capra says, 'A machine can
be controlled, according to the systemic understanding of life, but a system
can only be disturbed' (Capra 2002: 98). Lindblom's argument was that
you cannot model all the variables in an economic system and a policy that
changed one variable for the better (inflation) may have the unintended
effect of making another variable worse (unemployment). And when
applied to social policy he thought it difficult to rank competing values, for
example, whether you site social housing in one area or another. But
Lindblom did not explicitly distinguish between implementation of

policies, where one might experiment, on the one hand, and having a prior, clear, strategic intent on the other.

Lindblom maintained that a goal-oriented (or 'Root') method is *'for complex problems … impossible'*. But we need to consider the counter-argument, that goal-oriented policy-making – or strategy – is most required when working with complex problems. Because observations show that governments tend to muddle through doesn't imply they have rejected a strategic approach or that such an approach is impossible. It may just show that strategic approaches are thin on the ground. In other words, Lindblom's work in this area may best be understood as descriptive rather than prescriptive.

The choice for governments is not *between* problem-solving and identifying and pursuing desired outcomes (that is, acting strategically); the choice is between *only* problem-solving (as Lindblom recognized, common), or understanding the *dilemmas* that societies face and adopting both a goal-seeking and problem-solving approach. Governments have a bias towards problem-solving as Lindblom observes, but governments can do better than the successive limited comparison method when they adopt or supplement incremental analysis with a strategic approach.

In revisiting the topic in 1979 Lindblom acknowledged that 'the corrective to muddling through is not the suppression or neglect of incremental analysis, which remains necessary and useful … but the supplementation of incremental analysis by broad ranging, often highly speculative, and sometimes utopian thinking about directions and possible features, near and far in time' (Lindblom 1979: 522).

In 1972 Niles Eldredge and Stephen J. Gould noted 'punctuated equilibrium' in biology; long periods of stasis punctuated by step change, which Baumgartner and Jones applied to public policy in 1993. What is it that punctuates equilibrium in public policy? A 'bold and stretching' vision (Bichard 1999 and Dowdy 2000), 'a big hairy audacious goal' (Collins and Porras 1994) plus the determination afforded by robust plans to carry it through? Some social problems demand bold vision rather than incrementalism. Martin Luther King, Jr. opposed gradualism as a method of eliminating racial segregation. The US government was seen as procrastinating in its slow approach to racial integration. King said in 1963 'This is no time to engage in the luxury of cooling off or to take the tranquilizing drug of gradualism. Now is the time to make real the promises of democracy' (King 1963).

One might expect times of crisis to induce in governments their most extreme reflex mode, seeking to solve problems with little analysis or concern for the long term and simply trying to get through the exigencies of another day. This behaviour would be consistent with Lindblom's thesis. Yet President Franklin Delano Roosevelt's 1933 New Deal, the 1942 UK Beveridge Report and the 1948 Marshall Plan are all examples

BOX 4.2 German reunification: a case of muddling through?

The German economy has been the powerhouse of European growth for more than half a century. Although the German economy contracted by 4.7 per cent in 2009, it grew by 3.6 per cent in 2010 and though it fell back to 0.7 per cent in 2012 it was still the strongest performer in the major Eurozone economies. Yet Germany continues to experience post-reunification economic and social problems (OECD 2013).

There was a rapid improvement in economic performance of the eastern Länder in the five years following reunification, with per capita GDP increasing from 43 per cent to 67 per cent of that of the western Länder by 1995. But since then progress has been slow, with per capita GDP edging up to just over 70 per cent of that of the western Länder by 2009.

While the policy of reunification was bold and imaginative on one level, it was largely incremental in its execution. Measures were taken to respond to problems as they arose, rather than anticipated and planned for. In 2009 unemployment stood at 15 per cent in the eastern Länder, about twice as high as the rate in the western Länder.

Could the Federal German Government have adopted a different and more successful approach? Perhaps, according to Joachim Ragnitz (Ragnitz 2009):

> In order to explain the deficits of the 'economic reconstruction of the east'… it is necessary to look at the strategic decisions which were taken in the early 1990s. In doing so, the aim is not to denounce these political decisions. It is not only futile to argue about what could have been done differently – one also has to consider that many of the decisions at the time had to be taken under time pressure and without recourse to historical experiences or access to empirical economic research. In this respect, it was inevitable that developments initiated at the time appear problematic.

Ragnitz suggests that the immediacy of the crisis and opportunity presented by the collapse of the Soviet Union meant that decisions were taken that were almost inevitably incremental in nature. Lindblom would argue that this was the only realistic approach available to the German government. But other lessons from history suggest that a more strategic approach would have been possible, and that it might have yielded better results. The German predisposition to incrementalism almost certainly played a part in reaching the current position, with a strong German economy yet with persistent problems in the eastern Länder.

of long-term, comprehensive thinking produced under pressure, at pace and, on the face of it, at times when a scramble to deal with immediate problems would be forgivable. Each case offered a way through

---

BOX 4.3   The Beveridge report: goal-oriented policy-making

Sir William Beveridge, an academic and public administrator, was appointed in 1941 to chair the wartime Inter-departmental Committee on Social Insurance and Allied Services by the UK wartime coalition government. The Beveridge report, published in December 1942 in the midst of war, set out a bold vision of the future:

> The first principle is that any proposals for the future, while they should use to the full the experience gathered in the past, should not be restricted by consideration of sectional interests established in the obtaining of that experience. Now, when the war is abolishing landmarks of every kind, is the opportunity for using experience in a clear field. A revolutionary moment in the world's history is a time for revolutions, not for patching.
>
> The second principle is that organization of social insurance should be treated as one part only of a comprehensive policy of social progress. Social insurance fully developed may provide income security; it is an attack upon Want. But Want is one only of five giants on the road of reconstruction and in some ways the easiest to attack. The others are Disease, Ignorance, Squalor and Idleness.
>
> The third principle is that social security must be achieved by co-operation between the State and the individual. The State should offer security for service and contribution. The State in organising security should not stifle incentive, opportunity, responsibility; in establishing a national minimum, it should leave room and encouragement for

$\rightarrow$

---

profound and complex problems by setting ambitious goals. There were inevitably aspects of 'muddling through' in the implementation of all, but fundamentally each of these programmes entailed a strategic process of setting a vision and set of desired outcomes.

Why does this happen? Why is it that when governments have the time to gather analysis, to consider it, to think of the long term, to engage widely and offer contrasting visions of the future, to plan and act to achieve desired outcomes, they rarely do? Instead they lapse into 'casework', into waiting for problems to arise and dealing with them as best they can: they 'stick to the knitting'; they muddle through. Yet when an emergency strikes, when backs are up against the wall, when everything seems about to fall apart, governments seem to be required in some way to consider first principles. They begin to ask themselves: *what do we really believe (as a political party, as a government, as a community, a nation)? What is it that we stand for? What is our real aim? Why are we here at all?* The act of asking these questions brings about a further

→

voluntary action by each individual to provide more than that minimum for himself and his family.

Beveridge recognized that the moment of crisis in the midst of war was also the moment for strategic vision:

There are difficulties in planning reconstruction of the social services during the height of war, but there are also advantages in doing so. The prevention of want and the diminution and relief of disease – the special aim of the social services – are in fact a common interest of all citizens. It may be possible to secure a keener realisation of that fact in war than in peace, because war breeds national unity. It may be possible, through sense of national unity and readiness to sacrifice personal interests to the common cause, to bring about changes which, when they are made, will be accepted on all hands as advances, but which it might be difficult to make at other times. (Beveridge 1942)

The Beveridge report epitomized the strategic approach to policy-making. Harold Wilson, later to become UK Prime Minister, worked with Beveridge as a researcher. He had this to say of the Beveridge report: 'They underestimated their Beveridge ... He had presented his detractors with a highly embarrassing, forward-looking report, rapidly accepted as a blueprint for post-war Britain. It was seized on in Parliament. He became, for the first time, not a Whitehall expert, but a national figure, in some way the harbinger of the kind of postwar world people wanted to see. Public opinion forced the adoption of his report by Parliament' (Wilson 1986).

requirement: to test the assumptions that underpin these beliefs, to seek evidence, to consider different potential futures and to construct a vision that the party, the government, the community or nation can share.

It is generally easier for a large number of people to work towards a desired outcome than to ask them to decide between options to solve a problem, particularly when a population is enduring an economic crisis, a war or grappling with post-conflict recovery.

Meeting the needs of citizens depends on the interplay of the state, civil society, family and the market. In the UK it was not until the 1940s that public services and welfare provision moved away from a fragmented locally-based system towards a core function of the central state. Municipal and voluntary insurance schemes predominated until then, with services such as basic utilities funded through local taxation or contribution schemes. The Beveridge Report was a reaction to this (dovetailing with Keynesian economic orthodoxy which signalled a shift from *laissez faire* towards central demand management).

Although Beveridge expressed the role of the state in welfare in outcome terms in tackling the 'Five Giants' (Want; Disease; Ignorance; Squalor; Idleness) the post-war UK Labour government regarded the state as the main instrument of social change in the post-war vogue for central planning. It used its mobilizing capacity for delivery, offering an input guarantee not an outcomes guarantee, with universal access on the basis of citizenship funded by national taxation. The most effective mechanisms through which to deliver core services were seen as central Departments, elected local authorities and the new National Health Service. This administrative model represented a deliberate shift from the voluntary, localized and piecemeal organization of welfare provision in the 19th and early 20th centuries. It was taken for granted that the state had the dominant role as both funder and provider of services.

Seven years later Beveridge criticized the implementation of the Welfare State in his 1948 report on voluntary services. He was alarmed at its bureaucratic nature and the fact that people saw volunteering as unnecessary because of state welfare, but he was met with silence.

Short-termism

Electoral cycles, the demands of legislatures, the pressures of the media, the whims of presidents and prime ministers and mayors inclined to 'shuffle their teams' and move people into new jobs – all of these combine to pull politicians towards seeking 'quick wins' and 'visible results'. This makes it hard to find the space to develop strategy, let alone make the case for policies that will be resilient over the long term. Public officials are good at getting on with the activity at hand – dealing with casework, managing the budget, drafting the legislation – rather than planning for the future or in making sure that the plans are well executed and achieve desired outcomes. But better educated children, a healthier population, a more skilled workforce, a more sustainable economy – all of these are the work of decades, even of generations. It is hard to be strategic, to look to the long term to achieve those long-term outcomes if the system in which politicians work is itself an obstacle to achieving long-term change.

If all this sounds disheartening, don't worry. You don't have to fix these structural obstacles before you can be strategic if you recognize the constraints and difficulties in your way. You can quietly ask questions that challenge muddling through, with the confidence of knowing how public strategy should work in an ideal world. Chapter 5 outlines methods and approaches to help strategic thinking, even in difficult circumstances.

Personalities, agendas, competing institutions and parties are important in the world of politics, and can obscure or displace strategic intent.

Politicians who first entered politics to bring about change have to protect the interests of their immediate supporters who often have as much or more to lose than the politician. Politicians can be allergic to certain approaches to strategy and – rightly – detest jargon. Officials can all too easily interpret a politician's preoccupation with immediate problems, demands for quick wins and suspicion of the language and methods of strategy as a lack of interest in strategy. Officials will pick up signals and, whatever the pledges might be about 'governing for the long term', or 'a horizon shift to the long term', associate the signals of what is given attention as important, noting that a programme might be described as 'failing' in its first year, despite being approved on the basis of a return on investment over ten years.

In business the profitability of the company is a matter of interest to all of its employees; without profits it is unlikely that they will remain employed. The goals and ambitions of politicians similarly need to be of interest to all who work in government. Political goals and ambitions (or 'desired outcomes', or 'results', or 'change for the better') may become obscured by the demands of the day-to-day. In time the day-to-day demands can become more alluring than the difficult business of long-term change. A lot can seem urgent when holding elected office, especially when in the glare of the media or under the scrutiny of political opponents. Without political appetite for strategy it is as comfortable for officials to avoid acting strategically as it is for politicians. Both groups can collude or – worse – blame each other for lack of ambition, lack of direction, lack of clarity, lack of vision, the inability to see things through. But strategy needs politicians and officials to work together.

It's not the case that the short term necessarily obscures the long term, or that spending time considering and planning for the long term is inevitably a distraction from coping with the short term. Long-term thinking can be a diversion in organizations that don't make the links to the short term – those that do not give 'line of sight' from high-level outcomes to the actions of their own employees, residents and citizens. But when applied in a strategic context, long-term thinking enables short-term decisions to be taken faster and more effectively – one reason why governments and organizations that have planned for the long term tend to cope well in a crisis.

As well as conditions that can encourage an institutional short-term focus, we need to be aware of the individual psychological bias to the immediate future in the minds of the individuals who constitute the organization. The esteem in which we hold particular skills, such as consequential reasoning or the ability to defer gratification, acknowledges their relative rarity and our natural disposition to the immediate. People discount the future heavily when it requires sacrifices in the present. We prefer $100 today rather than waiting a month for $120 (the value of certainty – a bird in the hand is worth two in the bush – may play a part), although we are likely to prefer \$120 in 31 days to \$100 in 30 days. Behavioural and evolutionary psychologists call this 'hyperbolic discounting'. Rationally we know we should select commitment goods that involve sacrifice now and benefits later, but behaviourally we seek arousal goods we can enjoy now and pay for later. The closer you are in time to \$100 the bigger it looks. There's a switch from the larger but later reward to the smaller but earlier reward the nearer people get to it (Ainslie 1992: 78). That, and the incentives associated with the short term in which people find themselves more immediately accountable and in which rewards and punishments feature, leads to a 'we can worry about the future in the future' approach.

Mulgan (Mulgan 2009: 25), applying a 'three horizons' model, argues that competent and responsible public organizations that are ready for the future should strive to keep three different timeframes in focus:

- the short-term focus of day-to-day crises and issues
- the medium-term focus on programmes, policies and strategies
- the longer-term focus where new visions, scenarios and strategic innovation critical to survival and success are developed.

It's vital when considering this temporal dimension to take account of context. Pollitt (Pollitt 2008: 13) contrasts a state forestry agency with the job of maintaining biodiversity in the forest and compares it with that of a local community mental health agency. The former works over quite long periods of time, over wide areas and with fairly precise scientific measures of outcomes. The latter works locally, with individuals, sometimes for quite short periods, and finds it very difficult to disentangle its efforts from many other influences. Neither are routine bureaucratic operations with standardized procedures that are carried out in highly measurable ways over short time cycles. Both differ from easily measurable routine bureaucratic operations such as the issuing of driving licences or the registration of births, marriages and deaths.

Keeping in mind the short, medium and long terms connects the longer-term challenges and opportunities with the shorter time frames that are the preoccupation of most people within the organization. Curry and Hodgson (2008) extend this approach by presenting future challenges in terms of 'wave wars' where the current horizon and future horizons clash. The dominant present frames our current thinking about a domain (in electricity supply, for example, think of centralized generation based on fossil fuels). It will decline in influence as the external environment changes. The third horizon is a possible future which may become dominant over time; in the electricity supply example, one such future is a distributed network powered by renewable energy sources. There are clues already as to what these competing futures might look like, but they are marginal and often marginalized. In between, there is

FIGURE 4.2   *Seeing in multiple horizons (Curry and Hodgson 2008)*

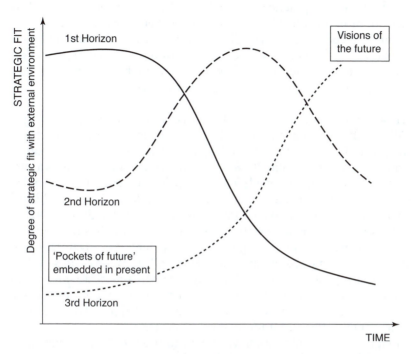

Reproduced by permission of Andrew Curry and Anthony Hodgson. First published in the
Journal of Futures Studies, 2008.

the second horizon. This is a space in which the current horizon – where the power, the influence, and the money, along with connections, relationships and prestige are to be found – adapts to signals about the future: sometimes incrementally, sometimes disruptively, sometimes destructively.

Curry and Hodgson trace the history of the development of the three horizons model from *The Alchemy of Growth* (Baghai *et al.* 1999: 4–7) pointing out that it doesn't deal with the transition between the dominance of the horizons and resembles the S-curve model popularized by Theodore Modis (Modis 1998).

The futures-oriented version of the model, shown in Figure 4.3, comprises:

- First Horizon: the current prevailing system as it continues into the future, which loses 'fit' over time as its external environment changes.
- Third Horizon: ideas or arguments about the future of the system which are, at best, marginal in the present, but which over time may have the potential to displace the world of the first horizon, because they represent a more effective response to the changes in the external

environment. Although the diagram suggests there is only one such third horizon, in practice, especially in the early stages, there will be several, or many, third horizon arguments being articulated.

- Second Horizon: an intermediate space in which the first and third horizons collide. This is a space of transition which is typically unstable. It is characterized by clashes of values in which competing alternative paths to the future are proposed by actors.

Horizon 2, then, becomes a space of both conflicts and options.

Pollitt calls attention to an implicit opposition to the past in change management literature which sees the past as basically a source of conservatism and resistance (Pollitt 2008: 9) and makes the case that time is a vital, pervasive, but frequently neglected, dimension in contemporary public policy-making and management and arguing for adding the past or historical dimension or horizon to the three horizons view (Pollitt 2008: 174), not least because where an organization has come from may constrain, through path dependency, where it can go. We usually think it is advantageous to take a 'blank sheet of paper' approach with no legacy constraints. Taking the perspective of a 'new entrant' (an actor new to a market with no path dependency) is always a useful check on your strategy, but this may ignore the value of experience and knowledge of what has happened during earlier similar events, or the preparation over the long term.

In Figure 4.3, the authors have sought to use the three (future) horizons model (Figure 4.2) in a slightly different way, by suggesting what techniques might be most useful for each horizon. Analysis of the first horizon of the near future typically uses forecasts, trend analysis, and extrapolation (see Chapter 5 for all techniques mentioned in this section). Looking further out to the second horizon will benefit from system modelling and scenarios to explore the medium-term future. Looking much further out to the third horizon benefits from random prompts that will derail linear thinking and stimulate new thinking. Schwartz recommends exposing yourself to different stimuli. 'Routinely pick up a dozen magazines from a newstand and scan them. Include magazines you would not otherwise read: an audiophile magazine, a literary journal, a gardening magazine, a car magazine, a political magazine opposing your own opinions, a magazine about a hobby you don't have, a fashion magazine. Don't be afraid to throw in a random-impulse purchase: odd magazines could turn out to be the most cost effective research dollars you spend' (Schwartz 1996: 81).

The more tangible, 'harder' techniques, like extrapolation, aim for certainty and control. They favour forecasting and behavioural simulations (for example, role playing external interests to flush out perverse incentives). They suit nearer timescales. Because they are rational and logical, public sector organizations may favour them, despite the risk that they lock themselves into the shorter-term horizons.

FIGURE 4.3 *The temporal dimension*

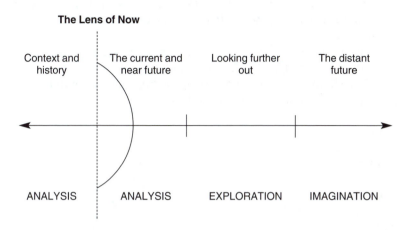

The 'softer' techniques (scenarios through to horizon scanning) lend themselves to looking further out, embracing ambiguity to support intuition, exploration and learning.

All are different kinds of evidence – the evidence will be richer where it's possible to combine methods. What constitutes evidence, and the evidence that is privileged or persuasive in different situations, is a construction by the organization. Quantitative evidence, using data, is convincing but by definition will be backward-looking. Extrapolating data carries the serious risk that it's unlikely to identify discontinuities, where a trend line abruptly changes, perhaps because another trend intersects.

As well as respecting other methods, we need to consider whose evidence it is, who's counting the evidence, who distributes it and whose voices are being heard. 'Evidence shopping' means people might select evidence in the context of securing grants or publication, to comply with regulation or for marketing. The scientific 'gold standard' of randomized control trials as the only version of the truth isn't possible in many disciplines (and in any case, science itself is a moving field). Evidence can embrace values and beliefs. Who represents the voices not being heard? Which section of civil society is providing the evidence? For instance, are the voices of women underrepresented in some contexts and cultures?

Pollitt looks at the often ignored importance of context and says a recent engine for decontextualization has been the fashion for 'evidence-based policy' commonly regarded as the pinnacle of research-based rational policy-making and management. But it may in practice become a way of absorbing or 'assuming away' critical contextual differences which are crucial to understanding why a particular programme or activity works reasonably well at one place or time but not at another. It aggregates results but not rationales (Pollitt 2008: 12). This means context and place must form part of the evidence for evidence-based, or evidence-informed, policy.

What is the length of each wave or horizon? Again, it depends on context. Brand (Brand 1999: 35–6) proposes seven significant levels of pace and size in the working structure of a robust and adaptable civilization, organized from fast to slow as follows:

1. Fashion
2. Art
3. Commerce
4. Infrastructure
5. Governance
6. Culture
7. Nature.

In a healthy society each level is allowed to operate at its own pace, safely sustained by the slower levels below. Culture declared it was okay to change clothing at fashion pace but not buildings, okay to change tenants at commercial pace but not buildings, okay to change transportation at infrastructure pace but not neighbourhoods (Brand 1999: 38).

Mulgan (Mulgan 2007), in the context of public sector innovation, also identifies four horizons, (short, medium, long, and legacy/generational for issues like pensions and greenhouse gases) and in this context is able to assign time periods from days, months, weeks; 1–3 years; 3–20 years plus, and beyond. Perez (Perez 2002) studied five technology ages, from 1770 to 2000 (industrial revolution; steam & rail; steel, electricity & heavy engineering; oil, automobile & mass production; information & telecommunications) and found regular cycles of two elements, an installation or growth period lasting 20 to 30 years, a bubble leading to a financial crisis, followed by a period of diffusion of 20 to 30 years of modernization as the technology matures because (in capitalist societies) the accumulation of production capital in the first stage has a long-term bias, whereas the financial capital used to allocate resources has a short-term bias. Each technological revolution gives rise to a paradigm shift and a 'New Economy'.

Nowotny (1994: 50) argues that today an 'extended present' eats up the future and some of the past. Instead of the future being a space where progress happens, she says it's a place of future problems to plan for now (the future becomes the extended present). These include global warming, new epidemics, the long-term management of ever growing quantities of toxic wastes, changing demographics and their negative impact on the welfare state.

BOX 4.4 The Marshall Plan: long-term thinking to solve a short-term problem

The 1948 Marshall Plan for US aid to Europe was a conceived as a long-term solution to the immediate economic and humanitarian crisis in Europe. Although around $12 billion of US aid had already gone to European countries in the three years following the end of the war in Europe (the Soviet Union declined to participate, and countries within its sphere of influence also declined or were obliged to decline to participate), it had become apparent that economic recovery was too fragile to be sustainable. In a speech at Harvard University on 5 June 1947 US Secretary of State George C. Marshall made the following comments:

> The truth of the matter is that Europe's requirements for the next three or four years of foreign food and other essential products – principally from America – are so much greater than her present ability to pay that she must have substantial additional help or face economic, social, and political deterioration of a very grave character.
>
> The remedy lies in breaking the vicious circle and restoring the confidence of the European people in the economic future of their own countries and of Europe as a whole. (Truman Library 1947)

The European Recovery Program Basic Document of 31 October 1947 made clear

> that if further aid to Europe were to achieve any really useful purpose certain definite prerequisites would have to be followed. First of all, the aid would have to be granted according to some overall, integrated concept which took into account the problems of European nations in respect to each other and not individually. Further piecemeal approaches would not do. (Truman Library 1947)

A further US$13 billion of aid was pumped into European economies by the time the plan ended in 1951. UK Prime Minister Winston Churchill described the Marshall Plan as the 'most unsordid act in history'.

In a 2002 Brookings Institution survey of more than 450 historians and political scientists, the Marshall Plan was selected as the greatest achievement of the US government of the 20th century (Light 2002).

We've shown that thinking and planning for the long term alone isn't enough. Plans have to be turned into action. The Marshall Plan was a long-term strategy, introduced at the moment when it could work best. At ministry and agency level this conversion of long-term thinking into action is just as important. In the UK, ministries have boards of management. A 2010 UK Institute for Government survey of the work of the executive boards of UK government departments suggested a negative correlation between the amount of time spent by departmental boards discussing strategy and their overall effectiveness '... we found that a focus on "strategy" actually had a negative relationship with effectiveness once focus on performance management was taken into account. This reinforced the sense that some underachieving boards were spending time discussing strategy when what they really needed to do was roll up their sleeves and manage the department, or perhaps go back to ministers and alter strategy' (Parker *et al.* 2010: 53).

This finding doesn't suggest that the management boards of ministries should not consider strategy at all. It recommends boards should engage with politicians when shaping strategy, because the strategy of a government department of state must be political. Having defined strategic direction, it is the board's job to make sure the strategic intent is implemented, moving from strategic thinking to action and managing the performance of the department in an accountable way.

Conclusion: the art of the possible

US Secretary of State John Kerry said (when a Senator): 'Politics has always been the art of the possible. Today it's too often the art of the probable – tinkering around the edges without any greater vision, without a sense of optimism and imagination.'

Being strategic does not require the ability to see into the future. We cannot know what will happen tomorrow, let alone in five or ten years' time. But the world does not present us with a binary choice between certainty on the one hand and fatalism on the other. We can plan for the future and, in planning, make it more likely that it will come about. When we create constructs for ourselves these can be liberating or constraining. The construct of a flat earth constrained navigation; the construct of standardized time eased communication and trade; the construct of a week helped the organization of work, markets, leisure and religious observance. We create a problem-construct of the big challenges most societies face, of child poverty, of longer-living populations, of energy insecurity, of climate change and in so doing lend to the notion that each one has a solution. In order to find that solution we drive hard to narrow the problem to the point where it is amenable to solution – sometimes a solution we have already chosen. A strategic approach makes this unhelpful narrowing less likely. It gives us better courses to follow.

The United States Commission on National Security/21st Century (1999) understood this: '"No man can have in his mind a conception of the future, for it is not yet", wrote Thomas Hobbes in *Leviathan*, "but from our own conceptions of the past we can make a future." Hobbes meant two things by this statement: most obviously, that the past is the only basis upon which to consider the future; more subtly, that social life tends to freeze itself into the conceptions we have of it. Hobbes was twice right. Absent the gift of prophecy, history's recurrent patterns, discontinuities and intimation about human nature compose our only means of reckoning ahead. It remains true, as well, that the very act of probing the future tends to shape it, for we often act on our anticipations in ways that invite their arrival.'

Chapter 5

Thinking Strategically: Methods and Approaches

Strategic thinking is, by definition, a particular category of thinking – the qualification 'strategic' shows it's not meant to be 'any old way of thinking'. Neuroscientist Iain McGilchrist points out that the kind of attention we pay alters what we find. 'A mountain that is a landmark to a navigator, a source of wealth to the prospector, a many-textured form to a painter, or to another the dwelling place of the gods, is changed by the attention given to it' (McGilchrist 2009: 28–9). Strategic thinking requires an approach requiring 'navigation, prospecting, painting and belief' among other qualities. To help this, strategic thinking has a number of disciplines that we examine in this chapter.

Strategic organizations think strategically by paying attention to the future in a way that develops an understanding of their likely operating environments in five, 10, 20 or perhaps 50 years' time and, depending on context, beyond (for example nuclear or transport). For governments, it is not a sufficient ambition simply to understand how to survive in a particular future. As we explored in Chapter 3, the job of government is to *change the future*, that is, to set out a vision of a desired future and through policies and achievement of those policies, to bring that future about. This is the key difference between strategy work in the private sector which looks to optimal performance and profitability in whichever future comes about ('surviving the future'), and strategy in the public sector – which aims to achieve better outcomes for citizens ('changing the future').

Strategic thinking needs imagination, many willing minds, a sense that the long term matters and a rigorous process that has at its end point a commitment to action. This means ownership is vital – whether by a minister, a cabinet, a board of management, a city council or mayor. Implementing strategy work without a clear commission carries the danger that it degenerates into a talking shop that doesn't lead to any choices being made or action being taken. The work needs to be undertaken to a meaningful deadline in the belief that change will be made to polices, programmes or services as a result of the strategy work, and that these changes will be measured in some way.

Brothers Kenneth and William Hopper make the case that the separation of design and implementation – which then prevents rapid review, reversal or alteration to meet new circumstances – has led to the down-fall of modern corporations. Strategic thinking shouldn't take place in an ivory tower, and the Hoppers make the case for the value of monitoring, adjusting and refining of strategy by following its implementation closely (Hopper and Hopper 2009).

In this chapter we look at a set of methods and approaches that, when applied in the right context, can help organizations to think strategically.

Pace of change: cracking the 'lens of now'

As discussed in Chapter 4, 'lens of now' thinking, expert bias and groupthink can stop strategic thinking before it has had a chance to get under way. One way to get people to start to question and expand their conceptual framework, however firmly held, is to ask them to think of the context for their organization, sector, city or country ten or 20 years ago – the time period is determined by the context. For a fast-moving industry or service even five years can be long enough; for a nation or region 25 years is usually sufficient for there to have been significant and sometimes dramatic change, but for some issues (energy, environment, infrastructure, defence) it may be helpful to think in longer timescales. By thinking about changes in living memory and then speci-fying and externalizing them – looking at the organization, sector, region or nation from the point of view of someone sitting outside it, and understanding that current trends tend to break – people begin to understand the rapidity and scale of pace of change. We call this a 'pace of change' exercise.

Once they have looked back over time, those involved can then be invited to speculate on the ways the organization or sector or nation might change over the next ten years. We ask people to think particularly of what the organization might be doing, or what a government might be doing that it has never done before (to try to avoid the tendency to simply frame their thinking as 'there will be more of this' or 'less of that'). People should specify and externalize their thinking. By exposing the range of *actual* change over the previous ten to 20 years, and then the range of *potential* change over the next ten years, people can see that what actu-ally happens is almost always more radical than they think would be the case without some prompting. It encourages people to shake off 'lens of now' thinking and works successfully to prepare people to think openly and understand that the future won't be more of today.

Figure 5.1 shows the result of a 'pace of change' exercise conducted by the authors with a group of international officials in 2008 looking at India, 25 years back to 1983 and forward ten years to 2018. Each group was first asked to think of the key features about India in the early 1980s.

FIGURE 5.1 *Pace of change exercise – India past and future here*

India – 1983

Politics	Economy	Global position	Pakistan-China
Delhi-centric	Poor, rural	No aspirations to Security Council	High tension
Higher castes filled senior social positions	Gap between rich and poor less obvious	Non-nuclear	Greater parity with Pakistan economically
Congress party and Gandhi family powerful	Closed economy	Bipolar order – India member of Non Aligned Movement	China not significant economic influence or threat
More social cohesion	State-owned/ regulated manufacturing		
Pre-Amritsar	Small service sector		
	Growth rates around 2%		

India in 2018 ...

Politics	Economy	Global position/ Pakistan-China	Demographic and environment change
More fragmented, with power shift to states from centre	More open economy, increased trade	Security Council member	Population overtakes China
Inter-communal relations strained more from economic than religious or ethnic tensions	Consumer boom fuelled by middle class	Energy needs drive alliances	Young, better educated population creates employment challenge
More domestic terrorism	Big increase in industrial capacity	Competing with China for resources	Gender balance worry, though girls better educated
	Weak infrastructure	Relations with Pakistan and Afghanistan still important	Still 25% of world's poor
	Divide between SW and NE		Less water/ biodiversity
	Increased inequality – declining agricultural sector		

Figure 5.1 illustrates a 'blue skies' thinking exercise which, by definition, isn't rigorous. Its purpose is to open up thinking and make people ease out of the 'lens of now'.

The next stage in the strategic thinking process is to begin identifying relevant streams of evidence that are likely to help connect the past, the present and the future. These are known as 'drivers for change'.

Drivers for change

'Drivers' are forces in the world outside the organization or external to the policy area. They may be worldwide – for instance the threat from new forms of influenza, or near to home – for instance, an increasing reluctance by insurers to cover homes exposed to risk of flooding as a consequence of climate change.

Drivers shape the context in which the organization or policy will work in the future. They are not internal responses to external drivers like a new board, resource accounting and performance management systems. Budget constraints likewise are not drivers because strategy is what you *need to do*, not what you can *afford to do*, though budgets become very important later in the strategic delivery process in considering the ways in which strategy can be implemented.

When encouraging people to think as widely as possible about potential drivers, a useful approach is to invite people to categorize trends according to whether they are political, economic, social or technological (PEST). This is simply a convenient framework for managing what might be a large number of trends – you don't need to worry too much about whether the category is right – whether something is really a technology driver or has become a social driver (because of the way people use technology, for example). Some frameworks add legal, environmental or organizational drivers too, though you can usually accommodate these in the existing PEST categories. Equally common are variations known as 'STEEP' or 'PESTLE' approaches, which group the drivers in the following way (PESTLE adds the category 'legal', though for government and government bodies, legal change is a response to change, not a driver of change):

1. **Social and demographic** – behaviours, values and demographics
2. **Technology and Science** – medicine, IT, materials, processes and products
3. **Economics** – globalization, GDP change, economic advantage
4. **Environment** – climate change, natural resources, green issues
5. **Politics and Power** – governance, participation, balances of power.

People working in the public sector can tend to overplay political and economic drivers and downplay the importance of social and demographic drivers. There's an inclination to privilege quantitative data, which can be used for modelling, over values and beliefs which we (wrongly) imagine stay the same and are in any case not easily susceptible to modelling. Behaviours and attitudes are especially important in the context of designing strategic policy because all policy is essentially about changing behaviour. Table 5.1 shows some typical social and demographic drivers for change.

TABLE 5.1 Typical social and demographic 'drivers for change'

The world population	*The family*
Size of world population	Alternative social structures
Geographical growth profile	Intergenerational solidarity
Age profile	Family support mechanisms
HIV/AIDS	Demands on state support
Type II diabetes epidemics	Choice for the individual
Cross-species epidemics	Responsibility devolved to the individual
Birth and mortality rates	Role of men
Population management	Matriarchies
Ability to migrate	
National population characteristics	
	Self-belief and individual values
The limits of human potential	Search for identity – place
	Search for identity – ethnicity
Reproductive capacity	Search for values – cultural
Feasibility of clones	Search for values – spiritual
Perfection of foetuses	Search for happiness
Genetic selection	Desire for privacy
Cognitive advances	Security and risk aversion
New limits to physical performance	Propensity to blame
Independent ageing	
Individual genetic susceptibility	
Education level	
Mood management	*Traditional values*
Addiction control	
	Deference to authority
	Deference to class
	Religious affiliation
Living in the global context	Political affiliation
	Clarity of right and wrong
Competing in a world job market	Attitudes to monarchy/presidency
Retention of skills	Manners
Exposure to other value systems	Service
Information quantity and quality	Order
Travelling impact on health	
Impact environment change on health	*New values*
Impact social class on health	
Impact migration on social structures	Post-scarcity viewpoint
Membership of diasporas	Tolerance
Need for security	Acceptance of diversity
Need for justice	Self-reliance
Need for welfare	Self-actualization
Social capital	Work–life balance
Living alongside poverty	Citizen of wider world
Protection of national identity	Compassion

The drivers shown above operate at various levels. When creating strategy at national level, high-level drivers, like 'family structures' and 'the role of traditional values' are likely to be important. A particular ministry, for instance a finance ministry, will focus on a slightly more specific set of drivers, for instance: 'enterprise-friendly tax', 'access to markets' and 'viability of worker skill base'.

Don't mistake a trend for a driver. For instance, the finance ministry, when creating a strategy for improving the tax take, might identify the following:

- recession
- increasing offshoring
- tax evasion/informal economy.

But 'recession' is a *trend* rather than a *driver*. The driver for change is 'economic growth' (in the case of a recession, expressed as negative growth).

Drivers operate in different ways at different times, and one aspect in designing strategy is to understand, monitor and anticipate variable trends that different drivers produce. To take another example from the list above, the *trend* of 'increasing offshoring' (of banking, investment, gambling, services, property or residence, often to low tax regimes or avoiding tax entirely) could reverse. For instance, growth in international regulation might limit the attractiveness of offshoring, but so might international cyber-crime, or instability or costs in previously hospitable low tax regimes. Offshoring call centres might become unattractive if it appears that customers are dissatisfied with offshored call centre staff. Identifying the driver and describing it as 'location of financial services' is more helpful than describing a trend that might be short term.

You should also recognize when something that appears to be a driver is more meaningfully understood as a combination of drivers. For instance, 'tax evasion' is produced by a range of different drivers, which include:

- attitudes to the state
- confidence in the fairness of the tax system
- belief in the extent to which others are complying
- belief in the will and effectiveness of the state to enforce compliance.

Identifying drivers at the right level for the context is a strategic thinking skill. One way of doing this is to assess the degree to which a chosen driver ('tax evasion') is actually a product of other drivers (for example, 'belief in the compliance of others'). This separates the dominant and dependent drivers, and helps you in identifying those that are both domi-

BOX 5.1 Bahrain: drivers of change

In 2011 the small Gulf Kingdom of Bahrain was gripped by domestic unrest, in part driven by sectarian tensions between Sunni and Shia, and in part a reaction to the slow pace of political reform.

In 2007 the World Economic Forum published a set of scenarios for Bahrain to 2025 (World Economic Forum, 2007). It identified a number of key drivers of change in the Kingdom:

The rule of law
Economic growth
Political reform
Regional pressures (as drivers for internal tension)
Diversification (away from state-run industries)
Education
Innovation
Participation in the economy by Bahraini nationals
New technology
Transparency in governance
Corruption

The World Economic Forum report suggested three potential futures for Bahrain: one where political reforms and investment in human capital lead to Bahrain being a flourishing regional centre, despite difficult global and regional economic and political conditions ('Oasis'); one as the regional hub for high-tech industry and Islamic banking ('The Fertile Gulf'), benefiting from global economic growth and political stability. In the third scenario (Sandstorm) regional tensions stall the political and economic reform process leading to domestic unrest, violence and a government unable to fund public services.

In 2013 the Bahrain Government published its economic strategy to 2030 (Bahrain Government 2013):

The overriding aim of the Economic Vision 2030 is to improve living standards for all Bahrainis. It aims to develop opportunities for the private sector, which has a pivotal role to play as the engine of growth and productivity in Bahrain. Meanwhile, the Government of Bahrain is committed to investing in its infrastructure as well as its people. We aspire to shift from an economy built on oil wealth to a productive, globally competitive economy, shaped by the government and driven by a pioneering private sector – an economy that raises a broad middle class of Bahrainis who enjoy good living standards through increased productivity and high-wage jobs.

nant and uncertain. Each of those contributory drivers may itself be the product of other drivers, for instance 'belief in the compliance of others' may be driven in turn by 'transparency of information', 'enforcement capacity' and so on (each of the hypothesized drivers will eventually need to be supported by evidence to avoid making toxic assumptions). The strategic thinker needs to apply her judgement in determining the correct level of regression.

The discussion of drivers can involve a large group of people; if discussing the work of a particular sector (for instance, children's services, or food production) or of a particular policy (for instance on road use or alcohol abuse), this can be a good moment to involve stakeholders and users of services. If the strategy process relates to an organization like a government department or local authority, or to an agency of that organization, it might still be appropriate to involve stakeholders in this phase of the discussion. It is helpful to identify as few as ten drivers and probably no more than 30 as of most importance to the organization, policy or sector; these will frame the strategic process. Disputes are likely to arise about which drivers are most significant – and about how they should be defined. The process should also recognize which drivers are dominant and which are dependent (on other drivers). The disputes are necessary and healthy; they are signs of engagement and increasing appetite for analysis – both vital elements in any strategy process.

Finding the evidence

Evidence-based strategy and policy-making is widely desired but often unrealized, largely because the appetite for evidence in government is variable – too often it's for 'policy-based evidence-making' – analysts, researchers and other officials are asked to gather the evidence that supports a course of action already decided on. This may be legitimate if it involves a hypothesis to be tested – for example, whether schools should be allowed to recruit teaching staff without any form of regulation. Evidence can be gathered from other jurisdictions where regulation is light or non-existent and assess the impact on teaching standards. You can also look at historical evidence of the changing impact of regulation on teaching standards. It's unacceptable (but sadly not unknown) to include only evidence that supports the hypothesis and exclude all evidence that doesn't support the hypothesis. This can arise from confusing and conflating two different things: *evidence* and *judgement*. Because evidence tends to point in more than one direction, we must make decisions about which piece of evidence is most reliable, and we must recognize *and make explicit* when beliefs and factual premises come into the equation in making judgements to decide which evidence to rely on.

Decision-making in the political realm relies as much on values and beliefs as it does on the evidence that shows whether policy change is likely to be more or less costly, more or less effective, fair, achievable, sustainable and so on. Strategic advice needs to take into account the political context (including the value and belief systems of politicians) as well as the evidence of practicability. There's a tension between belief, political players, institutional power, and dominating paradigms on the one hand and evidence on the other.

What people regard as evidence and which kinds of evidence they privilege will be a reflection of beliefs and culture including organizational culture or the culture within an expertise or discipline. There may be a bias against evidence about values and beliefs or in favour of quantitative evidence, or modelling. 'An accumulation of anomalies, policy failures and experimentation of new forms of policies will undermine the credibility of the dominant paradigm. This will make more easy the crucial shift in the "locus of authority over policy". In other words politicians and policy makers, fumbling around to find policy techniques that work, will lose confidence in the magisterial received wisdom of established gurus in the field and begin to listen to unorthodox voices, whose thinking on the policy area is based on quite novel intellectual assumptions. Of course, the particular pattern of the paradigm shift will be determined, not simply by the force of arguments but by political events and the institutional structures and "ancillary resources" of the competing factions' (Greenaway 1998: 906).

The way that we interpret evidence will always be understood to some extent through the lens of now, of expert or professional bias and political preference, and that evidence can only ever carry us a short way into the future. This recognition of the limits of evidence makes the clarity of our understanding of *why* a strategy is to be adopted even more important. If public strategy necessarily has a political dimension which may not always be amenable to evidence, then transparency about the reasons for a redistributive tax policy or deregulation of energy markets or raising the school leaving age become even more important, because governments and public bodies have accountability not simply for the performance of policies and programmes, but for their judgement (we examine the exercise of judgement in more detail in Chapter 8).

This exercise of political judgement relies, fundamentally, on the interplay of three forces: *evidence*, both observable evidence and evidence-based assumptions based on trends, visions of the future and plans; *beliefs*, which may be influenced by evidence, but which may be rooted in philosophy, in prejudice, in faith, in dogma; and by *context*, which places limitations on the interpretation of evidence and the application of belief through framing understanding in particular ways.

All evidence is questionable. It is worth asking these three questions of any piece of evidence: is it

FIGURE 5.2 *Triangulating evidence*

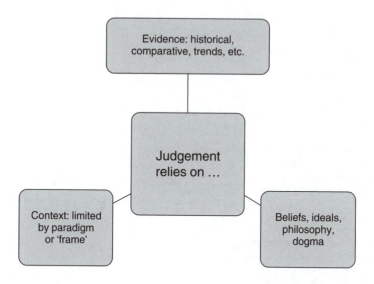

Reliable – objective and robust; can it withstand attack and criticism? Is it quality data from a reliable source?

Relevant – is it specific to the issue and up to date and suitable for the context to which it will be applied? Does it help to increase understanding of the achievement of the desired outcome?

Clear – is it unambiguous and comprehensible? Clarity is important if others are to be able to understand and act upon the evidence. Does it enable learning about the issue?

Don't take a narrow view of evidence – different people may privilege different kinds of evidence according to their profession, with double blind randomized control trials the gold standard. Scientists may prefer hard data and extrapolation to scenarios (which are themselves evidence: of considering different futures). Good evidence is both 'hard' and 'soft' (quantitative and qualitative). Evidential cases are more robust when they combine different kinds of evidence, and evidence can come from a wide range of sources including general sources of information like media stories, international comparisons, surveys, blogs, twitter and anecdotal evidence (including gossip and hearsay).

We need evidence so that we understand the context in which we are planning our strategy and so that we can anticipate its likely impacts. Evidence will help to give the process strategic robustness and if used objectively it will help decisions to be made; if it is used persuasively it will help win support from political leaders, senior officials and stakeholders, including citizens.

TABLE 5.2 Typical sources of evidence

Economists
Scientists
Statisticians
Social researchers
Librarians
Operational researchers
Anthropologists
Historians
Lawyers
Communications experts
Strategy Unit colleagues
Policy colleagues
Horizon Scanning Centre
Academia
Think tanks
Charities
Major accounting partnerships
Business and business consultancies
Futures boutiques
Gurus and futurologists
Professional associations
Pressure groups
Information services organizations
Consultations
Journalists
And ... the public

In some countries a draft legislative proposal is an essential precursor to any discussion about a change in policy, and the drafting of the legislation often brings different streams of evidence into play. European Union policy proposals usually involve a long period of evidence-gathering, engaging with a wide range of interested parties before the Commission puts a formal proposal to the Council of Ministers and European Parliament. In some countries legislation is needed only where the proposed action would be unlawful without it. Nevertheless there is a widely-held expectation that evidence will be considered properly before a policy is adopted. But even the notion of what constitutes 'evidence-based' is in dispute. 'Evidence can provide the rationale for an initial policy direction; it can set out the nature and extent of the problem, suggest possible solutions, look to the likely impacts in the future, and evidence from piloting and evaluation can provide motivation for adjustments to a policy or the way it is to be implemented ... This is not to say that most policy develops in such a linear way from first identifying the evidence, balancing the options and then developing and evaluating the resulting policy ... the idea of 'evidence-inspired' policy making might be more appropriate ... Amongst those interviewed, there was a

Box 5.2 Australia: evidence-based policy-making in action?

Several of the state governments in Australia – as well as the federal government – have adopted strategic approaches to public management, and have placed a high premium on evidence-based approaches to policy-making. Yet even where the political context for evidence-based policy-making is positive and the capability of public officials is broadly high, and even where a range of research evidence is available, it remains difficult to make evidence-based policy-making a reality.

The problem of obesity affects most countries today, especially the most economically developed ones. Obesity is an issue where strong empirical evidence about the nature and degree of the problem exists, taken from systematic medical records. But evidence about the most effective ways of tackling obesity is in dispute. The exploration for solutions therefore becomes an arena where opinion and beliefs play out in a strongly contested way. This was manifest in a 'Childhood Obesity Summit' held in New South Wales in 2002. One finding suggested that the contested nature of the evidence on the best solution meant that the demand for conclusive evidence increased – in order to refute the opinion-based arguments of one side or the other:

> In setting the agenda, formulating policy, and implementing and evaluating it, various forms of evidence are sought and utilised. While conventionally such evidence is conceived as being from 'scientific and objective' research, it is increasingly clear that a much wider range of sources and forms of evidence are influential. (Nathan *et al.* 2005)

Child welfare is similarly an area where evidence of the nature and scale of the problem is comprehensive, but evidence on effective interventions is contested:

> While the value of research is generally recognised, and increasing resources are being devoted to child protection related research, little is known about the extent to which research is used by policy makers in this or other human service fields ...
>
> Lack of time to access and apply research is a commonly identified barrier to research use across a range of professions, including health, education, social work and criminal justice (Hemsley-Brown and Sharp 2003; Walter *et al.* 2003). In our survey of Australian child and family welfare policy makers and practitioners it was noted that 79% of child protection practitioners and 62% of policy makers had little time to read research reports or to apply research findings (Holzer *et al.* 2008). (Lewig *et al.* 2010)

clear distinction between the theory or ideal behind evidence-based policy and the realities of making policy in the real world' (Campbell *et al.* 2007: 12).

Part of the difficulty is that evidence often points in two or more directions at once. Indeed, a thorough process *ought* to find evidence that is in conflict with other evidence: economic evidence might in any case sit in tension with scientific evidence; social research might sit in tension with long-term historical data. Inevitably politicians and administrators alike select evidence that supports a particular direction – so it's useful to ask 'whose evidence?' The problem–solution bias discussed in Chapter 2 encourages the sifting of evidence to support a narrow understanding of a problem and of its amenability to a particular solution. But evidence, and even the consensus on what constitutes evidence, changes because the world changes and, just as importantly, our understanding of the world changes. Policies informed by particular kinds of evidence can suddenly seem quite unsuitable on the basis of new insight. Evidence is usually backward-looking which means we can extrapolate what's happened before (not always wrong when dealing with the immediate future) without regard to discontinuities or the things that will break the trend.

Horizon scanning

A component of a strategic process is to have a wide range of historical and comparative evidence available, including evidence of potential futures. This latter category is what is sometimes described as 'horizon scanning', although horizon scanning should always include looking around you, not only peering into the future – as William Gibson (Gibson 2003), the writer who coined the term 'cyberspace', says 'the future is already here – it's just not very evenly distributed'. Horizon scanning and forecasting are different. Horizon scanning is where evidence is sought 'beyond the usual timescales and the usual sources'.

Governments have always had some capability for scanning the environment, whether for threats or opportunities, with a tendency to focus more heavily on threats than opportunities. Part of this capability is provided by the intelligence services which in many countries channel information through a National Security Council to the national cabinet. Terrorism, financial crises, the threat of a flu pandemic and successive energy crises all show the need for better information for contingency planning. Top-down pressure to think strategically, not just tactically, has been a further stimulus to get a better grip on understanding more about what's on the horizon.

The UK government has established a Foresight and Horizon Scanning Centre in its Government Office of Science whose role is to help the government think systematically about the future. As well as its Horizon Scanning centre, its Foresight programme also undertakes projects, in-depth studies examining major issues 20–80 years in the future, drawing together and synthesizing scientific research from across the world, for example on flooding, obesity, land use.

Horizon scans need to land somewhere on a spectrum between offering truly novel, surprising, valuable but occasionally 'wacky' perspectives whose novelty can often mean they are dismissed for lack of credibility (on one end of the spectrum) and predictable, well-known, unsurprising, broadly extrapolative 'lens of now' material that can be dismissed as uninteresting (at the other end). It can be difficult to strike the right balance. They always need to answer the 'so what?' question, so that whoever reads them will understand why they matter and be able to decide what to do with the perspective they have gained.

Forecasting

Clearly there can be no evidence of the future, because, in Thomas Hobbes' words 'the future is not yet'. But we have a wealth of evidence of potential futures, some of which may seem to us highly likely to come about, some highly unlikely. Strategic work needs a good range of plausible evidence, spanning both the probable and improbable for it is the improbable that catches us off guard. Forecasts are one good source of evidence for potential futures, though they should always be treated with caution. 'Like the weather, the political world has pockets of turbulence: political and financial crises during which we, the consumers of expertise, feel the greatest need for guidance but [when] such guidance will be least useful. Even the most astute observers will fail to outperform random prediction generators – the functional equivalent of dart-throwing chimps – in affixing likelihoods to possible futures' (Tetlock 2005: 41).

Forecasting comes in many shapes and sizes, including the following:

Analogous Data Forecasts: helpful where it is possible to find a historic example which has sufficient similarities. For instance, if a forecast is needed for the take-up of digital television, the historical data on the take-up of analogue television might be helpful.

Box-Jenkins: uses data about past behaviour to construct models which may explain future behaviour. The model uses past values of the data and past forecast errors. Best used when there are lots of data available for a short-term forecast. In the private sector the technique is popular for stock replenishment forecasts.

Curve Fitting: where groups of data points are linked together in a curve or line which is then extended into the future. This assumes that the drivers which caused the curve will be the same in the future as they have been in the past.

Decomposition Models: where series of data values are examined to see which underlying factors are influencing them. The effects of seasonal cycles, economic cycles, trends and specific events are unpicked to understand the likely relationships.

Delphi Forecasting: a form of judgemental forecasting, developed by the RAND Corporation in the 1950s. It is a method for gathering information or beliefs from a panel of experts about the timing, probability, importance, implications, trends and events relating to the subject under consideration. Delphi surveys are usually an anonymous process carried out over several rounds. The main result of the Delphi Survey is typically a consensus forecast that also identifies key areas of disagreement to thus highlight uncertainty. There's more on Delphi forecasts, their advantages and potential drawbacks in Chapter 6 which looks at their role in building strategic appetite, and includes examples.

Exponential Smoothing: where values in more recent times are seen to be more relevant than older values. Previous forecasts are compared with actual outturns. A smoothing constant is applied until past forecasts and actual outturns converge.

Extrapolation: perhaps the riskiest form of forecasting, because in its most basic form it sees the future through the lens of now. It's suitable for short-term forecasting but won't identify discontinuities, or where another driver intersects with the forecast to change its direction. One example of over-reliance on trend lines was the emergency conversion in 2001 of a pioneering new male prison in Rochdale, in England, to take female inmates. The Director General of the Prison Service described the rise in the female prison population as 'simply incredible'. A result of social changes in drug use and violence, he claimed it was 'something you can't plan for. The statisticians didn't predict it.' The planners had relied on historical trend lines. Anyone can be caught out by such rapid changes, but this illustrates the limitations of predictive techniques, and the danger of steering a ship by reference to its wake. Trend lines need not be straight lines, of course. Raymond Kurzweil (2006) makes the case that projections of technology progress that are linear miss the fact that they are logarithmic which means technology is exponentially accelerating such that humankind and computers will combine within 30 years (the 'singularity'). However, note that Theodore Modis (Modis 1992) advocates the S Curve, where an acceleration in growth tails off.

Judgemental Forecasting: where small groups of experts confer – and produce forecasts. Sometimes there is no alternative – for instance, in forecasting the future rate of discovery of oil reservoirs. Companies sometimes are forced to rely heavily on these forecasts, but try to do so only once they have been tested against others. The judgements of one particular group of experts can be collected alongside other specific group views. For example, the collective forecasts of customers may be considered valuable, particularly in comparison with the views of technical experts.

Leading Indicators: can be identified to foretell an impending change. For instance, an increase in the demand for seats on the London to Edinburgh Railway service was used as a leading indicator to identify an upturn in economic activity in the UK – spotting the 'green shoots of recovery'. More direct leading indicators are easier to identify – for instance forward contracts for bricks gives an indicator for future house building. When using trend analysis (see next section) these are events that we can identify that sit outside the main trend but which will be an indicator that a particular trend (and its outcome as described in the narrative) is coming about. For rising house prices in a previously down-at-heel city neighbourhood, the *lag indicator* is the increase in price itself. But a *leading indicator* is, typically, the opening of one or more coffee bars or bistros. For tracking the increasing use of Colombia as a hub for the heroin trade (as it uses its well-developed knowledge of consumers and markets gained in the cocaine trade to diversify into other profitable products and markets), the *lag indicator* might be seizures of heroin on routes that originated in Colombia. But a useful *lead indicator* would be the amount of telephone and internet traffic between Colombia and Afghanistan, or the number of Colombian visitors to Afghanistan.

Moving Average Forecasting: where future values are forecast on the basis of a linear combination of past values. A three-month moving average will smooth out monthly variations which may distort a view of a trend where large individual movements are eccentrically distributed, for example, the seasonal variation in sales of aircraft or of strawberries.

Neural Nets: IT systems which mimic in some ways the way the brain operates. Many instances of data sets are passed through the system which then can identify associations and dependencies. In doing so it builds up patterns from data, which can then be used as hypotheses on which forecasts can be developed. Neural nets are particularly useful when dealing with multilayered complex data. For example, the price of stocks and other investment vehicles such as bonds, derivatives and options are influenced by many different factors that are often interrelated. Traditional forecasting methods can be limited in their effectiveness as they make assumptions about the distribution of the underlying data, and often fail to recognize the interrelatedness of variables. Neural nets are ideally suited for making predictions in other financial areas, such as foreign exchange trading, financial planning, commodity trading, currency trading and oil and gas trading.

Regression Analysis: a technique for establishing the relationship between variables. In a simple Regression Analysis there is one dependent variable (for instance, number of people smoking) to be forecast, and one independent variable (for instance, the price of cigarettes). The values of the independent variable are suspected to affect the values of the dependent variable. This will involve hypothesizing then testing the independent variable.

Time Series Analysis: where historical data, defined and collected on a consistent basis, can be extrapolated on the same basis to give a good idea of future data. A standard example in econometrics is the opening price of a share of stock, based on its past performance. Time Series Analysis is a broad category of forecasting – a lot of other types of forecasting, such as Moving Averaging, Smoothing, Curve-fitting and so on are all different examples of time series analysis.

Presenting futures analysis

Because it is not possible to have evidence of the future, only of *potential futures*, it is helpful to present evidence of those potential futures in a way that connects the short-term and immediate world in which politicians typically operate with the long-term articulation of what it is the department or organization or policy is trying to achieve. Evidence and analysis must be 'bought into' by politicians and others who create the authorizing environment for strategy – from Board members to citizens. Evidence must resonate with the short-term pressures and political reality of daily life, rather than simply appear to be fascinating but disconnected – a common complaint about futures exercises. To overcome this you can present the analysis in three 'waves' or 'dimensions', whether in a one-page document or a 200-page report, whether in a ten-minute presentation or a two-day retreat. See also the section on short-termism and the presentation of temporal waves in Chapter 4.

Wave one: shorter-term strategic analysis, largely trend-based and offering evidence to support and question current strategic direction and policy sets. Ideally this work should also offer counter-trends and be cross-disciplinary (that is, it should deal with the social, cultural, technological, scientific, environmental and political as well as the economic perspectives). Diversity is an important quality of strategic analysis: historians are as important as scientists; social researchers as important as economists; anthropologists as important as statisticians; and librarians and archivists as important as operational researchers.

Thorough trend-based work commands attention as the most accurate statistical information about potential futures available and is the sort of evidence that experts and 'lens of now' thinkers are most likely to

BOX 5.3 Climate change: evidence and doubt

The Intergovernmental Panel on Climate Change in 2007 published a synthesis of the latest evidence on climate change. The evidence was:

> Eleven of the last twelve years (1995–2006) rank among the twelve warmest years in the instrumental record of global surface temperature (since 1850). The 100-year linear trend (1906–2005) of 0.74 [0.56 to 0.92]°C is larger than the corresponding trend of 0.6 [0.4 to 0.8]°C (1901–2000) ... The linear warming trend over the 50 years from 1956 to 2005 (0.13 [0.10 to 0.16]°C per decade) is nearly twice that for the 100 years from 1906 to 2005. (IPCC 2007)

The International Energy Agency estimated that emissions of carbon dioxide increased by 5 per cent from 2009 to 2010. Most scientists and many politicians were convinced that the world was heading for a climate catastrophe beyond 2100 but public concern in most countries was falling:

> [In a] 26-country poll, conducted by GlobeScan, a total of 13,389 people were asked to rate the seriousness of a range of environmental problems including climate change.
> Results from the 14 countries where GlobeScan has tracked opinion regularly since 1998 reveal that concern has fallen away particularly sharply on climate change. The proportion of people rating climate change as a 'very serious' problem fell from 61 percent to 53 percent this year [2010], after many years of increasing concern.
> While concern about climate change fell in many industrialised nations including the UK (down from 59 percent to 43 percent 'very serious'), the USA (down from 45 percent to 41 percent), and Germany (down from 61 percent to 47 percent), the findings also show that concern has risen in the last year in two major emerging economies: India (up from 45 percent to 53 percent) and Brazil (up from 86 percent to 92 percent). (GlobeScan 2010)

Why might this overall decline in concern be the case? For evidence to be compelling, it must be relevant. It must relate to clear desired outcomes. It must be given in terms that are comprehensible to those expected to act upon it. One of the fundamental difficulties with evidence of climate change is that citizens and governments are uncertain how to act upon it. This uncertainty acts in turn to build doubt about the evidence itself – because people cannot act upon their understanding, some question the understanding and, in turn, doubt the original evidence, along the lines of: 'This seems to be a very big problem, and it will probably badly affect future generations. I ought to do something about it. But I can do very little ... Perhaps the evidence is wrong.'

accept. But over-reliance on trend-based analysis is vulnerable to missing 'weak signals', 'wild cards' and 'strategic shocks'. (*Wild card* is a high impact but apparently unlikely event, for instance an asteroid strike or multiple hijacking of airliners by terrorists who then fly them into centres of government and commerce. A *weak signal* is a sign of an emerging trend, particularly attitudinal shift. *Strategic shock* is an alternative expression for a 'wild card').

Wave two: medium-term strategic analysis, which uses mainly modelling and systems techniques to surface the 'cocktail effect' of different drivers for change (as opposed to trends) – that is, their various permutations – and to surface some of the assumptions underlying our understanding of future developments. Much of this will relate to future developments in the four- to ten-year perspective (but can also be appropriate for much longer-term analysis work). Governments are more comfortable discussing the shorter-term and longer-term time horizons than the medium term, where trends are less certain but where the effects of policies are more certain, so this 'second wave' of futures work can often be the most controversial to present.

Wave three: longer-term analysis based on horizon scanning as well as trends and models and often presented as contrasting scenarios. These scenarios usually carry indicators of different futures developing, typically, over a ten- to 30-year time horizon. This enables politicians and administrators to

- think about the effects of those futures on their own organizations and how they can make them more resilient and responsive to such futures
- to construct leading indicators to track which future appears to be emerging
- to create a strategic vision of the *desired* future from the components of the scenarios.

Presenting analysis in the three waves means there's a mutually-reinforcing connection between each wave. The relevance of each type of analysis is clear, and you can use the appropriate analysis for each wave, rather than compromising.

Trend analysis

Having identified and agreed on the most important drivers for change, and gathered relevant, objective and clear evidence for each driver, the next stage in a strategic thinking process is to consider what the evidence suggests in terms of potential trends and counter-trends and to identify those that are dominant, and those that are dependent on a dominant trend. Trend analysis is used extensively in business, in science and in government. By analysing past and current trends and extrapolating a range of future trends it enables an organization to monitor which trend is developing and it also enables planning and preparation for the forecast trend.

The Scottish Government commissioned a series of Trend Analysis Papers in 2004–6 under the title of The Futures Project (Scottish Executive 2006). See Box 5.4.

BOX 5.4 Scottish Government Trend Analysis Paper

In 2006 the Scottish Government (then known as the 'Scottish Executive') published a paper analysing various national trends. Here is an extract:

Trend 3: More solo living: Why will this trend be significant for the people of Scotland?

The trend for more people to live alone is significant because of the policy implications it raises in terms of community and social care, pensions, employment, health and an increased demand for housing. Recent evidence suggests that there is a high expectation of childlessness amongst solo women; that those living solo report poorer health and are more likely to smoke and drink than those living with others; there are lower rates of economic activity amongst those of working age living solo than living with others; and those making a transition into solo living believe they are financially worse off afterwards.

This trend can be understood either optimistically or pessimistically in terms of relationships. Viewed pessimistically, the trend is symptomatic of a loss of connection to others. This may flow from excessive individualism or a pervasive sense of risk. Viewed optimistically, it can be seen as an aspect of the democratisation of personal life, creating a base from which equal and intimate relations with others can be sustained.

Solo living has become a common phase, with one person households now making up one-third of all households in both Britain and Scotland. This is a rising trend, with the percentage of 16–59 year olds living alone trebling in Britain from 5% of all households in 1971 to 16% in 2002 (26% in Scotland). It is proportionally more common amongst older people, which means that we can expect people to live a much greater proportion of their lives alone as they live longer. Older women (aged 65 and over) are twice as likely to live alone as older men, whereas young men (24–44) are more likely to live alone than young women. Solo living amongst adults aged 30–74 is higher in Scotland (18%) than the rest of Britain (15%). It is also much more common in cities than rural areas. It is often a temporary phase in the life-course, although there are far more transitions into it than out of it.

(Scottish Executive 2006. Reproduced under the terms of the
Open Government Licence)

The Scottish example highlights a fragility that can arise in a strategic process that relies too heavily on trend analysis. Officials and politicians can, without realizing it, make the assumption that well-established trends are bound to continue (a form of 'lens of now' thinking) and thus limit their analysis of potential *counter-trends* or they can fail to analyse counter-trends at all. In the Scottish 'solo living' example, for instance, the counter-trend would be a shift back to multiple-occupancy house-holds, which could be the product, for instance, of children staying with parents for longer – perhaps because of unemployment or reductions in availability of affordable housing; or it could be the result of aged parents being cared for by their children – perhaps because of the cost of care or because of a shift of attitudes. Even if a counter-trend is unlikely it should not be dismissed as long as it is *plausible*. Almost every trend in human history has broken at some point. The strategic approach is less concerned with the moment and nature of the break, a preoccupation of forecasters; the strategic approach must, however, understand that the trend will break, and examine the possible causes of the break and what the consequences might be. Understanding counter-trends helps the creation of scenarios (see later in this chapter), the development of desired outcomes and exploration of policy options.

Figure 5.3 provides an example of how a trend analysis on resistance of bacteria to antibiotics might look. In this case resistance of bacteria to antibiotics, therefore diminishing the efficacy of antibiotics, is one trend, and much reduced resistance of bacteria to antibiotics is another. The enhanced efficacy (for instance, resulting from rapid personalized treat-ments made possible by genetic profiling) is a counter-trend. Both are plausible. But a group of people working in this area might be familiar with working only in the context of one likely trend – and that trend

FIGURE 5.3   *Trend and counter-trend on resistance of bacteria to antibiotics*

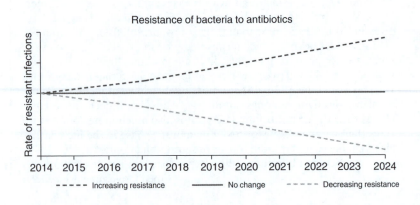

might frame all their work. One of the first things to do in a strategic process is gather more evidence of the counter-trend. Having gathered the evidence for each trend, a helpful next step in a strategic thinking process is to bring the available evidence together in the form of a narrative. This can create a plausible and meaningful picture of the consequences of both trend and counter-trend for a board, group of politicians, for stakeholders or the public.

BOX 5.5 Two imagined narratives of potential futures

Bacteria become increasingly resistant to antibiotics
Today in 2024 fears which we thought were consigned to history have returned to haunt us. Mrs Ruby Kansat yesterday saw her son Ambrose die from a cut finger – dying in a ward where seven others are awaiting death from small wounds. Twenty years ago penicillin would have made Ambrose's cut finger a minor inconvenience, but as year by year the various forms of bacteria have become resistant to antibiotics, avoiding infection has become a more and more important feature of our daily life. Ambrose played rugby, and his protective suit had always kept him out of harm's way. He cut himself by sliding his hand along a wooden seat – which had already been identified as due for replacement due to the risks of wood. Our ultra-hygienic, risk-controlled environment cannot save us all the time.

Example of a possible leading indicator from 2018
City hospital reports for the first time that for most common bacterial infections it has no effective response. GP referrals for such infections for the elderly, vulnerable and babies would be best left to homecare – or hospices.

Antibiotics become increasingly effective against bacteria
Today in 2024, Emily Williams' earache has caused her 50 minutes' pain. The doctor explained to Emily's mother that it was worth waiting the extra 20 minutes to prepare an antibacterial agent which was genetically tuned to both Emily and the bacterium. Such a targeted approach, he said, would mean that Emily could be treated effectively the next time she got a similar bug. He said to Emily's mother that he was worried that Emily had had so few infections in the last 18 months. Mrs Williams seemed hurt: 'My house really is quite dirty', she protested, and 'Emily has had plenty of chances to catch infections. She has had a high temperature and rash twice recently, and I sent her off to school with them as usual. The other parents were pleased that their child had had these chances to boost their immunity.'

Leading indicator 2018
GeneAppTech plc announces tailored antibacterial infection control agents, where the cycle time of reformulating and applying the agent is less than the cycle time of mutation of the target bacteria.

Narratives of potential futures

Narratives should be compelling stories that make the trends and counter-trends and 'strategic shocks' and 'weak signals' meaningful to a wider audience. Narratives should be written in journalistic form, in the present tense but from a future perspective. To avoid abstraction it is a good idea to populate the narrative with individuals rather than with generalized communities.

Box 5.4 shows two polarized narratives, one describing antibiotic resistance, the other more widespread and effective use of antibiotics. These two narratives 'tell a story' of the future. Each component of the story can be traced to an evidential source that reflects something that is either happening now or that has been identified by authoritative sources as a potential risk or opportunity given current trends, or 'weak signals' of future trends. This robustness in narratives is important – they are not 'blue skies thinking'. Narratives should invite challenge and be able to withstand challenge. Accessibility is almost as important as robustness. The ability to describe a future that can be 'seen, heard, felt and smelled' by those who read it is one of the keys to getting people to understand future scenarios and visions. It is creating *contrasting* narratives of futures relating to a particular issue – typically expressed as the product of a trend and a *counter-trend* – that is one of the essential steps in developing scenarios.

Identifying drivers, gathering evidence, including from forecasting and horizon scanning, identifying trends and counter-trends and finding ways of offering narratives of the future are all important stages in strategic thinking. However, the current and future environment is not made up of a series of component drivers and trends, but is a complex and ever-changing *system*, in which understanding the relationships between the different components is at least as important as understanding the drivers and trends themselves.

Systems, not machines

The machine view tends to prevail in the world of government. People talk of 'levers' which can be pulled, and make untested assumptions about causal relationships between a particular action, for instance the banning of a particular product, or an increase in tax or the creation of a particular service or agency, and the effects it will have. Yet these causal relationships are often imagined, rather than evidence-based. One of the main reasons that policies so often have unintended consequences (or no consequences at all) is not because of hurried implementation, or under-funding or poor project management (although these can all be problems), but because those who designed the policy or service or agency didn't understand that the business of government and other public services is conducted inside a complex adaptive system, not inside a mechanism. 'There are many implicit assumptions associated with mechanistic thinking and scientific management, but the two that are at the root of so many current difficulties are: the assumption of control – that organizations can be controlled in the way that machines can be controlled, to behave differently and produce different outputs: the presumption that the organizations involved in "delivery" behave in a predictable fashion so that the effects of interventions and policies can be predicted' (Chapman 2003: 51).

These assumptions do not simply impede the effectiveness of officials in framing policies and working for their delivery. They create an unhelpful construct in the minds of those who work in government – as unhelpful, in its way, as was the construct of a flat earth to early navigators. The construct results in actions that are damaging, in much the way that those who remove the parts of a frog assuming it can be reassembled as easily as a bicycle will seriously damage the frog: 'Intelligent leaders understand that complex systems are more like frogs than bikes. You can disassemble a bicycle completely, clean and oil the separate parts, and reassemble it confident that it will work as before. Frogs are different. The moment you remove any part, *all* the rest of the system is affected, instantly, in unpredictable ways, for the worse. Binary "leaders", and quite a few management consultants too, really do think that complex organizational systems will respond to the bicycle treatment. They think you can get a realistic picture of the total system by simply aggregating its *component* parts' (Mant 1997: 54).

Politicians and leaders sometimes complain that when they pull a lever nothing happens ('the levers aren't connected to anything'). Understanding an organization as a system in part of a wider system, as bundles of conversations or dialogue, which create value and depend on emergent behaviour, shows why perturbing the system can have more effect than seeking to command it. In the industrial era, or in industrialized nations, machines surpassed the productivity and efficiency of manual labour to the extent that the machine became a metaphor for efficiency. Today complex adaptive systems offer a better understanding of how economic, social and political processes actually function and change. That includes organizations – what Eric Beinhocker (2007) termed 'social technologies'. Axelrod and Cohen put it this way: 'Just as the clock and the steam engine provided powerful images for the metaphor of society as a machine, distributed information technology can provide a powerful image for society as a complex adaptive system. Already the internet provides an example that has begun to capture the popular imagination in the way that the early advances of the industrial age captured the imagination of social thinkers and the broad public. The fact that the internet functions without a central authority is widely marveled at today precisely because it challenges widely accepted notions of how large systems are "supposed to work"' (Axelrod and Cohen 1999: 30).

Axelrod points out that Adam Smith's 1776 description of a market introduced some of the key concepts of complex systems including the notion of a hidden hand and market clearing, concepts that would now be called emergent properties of the system. Emergence is a feature of systems, a property that you can't deduce from the system's component parts. For example, consciousness that emerges from 100 billion neurons of the human brain, or a whirlpool that emerges from trillions of water molecules are both emergent phenomena. Darwin's 1859 theory of evolutionary adaptation is another example. 'Most people in industrial nations have worked with machines and have been exposed to the discipline of the factory or the office. This has had a powerful influence on our way of thinking about politics and society. Today more and more people are becoming personally familiar with the flexible, adaptive and dispersed nature of information technology. This metaphor will make the metaphor of the complex adaptive system more compelling as a guide to thinking not just about information technology itself but also about how business, society and government can and should function effectively' (Axelrod and Cohen 2001: 30).

Systems approaches are able to help people to work more effectively when developing strategy or designing policy or working out how to deliver a service by obliging them to consider a much wider set of relationships than they might otherwise. Asking people to create system maps requires them to do a number of things that might otherwise be overlooked:

- consider the relationships between different drivers for change
- consider the nature of those relationships, and what assumptions are made about the relationships (for instance, that more urbanization leads to more traffic congestion)
- determine which drivers are the most important in the system under examination and whether some drivers are in fact not drivers in the context of the system but are instead products of other drivers
- consider whether there are causal loop or feedback loops between drivers.

A visual representation of the dynamic system in which the different drivers operate is a systems map, sometimes described as a logical model. The figure below is the result of a mapping exercise run by the authors with a group of policy and policing officials.

In Figure 5.4 the systems map shows the relationships between key drivers, for instance the degree of trust in authority and the age of population. It makes an assumption that an older population will have a

FIGURE 5.4   *A systems map for neighbourhood policing*

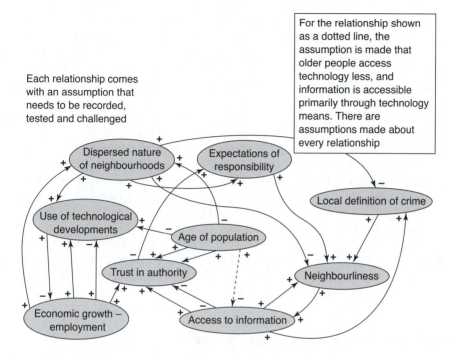

Each relationship comes with an assumption that needs to be recorded, tested and challenged

For the relationship shown as a dotted line, the assumption is made that older people access technology less, and information is accessible primarily through technology means. There are assumptions made about every relationship

greater trust in authority. But you will see that the group working on this systems map argued that there was also a relationship between older people and decreased trust in authority, for instance where authority is seen to favour younger people's rights, or where the group of older people are from a community traditionally resistant to authority. Systems maps can show quite complex sets of relationships and provide a good way of identifying relationships and gathering evidence to test relationships. But systems thinking does not always earn itself a good name. Systems approaches on their own cannot provide a whole strategy – they should be used to understand the landscape rather than build a new landscape. Systems models can sometimes seem baffling.

A systems map showing interdependencies in the security situation in Afghanistan entitled 'Dynamic Planning for COIN in Afghanistan' prompted the following from US General Stanley McChrystal: 'When we understand that slide, we'll have won the war.' These comments, made in mid-2009 but only reported widely in May 2010, shortly before the General's resignation, were seen as a condemnation both of the impenetrable complexity and irrelevance of a systems map, and at the same time of the dangers of over-simplification inherent in PowerPoint™ presentations.

The point of systems maps like the one attempting to map counter-insurgency dynamics in Afghanistan is not that it should provide a snapshot and instant understanding, but that it should help to surface, challenge and test some of the assumptions underlying the relationships between different drivers. Being part of the process that creates the systems map is far more useful than having it presented to you. The full presentation explains this rather better than the extracts published in the world's newspapers in May 2010. The diagram is widely available on the Internet under Afghanistan COIN dynamics, and see the bibliography – Afghanistan.

Systems thinking isn't new. Checkland, an advocate from the 1960s onwards, defined it in the following way: 'The central concept "system" embodies the idea of a set of elements connected together which form a whole, this showing properties which are properties of the whole, rather than properties of its component parts. (The taste of water, for example, is a property of the substance water, not of the hydrogen and oxygen which combine to form it.) The phrase "systems thinking" implies thinking about the world outside ourselves' (Checkland 1981: 3).

Having identified drivers, evidence, trends and counter-trends, narratives and systems, the strategic thinking process now has the elements it needs to build one of the most well-known instruments of strategic thinking: scenarios.

Scenarios – pictures of the future

Scenarios have been a core part of strategy work for more than half a century. Among the first to use them were the RAND Institute (www.rand.org) in the 1940s, followed soon after by the Stanford Research Institute. They were adopted and adapted by the Hudson Research Institute in the 1960s. Since that time they have been the relatively unchanging core of strategic thinking and planning. Some well-known users of scenarios include:

- Royal Dutch Shell (www.shell.com), which produces scenarios on a three-year cycle which inform a range of corporate decisions
- The World Economic Forum, which produces scenarios for particular countries and regions (www.weforum.org)
- The US National Intelligence Council, whose scenario work aims to increase US resilience to strategic threats (www.dni.gov)
- UK Government's Foresight projects (www.foresight.gov.uk).

Scenarios build contrasting pictures of the future operating environment for a business, for a government, for a government department, local authority, agency or other organization. They can be used to bring people together to create shared understandings of the future. Scenario-building processes have played an important part in peace processes, for instance the South African *Mont Fleur* scenarios and, more recently, in Guatemala's *Vision Guatemala*. The most useful scenarios contain sufficient specific detail to enable indicators to be put in place which can be monitored so that the organization knows which future appears to be coming about and can respond early and appropriately, thus increasing resilience.

BOX 5.6   South Africa: building post-apartheid scenarios at Mont Fleur

Nelson Mandela was released from prison in 1990, and the ANC, the South African Communist Party, the Pan African Congress and other parties were 'unbanned' by the apartheid regime. In the three years that followed many informal groups were created alongside the formal negotiations that led to the 1994 elections that brought the ANC to power and made Nelson Mandela South Africa's first majority-elected president. One informal group was the diverse set of 22 South Africans from across the political spectrum who met three times during 1991–92 at Mont Fleur, near Stellenbosch, to create four scenarios that described potential futures for South Africa. The four final scenarios were:

'Ostrich' – a non-representative government, the product of no settlement or failed negotiations

'Lame duck' – an incapacitated government, the product of an insufficiently rapid and decisive transition

'Icarus' – macro-economic populism, resulting in government policies being unsustainable

'Flight of the flamingos' – inclusive democracy and growth, the product of decisive transition, coupled with prudent macro-economic policies (Kahane *et al.* 1997).

The scenarios did not attempt to predict a future, nor did they resolve all disagreements among the participants. But the process did enable those who participated to reach a shared vocabulary and an understanding of the problems that faced South Africa in the coming decade. At the end of the process the scenarios received widespread coverage in the South African media and helped to stimulate a wider national discussion about the future of South Africa, prompting the President, F. W. de Klerk, to say 'I am not an ostrich.' While one scenario *Flight of the Flamingos* was clearly preferable to the other three, it was not intended to be a blueprint. The role of the scenarios was to help everyone involved in the transition process to look out for signs that one scenario was developing rather than another and to understand that there were many possible outcomes from the negotiations and majority rule (Kahane 2012).

Organizations can also prepare risk mitigation strategies for different scenarios or stakeholder engagement strategies or innovation strategies. Because they are contextualized for a future operating environment rather than the current one, strategies developed using scenarios are likely to be more robust than ones developed without – and because the future is uncertain, scenarios are developed not for a single conceived future but for several. Scenarios can be used not only for organizational or national/local strategy development but for policy areas or sectors (for example, childcare; public health; national security; energy). Scenarios can also be used to engage and motivate a workforce or stakeholders or citizens – both through increasing awareness of a future situation, perhaps one that is undesirable, and through increasing the appetite to move towards a future that is seen as desirable.

When to use scenarios

- If there is a need to understand possible futures
- In an environment of uncertainty
- In dealing with complexity
- To inform a new strategy or strategic direction
- If there is a need to prioritize action
- To stimulate creativity, to open up thinking.

The method adopted to build the *Mont Fleur* scenarios comprised of an initial brainstorming workshop in September 1991 in which 30 ideas, many of them sharply conflicting and sharply disagreed by participants, were produced. Following this research was conducted and nine preliminary stories were produced. A second workshop took place in November 1991 and, following further consultation four draft scenarios were produced. These were refined in a third workshop in March 1992 to become the *Mont Fleur* scenarios.

There are many other methods of scenario building.

Royal Dutch Shell and scenario planning

It's hard to unravel causal effects in a complex adaptive system like a multinational corporation – even those involved will have different perspectives or will believe they know 'what really happened'. There are lots of academic descriptions of the Shell scenario process, most famously Pierre Wack's two articles in the Harvard Business Review (Wack 1985). An absorbing account of what went on behind the scenes is Art Kleiner's description in *The Age of Heretics* (Kleiner 2008), which also paints a picture of the perils and pitfalls of trying to use scenarios in a numbers-run corporation. Scenarios are evidence, even if they are not traditionally seen as such.

Kleiner describes how, in 1964, Royal Dutch Shell decided it should have its own futures team led by one of its planners, Ted Newland. The oil price had been around two dollars per barrel for a couple of decades. Yet worldwide demand – for supplies of oil that were finite – was rising steadily. If economic growth continued, then oil prices would have to rise with profound shocks to industrialized economies.

How would oil-producing states behave? Would they leave oil in the ground, appreciating in value, rather than in the bank, depreciating? Did they have large populations and the need to invest in infrastructure and so require cash from increased oil extraction? Would they use oil as a political weapon? How might they react to control of oil production by wealthy Western industrialized countries whose economies were dependent on their oil reserves?

Newland used scenario techniques pioneered by the RAND Corporation and Herman Kahn's Hudson Institute and, aware that convincing a single executive can't change corporate policy, Shell chose a compelling storyteller, Pierre Wack, to speak to Shell managers throughout the world about Newland's analysis. Wack was a remarkable packager of ideas into coherent storylines and had an ability to find phrases that fixed his points in the imagination of listeners. He showed that across six scenarios Shell would need fewer tankers and different types of refineries (see Jefferson 2012 and Wack 1985 for more on the Shell scenarios story).

It is worth considering the Shell scenarios case in more detail. One scenario showed that free-market forces would solve the problem, another that industrial governments might act together and negotiate with the Arab world. A muddling through scenario relied on energy saving. A low-demand scenario posited that people would voluntarily consume less, and governments would promote energy efficiency. A high-supply scenario suggested oil companies would develop enough new oil to keep on top of the world's demand – a scenario that would appeal to the instincts of oil companies to explore, drill, refine, ship more oil. We saw in Chapter 4 the risks of selecting futures that align with particular worldviews and existing capabilities. Kleiner points out that as long as Shell felt the best policies were to 'explore and drill, build refineries, order tankers, and expand markets' they could not help perceiving evidence in support of these policies wherever they looked.

Wack addressed this by showing the high-supply scenario would require three miracles. Oil companies would rapidly have to find reserves in new regions. OPEC (the cartel of Oil Producing and Exporting Countries) countries would have to become willing to sell as much oil as they could produce, happier with massive amounts of money in the bank than with oil in the ground. Finally, there would have to be no extra strain on oil demand – wars or extra-cold winters. And any single small accident could upset the whole system.

The scenarios had an effect on managers. A few Shell engineers began designing refineries that could switch from Kuwait crude to Saudi or Iranian (they had different technical requirements), depending on what was available. But before refined scenarios could be adopted by group planning to guide investment and strategy in late 1973 OPEC had announced they would set the price of crude oil themselves. The oil companies could take the arrangement or leave it, and the OPEC countries would find other commercial partners. The oil price quadrupled.

One of the scenarios had suggested that the price of oil might jump fivefold to ten dollars a barrel. This was too extreme for Shell's managing directors, though within a year, the price would rise above 13 dollars and fluctuate between 40 dollars, back down to seven dollars, and ultimately rise to over 100 dollars.

Jefferson notes that although the scenario work had many brilliant and insightful features, 'There was serious failure up to early 1974 to understand fully and take due note of forces "already in the pipeline"; failure to draw on past experience – from economic and social history, from past financial crises, from the operation of business organizations and industrial cartels, from past military and religious conflict; from the history of the Middle East (especially the Gulf); and failure to assess sufficiently the risks of taking one's eyes off the short and medium term for whatever reason' (Jefferson 2012: 187).

In particular Kleiner and Jefferson point to the particular dependence for success on certain personalities and, of course, for every scenario exercise that produced a rational link between scenarios and strategies pursued there will be many that don't succeed. The product is not the scenarios, but the conversations they stimulate and the way these influence decisions, or the visions developed, as a consequence of broader thinking.

The oil industry was, until this point, muddling through on two assumptions; that oil would remain plentiful and prices would remain low. Wack presented the Shell senior management with stories or scenarios that would change their perception of the need to plan for many different possible futures. Senior managers decided to question initial assumptions and discovered that OPEC were intending to increase their oil prices. Although the Oil Shock of 1973 overtook the conclusion of the process Shell was the only major Western company (or nation for that matter) that was prepared. Within two years, Shell moved from the eighth biggest oil company to the second.

The Shell method became an established approach in Shell with a scenario team preparing scenarios every three years. It uses the following steps:

- Decide drivers for change/assumptions
- Bring drivers together into a viable framework

- Produce initial (7–9) mini scenarios
- Reduce to 2–3 scenarios
- Draft the scenarios
- Identify the issues arising.

Today Shell uses its scenarios to increase awareness of policy options through 'scenario excursion' – publicizing and presenting its scenarios to governments, so that some scenarios can almost become self-fulfilling prophecies, 'colonising the future' as Barbara Adam puts it (Adam 2004: 1) – Shell (not alone among major corporations), in this respect acting more like governments than governments themselves, adopts a public strategy urging the creation of better futures.

The 'two axes' scenarios method

One way of building a scenario is to use the axes (or 'dimensions') of uncertainty method (see Figure 5.5). Two axes cross to produce four quadrants. This method can be used to produce four strongly contrasting scenarios. The method takes two drivers or trends and produces in each quadrant a scenario. You must choose as your axes drivers or trends that are both important AND uncertain. It is also helpful to have at least one driver that relates to social attitudes and change; these drivers are too often overlooked or undervalued because the data aren't as easy to manipulate as quantitative data and because we live through and gradually adapt to social change, often without realizing it.

The systems modelling process (discussed in the previous section) can help us to identify the key drivers in the system – these will often translate into our axes of uncertainty. It's also possible to 'cluster' drivers together to create an aggregated dimension of uncertainty.

Making use of scenarios

Scenarios can be 'normative' – projecting forward from permutations of drivers as above, or use backcasting, where the scenarios start with a particular vision and work back to see what needs to happen to lead to it. In the case of normative scenarios, too, it helps with plausibility if you can identify the events, or milestones, that lead to the story described in each quadrant.

Scenarios are a useful way of developing dialogue and creating a shared understanding of an organization's current and likely future context, to increase awareness of uncertainty and to create the environment for more innovative thinking. Scenarios are a method of sensitizing an organization to 'weak signals' in the wider world, signals that may either disappear or

142

FIGURE 5.5   *The two-axes method of building scenarios*

In the following example scenarios are created using the axes/dimensions of 'reliance on the state by the citizen' and 'equality of society'. Each end of the axis will express one extreme of the chosen driver (or 'dimension' or 'trend'). For example the extremes for reliance by the citizen on the state could be either 'citizens dependent on the state', or 'citizens self-reliant'. The extremes for equality within society could be either 'a society of equality' or 'a society divided between rich and poor'. The axes should be selected from previous exercises, in which the most uncertain and most important drivers have been identified both from 'drivers for change' exercises and from systems thinking exercises.

Stage 1:

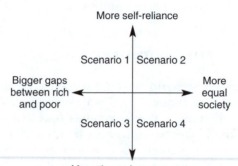

Stage 2:

Now the axes of uncertainty are labelled which gives the basis of four contrasting scenarios. They are:

Scenario 1: More self-reliance, with bigger gaps between the rich and poor
Scenario 2: More self-reliance, more equal society
Scenario 3: More dependent on the state, and a more equal society
Scenario 4: More dependent on state, and bigger gaps between the rich and poor

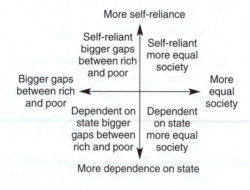

Stage 3:

Two of the fuller scenarios (which would draw on strategic thinking and analysis of drivers, trends, counter-trends, forecasts, horizon scanning and systems thinking) for scenarios 1 and 3 would look something like this:

Scenario 1: Self-reliant – bigger gaps between rich and poor, entitled *Life, liberty, and the pursuit of happiness*

Today in 2022, our material standard of living is as high as it has ever been, and we are increasing our lead over other developed countries. The entry of China and India into the global economy has provided us with many opportunities to create new industries. The developments in biotechnology have given our companies a firm grip on new and heavyweight world markets. Old economy activities still produce in volume terms the same as ten years ago, but with a fifth of the workforce. Unemployment is low, but persistent in those parts of the workforce who worked in businesses short-circuited by the internet, and the middle managers of the past struggle to find a role. Crime is at the same level as in the past, and confined to the same sectors of society. Despite increased retirement ages, public pension, and benefit deficits continue to grow. The unsustainable nature of these is now so severe as to be beyond the capacity of policy-makers to confront (and so on ...)

Scenario 3: Dependent on state – more equal society, entitled *Peace, order and good governance*

Today in 2022, our material standard of living is almost as high as it ever has been and unemployment is relatively low with the adoption of on the job training. The gap between the advantaged and the disadvantaged is narrowing. International competition has made life difficult for many of our major companies, but they focus on areas where they have unique and deep knowledge to deliver products and services not easily available elsewhere in the world. The role of the government in underwriting risk has enabled us to find our niche in the world economy. The reduction in unemployment and income inequality has brought down crime – and the reduction of the costs (for example security guards, insurance) have benefited the budgets of both public and private sector. Despite increased retirement ages, public pension and benefit deficits continue to grow. Public policy-makers have the support of their citizens in making the necessary changes ... (and so on ...)

suddenly amplify. They are a starting point for provoking conversations, not a product in their own right. It's astonishing how this happens at the level of the individual – you notice the pieces in newspapers that could be weak signals you might otherwise skip. They prime conversations so that discussions about the future don't take place at cross purposes as a result of people having different implicit perspectives they otherwise have no opportunity to synchronize by making explicit.

Scenarios are practical tools that are too often used as 'adornments' to management consulting when they could be used for more robust purposes, for instance:

- to test current policies of a government or an organization against potential futures, identifying in which future existing policies will perform best and in which worst. If the most likely future is that in which existing polices will fare worst then some mitigating strategies need to be developed

- to test in the same way current stakeholder relationships and resource allocations against different futures
- to run a gap analysis to establish what new measures, policies, resources, capabilities and relationships will be needed or will be superfluous in particular futures, and which are common in all futures
- to develop leading indicators which the organization can track to help identify as early as possible which likely future is developing
- to 'windtunnel' or 'future proof' planned future policies, resource allocations and so on against particular futures.

Scenario building stimulates thinking and helps planning, and shares possible futures more widely. Scenarios are not forecasts. The future is likely to contain elements of all of the different scenarios, and none of them. They are necessarily speculative and have to survive sceptical readers by being based on a rigorous process, deriving the components of the scenarios from horizon scanning and other strategic thinking techniques. Some audiences will see their purpose and simply accept the premises in order to consider implications for their area of business. Much of the value of scenarios is in the process as well as the result. Scenarios can also help us create our visions of the desired future, being an evidentially-based source for that vision (sometimes called a 'fifth scenario', based on aspects of each of the quadrants) from which the desired outcomes that will be the destination of the strategic thinking process can be derived (see Chapter 7 'Building a vision of a desired future').

Conclusion: it's a state of mind

'[Strategy is]...a state of mind. It's a constant reconciling of possibilities, means and ends and it requires, in a very complex world that we now live in, a lot of analysis and judgement and assessment' (UK Member of Parliament Bernard Jenkin speaking on 18 October 2010, interviewed on BBC Radio 4's *Today* Programme).

Strategic thinking does not come to us naturally – we need some approaches and techniques to help us to adopt the discipline of strategy. Scenario thinking, for instance, is helpful because it nudges people out of the default position – imagining the future is 'more of today' – and into the exploration of alternative futures. This is the cornerstone of strategic thinking, embracing uncertainty and shaping uncertainty into positive ideas and plans for the future. Scenarios and visions (see Chapter 7) also help to bring conversations about the future to the same starting point, by synthesizing our different conceptions and models of the future instead of leaving them sitting unexplored and a potential source of confusion and disagreement.

Strategic thinking does not create an illusion of control and certainty where it does not exist. This can make it hard for some people to embrace or even to understand, because for many the fact that no one is ultimately in control – whether gods or governments – is distressing. The hard message of strategic thinking is – or should be – that we shape our own destinies. It is worth reminding ourselves again of the Final Report of the National Commission on Terrorist Attacks on the United States: 'We believe the 9/11 attacks revealed four kinds of failures: in imagination, policy, capabilities, and management ... It is therefore crucial to find a way of routinizing, even bureaucratizing, the exercise of imagination' (National Commission on Terrorist Attacks on the United States 2004).

Strategic thinking is ultimately an act of imagination. The techniques we have described in this chapter help us to 'bureaucratize' imagination, to organize the process of imaginative thinking into something that can be shared, understood and melded purposefully. For without imagination there can be no progress.

Chapter 6

Acting Strategically: Building Strategic Appetite

In Chapter 4 we considered a range of obstacles to strategy-making and the advantages of recognizing these. Chapter 5 discussed a process for strategic thinking that would help to produce a strategy. But strategies are only effective in the right circumstances. In this chapter we recommend ways to create the right institutional conditions for good strategy development and implementation, and offer suggestions on how to stimulate an appetite for strategic thinking in the first place. Without appetite there is little point in a strategic thinking process, investing in strategy teams or a horizon scanning centre, buying in analysis from consultants, reorganizing an agency or taking the management board or political leadership on awaydays. The organization has to *believe* that strategy matters.

Building strategic appetite

Most approaches to working strategically begin with a textbook, a website, a Masters course, a training programme, a facilitated event, a new organizational design, a new recruitment and performance management system or with consultants. These may produce interventions based on a particular model, diagnostic tool or methodology for strategy-making. These are all valid approaches but they are unlikely to be helpful in isolation from other institutional changes to increase appetite. Building capability (in its narrow definition of knowledge and skills) without first building the desire and confidence to work strategically (to ensure, first, that *appetite* to work more strategically is present) won't create more strategic organizations in government and the wider public sphere.

Governmental bias towards problem-solving rather than goal-seeking, combined with the tendency towards short-termism that we explored in Chapter 4, can produce a strong counter-current against strategic working. 'Firefighting' jobs are often seen as glamorous – people notice the 'goals scored not goals saved'. Those who excel in a crisis can develop a habit of creating or finding a crisis to excel in. Another rationalization is that the pace of change renders planning pointless, but this attitude overlooks long-run socio-cultural trends that have profound consequences on how people behave and the economic implications of their behaviour. It's the long cycle changes that creep up on us and change our environment completely. In this context receptiveness to capability-building approaches that don't first increase appetite is likely to be low or superficial. This is one reason why people can *appear* to be highly receptive to a training programme or series of events, but revert to tried and tested ways of working as soon as they get back to their offices. In other words, the enthusiastic embrace of a training programme, or even the development and publication of a new strategy, can be like a kind of religious ceremony, where supplicants are gathered in a special place, follow a liturgy led by a shaman or priest, make a number of vows, with the net effect that, suitably 'cleansed', they return to their normal way of doing things. The *Theory of Rituals* can be helpful in understanding the relative ineffectiveness of many consultancy or training interventions (Bell 1992).

Increasing 'capability' without also increasing appetite at best leads to better-informed inaction. We know something previously unknown to us, but our comfort zone is for familiar ways of working, reinforced by the expectations others have of us. This makes bravery, courage and doggedness important qualities in the strategic field. Consideration of preferences and what drives them (and steering a course that takes account of them) too rarely happens – partly because public sector commissioning of training, learning or consultancy have incentives that favour activity over achieving the outcome.

At worst strategic interventions can build a hard shell of resistance, cynicism and blatant opposition to strategic working – 'inoculation against strategy'.

Models, methodologies, toolkits and so on can have the effect of switching off the very thinking that they are supposed to switch on. Public officials are often keen to adopt checklists, processes, scorecards, seven-step approaches where they can check off each stage. It's a way of simplifying complexity and making sense of the world. Well-defined procedures suggest transparency in the selection of priorities, but run the risk of compartmentalizing strategic processes, which in turn disconnects them from the larger strategy. They seem to offer a way of depersonalizing processes – allowing officials to present a model or method as something they are obliged to follow and that – at some level – has 'nothing to do with them'. The cumulative effect of these frameworks for strategy-making can be to decrease levels of engagement with the current and future positions and the journey that needs to be made between them.

Overcoming the obstacles to working strategically described in Chapter 4 begins with increasing the desire and confidence to work strategically, whether for a government as a whole, an authority or agency, of those working on a particular programme or across a particular sector. There's no template or 'checklist' for how to go about this, but leadership through emphasis on outcome, change, challenge and accountability are crucial. Let's look at each of these areas in turn.

Leading with outcomes

Leaders in government – both elected and appointed – can overestimate their ability to get things done through direct action. They can see themselves hampered by a lack of strategic capability among their staff and seek alternative ways to get the job done in order to fulfil their strategic ambitions for the organization. They may try to focus on increasing knowledge and skills (superficial capability), or buy capacity (outsourcing, consulting) or turn the process of realizing their ambitions into a set of projects (input/output working; 'pushing on a rope'). These approaches further *diminish* the strategic capability of their organizations, placing more reliance on the same measures that have already reduced strategic capability – a classic vicious cycle. The same leaders can, conversely, underestimate the *influence* they have on their staff because people may take a casual, offhand observation or throw-away remark as an indication of strategy.

You can get things done as a leader when you are clear about the outcomes you are trying to achieve. As we saw in Chapter 2, some people distinguish leadership from management when it comes to problem-solving, because the leader deals with 'wicked problems' (problems which are novel rather than familiar, and have no clear cause and effect). Leading strategically means leading with outcomes, and is goal-seeking rather than primarily problem-solving although a strategy will have to identify and explicitly address barriers to achievement of outcomes.

Clarity, consistency and persistence in both messages and signals about the future is vital. The more contradictory the signals the more confused staff will become and ultimately people will stop acting on any signal in the expectation that it will be contradicted.

By concentrating first on building desire and confidence to work strategically, leaders can quite quickly build greater capability.

Leaders need to recognize where the organization has come from and where it is at present. Recent problems need to be talked about honestly, as do the successes. People respect leaders who show they have a grasp of what has gone well and what has gone badly. Leaders need to give credit to those individuals and teams within an organization who have achieved results, and also give credit to those who have worked hard but been less successful, while showing that they understand the difference between the two. There are incentives in government to present recent history as an untarnished triumph or, if there has been a recent change of government, an unalloyed disaster. Neither position is likely to be true, and will certainly not be credible. People identify this as insincere or dishonest. It can undermine what follows. Political leaders often find it difficult to speak critically of the recent past if their own party was in control, and equally find it difficult to speak in praise of achievements where an opposition party was in control. But where leaders do speak honestly and objectively it is almost invariably well-received and lays important foundations for subsequent success.

Having spoken in a balanced and objective way about the recent past and the present, leaders need to start talking about the future. A popular and successful Chief Executive of one government food safety agency began his tenure by talking to staff individually as well as in small groups and observing 'We're very focused on today, aren't we ...?' and asking whether people felt that the organization was too concerned with the day-to-day, and not on the long-term effects the agency wanted to achieve. He prompted extensive discussion about where the agency was headed and about the future operating environment that helped to increase the organizational appetite for strategic working. Talking about the future does not mean that leaders themselves provide the analysis of potential futures for their staff (that needs to be an inclusive process), but it can begin to provide the framework for building capability in strategic thinking by showing that they are interested in the future of the organization or programme they are leading five or ten years hence.

There is no point making the effort to talk objectively about the current situation but describing the future in platitudes and clichés, for example terms like 'world class', 'leading edge' and 'centre of excellence'. Equally, starting the process of convincing people that the organization is going to be more future-focused but sending signals about 'quick wins', or the urgent need to meet a budget target or make an efficiency gain will seem inconsistent and confusing, even though short-term imperatives must often be met even when trying to focus on the longer term: it is a matter of signalling what is important. If the signals are confusing, people will tend to respond either by playing safe and waiting until they are clear what the leadership really wants or by growing cynical and failing to engage. The result in either case will be no appetite for strategy, preventing the development of strategic capability.

None of this is to deny the importance of the quick wins that are often needed, or the budgetary targets and efficiency gains that are nearly always necessary and important. But the chances are these are already more than familiar to the people who work in any organization. People understand that they have not gone away simply because the leadership talks less about them and more about the future. There is an unhelpful and quite mistaken belief that there has to be a 'trade-off' between present demands and future resilience. In fact the two are mutually reinforcing, or can be when developed with 'line of sight'. Developing the appetite and capability to think, plan and act for the future does not limit the ability to work quickly and effectively in the present. But a preoccupation only with the present without the desire and confidence to think, plan and act for the future does impair the ability of organizations to respond to and shape the future.

Early signals to the organization that leaders mean what they say about the future need not be time-consuming or difficult. Useful signals include praising staff who show a keenness to identify future trends, counter-trends and scenarios, and who focus on outcomes. Notes issued from time to time from a chief executive, a minister, a council leader (or from their offices) saying, for instance, 'The Chief Executive was pleased to see the future focus of this work, and its identification of potential outcomes for the organization in five years' time' can work wonders. People will discuss this among themselves and it will underline the belief that the talk from the top about the future is serious. Why? Because staff are in any case already attuned to the signals that 'quick wins' are valued, and that praise is given for cost savings achieved or useful briefs produced at short notice. Those things get taken seriously anyway, and (because they so rarely see reward for longer-term advice or orientation) it is one of the reasons staff see longer-term thinking undervalued by leaders.

Change

Minor institutional changes can be totemic. Board meetings have a habit of focusing on the immediate, looking at current performance, short-term trends and tackling problems affecting the organization or its operating environment. Boards – and their political equivalents at cabinet and committee level – are often also the places where departmental interests are on display. Even strong leaders can't prevent this – nor should they, because the senior leadership team needs to discuss problems and reach agreement on how they will tackle them. But if they do *only* this they don't offer direction to the organization or play a role in building organizational capability for strategic working. One way is to get boards to discuss strategic issues to the exclusion of other issues regularly. These strategic discussions need to include politicians as well as administrators and should exclude the usual discussion of current performance and problems (because they will crowd out all other discussion) and focus instead on analysing the organization's future operating environment and identify medium- and long-term outcomes, and consider identification and adjustment of existing objectives and programmes. This sends a signal to the wider organization that it takes strategy seriously.

An alternative approach is a separate 'strategy board' or 'policy commissioning board', ideally chaired by the most senior political and

BOX 6.1 The UK Foreign and Commonwealth Office 2006–10: building strategic capability

Following a rapid strategic review conducted in late 2007 the Foreign and Commonwealth Office (UK foreign ministry known in Britain as the 'FCO') moved from ten strategic priorities to four policy outcomes, with four supporting objectives, with clear line of sight between each. For each of the new objectives the Foreign Secretary (the most senior foreign affairs minister) commissioned a 'sub-strategy' that was compiled by a combination of Strategy Unit and other FCO staff with relevant external consultation.

With the refreshed objectives came more tangible changes in the FCO's alignment of resources and work, including resource shifts from Europe to the Middle East, Asia and parts of Africa to reflect changing government priorities; establishment of a $60 billion trade target with China and £10 billion worth of future contracts with India in January 2008 in support of the UK economy; a 'Know Before You Go' campaign to support UK nationals travelling abroad; the launch of a new migration strategy entitled 'Managing Global Migration' to support the aim of managed migration for Britain; and a significant increase in resources allocated to countering terrorism and weapons proliferation by the 2008–09 Comprehensive Spending Review (national budgeting process). In the words of a senior official involved in the process: 'This [the strategy] did drive resource allocation. We moved people out of some offices and into areas like climate change, and regions like China and Brazil that were pivotal in achieving our refreshed objectives.'

The FCO created a Strategy & Policy Commissioning Board chaired by the Foreign Secretary. The creation of the Board sent a signal through the organization that strategic thinking was a valued skill in the modern FCO.

The Strategy & Policy Commissioning Board commissioned the Strategy Unit to provide strategy support to wider teams and departments at the FCO. Project teams generally consisted of a Project Director, the 'project owner' (from a particular team or directorate), a 'post' (or country) expert, a functional expert, a research analyst and one or more cross-government participants, with external 'red teams' providing a challenge function.

The Strategy Unit's projects included emerging issues such as the implications of melting Arctic ice caps for national security; international maritime law and UK shipping paths; and using the Afghan Diaspora in the UK to better understand and influence the outcomes of the UK's involvement in Afghanistan.

most senior permanent official in the organization, to meet and respond to proposals from the organization on the major future issues that it will face, looking ten years or so ahead. The board can commission further analytical work on some of those. This embeds futures analysis within the organization and increases appetite. Is shows the leadership is not just paying lip-service to long-term thinking. Strategy discussions should not take the place of action, they must translate into strategy processes (Chapter 5), and into implementation and performance monitoring (Chapter 7).

Urgency can generate a desire to change. Beckhard and Gleicher's model (Beckhard and Harris 1977: 25) suggests that change requires a degree of dissatisfaction with the current situation that is greater than the resistance or cost of change, expressed in their 'change equation':

$$C = (ABD) > X$$

where   C = change
         A = level of dissatisfaction with the status quo
         B = clear desired state
         D = practical first steps towards the desired first state
         X = cost of change.

A, B and D must all have roughly the same value for change to occur. So even where there is a very strong vision of the desired state, if dissatisfaction with the current state is low, or there is no sense of what the first concrete steps towards realization of the desired state are, change will be blocked. Equally, if there is a strong dissatisfaction with the current situation and a sense of first steps but a weak vision, change will be unlikely. And in all cases the elements in favour of change must amount to more than the weight of resistance to (or 'cost') of change. Beckhard's work focuses primarily on organizational change, but the change equation can be a helpful way of seeing systemic or societal change, too, and whether the organization lags behind.

A sense of how long it will take to get to the new and better position will gain commitment of staff to invest time in a process that identifies a vision of the future and what first steps they must take. People wary of making open-ended commitments can feel comfortable with a process that will take ten weeks, ten months or longer, if that's specified. They will expect their contribution to be used, that there will be difference at the end of the process and that the change, whatever it is, will stick. Leaders create that energy and sense of defined journey. If they do, then appetite is likely to be high – though if tangible progress is not made then people can quickly become disillusioned. In practice the most successful strategic reviews seem to last between three and nine months, followed by implementation, resource reallocation, and regular review and adjustment of strategic direction.

Many of these approaches should embed an appetite for strategic thinking and action and affect the culture of the organization or 'the way we do things around here', based on self-reinforcing behaviours, beliefs and values. This gives an organization a sense of identity – 'who we are', 'what we stand for', 'what we do'. The fact that organizations build up their own identity through tradition, history (an organization's culture encapsulates what it has been good at it in the past) and structure means that changing the culture takes time and sustained effort. The culture, and its readiness to think long term, is a key factor contributing to an organization's success or failure.

Although culture seems nebulous it is readily visible in the language an organization uses, as explained by Gill Ereaut (Verity 2012). The relatively new discipline of behavioural economics includes the use of 'framing' or 'priming' often by using language to shape automatic behaviour (Kahneman 2011). The concept of positive deviance (Pascale *et al.* 2010) shows that once people begin to act differently, they induce different responses from those around them, creating a reinforcing loop that can act as a catalyst for culture change.

Challenge

Diversity of thought and experience help to develop strategic capability. Conformity can suppress strategic appetite if it inhibits challenge. Sometimes a misplaced loyalty to the organization, in the form of conformity to its processes, will conflict with a greater loyalty to the interests of the public. Statements like 'there's no point in trying that because we tried it once before …' or, 'we must do this because it's what the minister has asked for …' should not go unchallenged. Politicians are often as frustrated by the lack of constructive challenge from officials as they are by the fact that things don't seem to be delivered on the ground.

While it's important to follow recognized ways of 'doing business' – for instance, which departments or agencies are routinely consulted on proposals, or how parliamentary questions (questions from elected representatives to ministers responsible for departments of government or outcomes) are dealt with – these processes should not constrain the ability to question current policies and programmes; if anything they should provide a framework to encourage that questioning. Government often recruits people into senior jobs to bring fresh approaches and a sense of challenge to the *status quo*, yet then seems to do all it can to get those same people to conform.

One good way to encourage challenge is to *celebrate the outliers*. Public organizations often seek to anonymize and collectivize ideas for new initiatives or for the delivery of programmes. In many ways this is helpful – it can encourage shared responsibility when things don't go as planned and shared credit when things go well. It can also mean that individual good ideas get lost or are credited to a senior official when they actually originated with original thinkers in the organization, often someone with strong strategic appetite – not a 'groupthinker' but, typically, an 'outlier' who has picked up and responded to a sign of impending change that others have missed. Giving space to outlying opinion, analysis and proposals, and giving credit when the organization adopts that thinking, is an effective way to reinforce healthy challenge. It is a lesson that can be learned from successful and innovative firms, who – like Google and 3M – encourage staff to spend 15–20 per cent of their time working on 'own projects', in order to reinforce an appetite for thinking, experimentation and innovation. These firms and others, like Procter & Gamble, know that new ideas give them resilience in changing markets and the potential for competitive advantage.

Outliers who achieve results using only the same resources that their colleagues have, who take personal responsibility for outcomes and who interpret the rules of the organization in ways that will let them contribute to the outcomes are sometimes referred to as 'positive deviants'. Surgeon Atul Gawande (Gawande 2008) has five suggestions for becoming a positive deviant, which include asking an unscripted question 'where did you grow up' rather than 'where's the pain'. This helps a surgeon connect with their patient as a human rather than as a case, but can also have the positive effect of knocking the patient's or the surgeon's thinking off the tramlines framed by the institutional environment. Gawande provides the foreword to Richard Pascale's book *The Power of Positive Deviance* (2010) which describes case studies of unconventional approaches to solving social problems like childhood malnutrition, infant mortality and hospital acquired infections.

Delphi forecasts can be another useful way to discover outlying thinking. The Delphi Method as developed by the RAND Corporation aimed to use the knowledge of staff in the process of forecasting without the effects of groupthink. The process is a method of asking opinions on a set of questions and feeding back aggregated results anonymously in a series of iterations, noting consensus and areas of disagreement. This has the additional role of building strategic appetite. Asking staff throughout an organization a set of standard questions regularly, they become used to giving their opinions about the future. It can also encourage people to learn more about the issues they are being asked about.

Valerdi (2011) warns 'numerous threats to validity come from cognitive biases in Delphi participants'. Although the Delphi method was developed to eliminate biases that emerge during group decision-making, the facilitator must remain vigilant against any that do appear. Quantitative consensus must not be mistaken for practical consensus. If an individual chooses an answer choice just to match his or her peers, then the resulting estimate is of little practical use.

BOX 6.2 NISTEP: Japan and Delphi forecasting

The Japanese National Institute of Science and Technology Policy (NISTEP) is a national research institution that informs the Japanese government's science and technology policy-planning process. It conducts a Delphi survey every five years. Japan has a 40-year history of foresight activities looking at the contribution of science and technology to future society and conducted its first Delphi survey in 1971. The Delphi method iterates two or more rounds of the same questionnaire to the same respondents, until the answers converge. In the second and subsequent questionnaires, the respondents can change their answers based on the summary of the previous round. 2,900 experts responded in the ninth survey in November 2009 and February 2010 looking at the future of 832 topics in the 30 years until 2040 (NISTEP 2010).

The survey sought to identify developments in major areas of science and technology and define 'what we should do from now onward' to attain future goals and resolve the global and national challenges. Global and national challenges were identified as energy, resources and the environment. In the health and medical areas, these were identified as prognosis and preventive medicine and therapy. Other areas included ICT infrastructure, human resource development and management, and fundamental technology.

NISTEP uses this Delphi forecast to produce a dozen scenarios, for example for 'Maintenance and promotion of health in an aging society with fewer children.'

Japanese scientific research has been criticized for lack of R&D investment, and Japan has slipped from second or third place in international rankings for scientific research to around sixth since 2005. 'Progress in science and technology depends not only on money and people but also on supporting systems and institutions. And the systems and institutions are flawed in a number of ways' (Yukihide 2013).

Although Delphi forecasts often relate to technology areas, they can be used in a variety of contexts, for example tourism forecasts from Botswana to South Australia, where opinions on what is likely and desirable can help align people to outcomes.

In addition to encouraging appetite, Delphi forecasting can give an organization a useful database from among its own staff, whose knowledge and expertise is often underused. One easy way to guard against expert bias in this process is to investigate the views that are outliers – in a positive way – by watching for patterns of results in a Delphi forecast, either from individuals or groups within an organization that deviate from the norm and finding out why they think what they think. This can be a good indicator of evidence of trends that would otherwise have been missed. For instance, public-facing staff might consistently report that

BOX 6.3 Extract from a Delphi forecast run by the UK National School of Government

For many years the authors ran a Delphi forecast for all those who participated in strategy courses at the National School of Government – mostly students drawn from the middle and senior ranks of the UK Civil Service. In this forecast we tested a set of propositions, including the following ones.

In ten years' time will these propositions be true?

Please enter a tick in the box if you agree with the proposition.
Assume that the questions relate to the UK unless indicated otherwise
By 2019:

People – social and demographic
Genetic scanning of foetuses for abnormalities will be routine.
The Ministry for Men will have replaced the Ministry for Women.
Nationalism and the desire to be associated with regional and local institutions will increase.
Traffic signs will be scarcer as drivers take more responsibility for their actions.
Social mobility will slow as higher social classes prosper in a global economy.
People will increasingly opt for security rather than privacy(CCTV, databases etc.).
The compensation culture will increasingly dominate business transactions.
People will demand more personalisation, of both services and products.
Obesity will rise.

Environment
One developed nation will have become carbon neutral.
Technology will overcome environmental problems.
Nuclear power will be the dominant new source of energy in developed nations.
Travel will be reduced by road pricing.
Towns and cities will increasingly be seen as environmentally helpful places to live.
Personal Carbon Accounts will be supported by major political parties.
Disputes over physical resources will outrank religion, politics and power as a cause of war.
Developing nations will insist on per capita emissions caps as basis of emission trading.
Loss of key species (e.g. bees) will increasingly disrupt agricultural economies.

Economics
Sovereign wealth (investments by National Governments) will reshape world stock markets.
Private equity investments will reduce the size of world stock markets.
The financial institutions of London will become foreign owned and operated.
University education will be a more important part of international traded services.
Creative industries will become more important to the UK than financial enterprises.
UK employment will show growth for top earners and bottom earners.
Energy intensive businesses will relocate to environmentally unregulated parts of the world.
Britain will increasingly lose control of its corporate tax base.

the compensation culture is on the decline, whereas others see it on the rise. Investigating the difference could expose a seam of evidence (let us say, on attitudes to services) that would otherwise be overlooked.

Another good way of encouraging challenge is to *use Non-Executive Directors to encourage challenge*: most Boards of government departments, agencies and other public organizations have non-executive members who can bring alternative experience and perspectives to the board's work. But non-executive directors (NEDs) can often feel underused. One good way to make better use of NEDs (who often have only a limited amount of time to give to the organization) is by reinforcing their challenge function, for instance by asking them to sponsor networks of staff from within the organization in order to give voice to informed challenge and new ideas at board level. This can also give NEDs more influence within an organization.

Another method used successfully in some governments and agencies is to have *shadow boards*. Invite a cross-section of staff from within an organization to participate for a set period (a year, for instance) on a shadow board. These bodies can be used in a variety of ways. Many private firms use shadow boards to capture the views of the 'future leaders' of the business. People who might otherwise grow frustrated with the direction of the firm are, instead of quitting or leaking or complaining, able to put their views directly to the board and exert influence over it. The Welsh Government used a shadow board primarily as a means of staff development.

Expert panels are another means of embedding challenge: formal advisory groups have long been used by government to offer analysis or to make recommendations. Used less formally, sets of panels can strengthen the challenge function, bringing in outside expertise and peer-reviewing work done in-house. Some government departments and agencies ask its expert advisory panels to critique policy proposals made by its own staff, and these views are taken at board meetings (sometimes publicly – see 'Accountability' section below).

Perhaps the most effective way of all to embed challenge and questioning of assumptions and to develop appetite for outcome-focused working is to ensure that all staff regularly *get out and about into communities* and see the effects of policy proposals in action, seeking the views of those who deliver policies in partner organizations and of those who use services or who contribute to outcomes, whether teachers, schoolchildren, parents, doctors, cleaners, tax inspectors, farmers, highway engineers, community support officers, housing association tenants, soldiers, shopkeepers or taxi drivers. This is particularly valuable in central government which is usually at the greatest remove from the effects of the policies and programmes it devises, but it applies to all organizations in the public sphere.

Most organizations express a vague desire to be connected to public-facing staff and members of the public and many will encourage staff to get out of the office from time to time. But, without systematic enforcement, the daily pressures of work tend to get in the way of the 'luxury' of seeing policy in action. Organizations need to insist that all staff spend a minimum number of days out of the office visiting – one day a month is a good average. The next problem is how to prevent these visits themselves becoming an exercise in bureaucracy, either by over-formalizing the visits so that the schools, hospitals, housing estates, etc. that are visited suffer from 'fresh paint syndrome' (as with visits by royalty, where everything is presented at its best), or become 'habitually visited'. One way is to keep visits informal and personal. Another is to avoid formal reports of such visits. One city council insists that all its staff spend a day a month in the community. Afterwards they are required to write a letter to the organization or individual with whom they spent the day; a simple (and courteous) way of recording what has been learned.

Accountability

Awareness and focus on desired outcomes and accountability for their achievement is one of the best ways to create appetite for strategic working in a public organization. It is the equivalent of building passion for product, service or new markets and shareholder value in a firm, but it is often overlooked – and sometimes an emphasis on organizational performance can squeeze it out.

Organizations that have identified the outcomes they seek to bring about in society, as described in Chapter 3, are more likely to develop their sense of public value, created through a strong authorizing environment and organizational capability – they will have a greater appetite for strategic thinking, planning and action than those that do not. Strategic capability in turn creates more public value.

For those working in central government traditional avenues of accountability to the public are mainly through ministers and parliament; for those working in local government, mainly through elected councillors; in other organizations relationships are usually a mixture of direct accountability and accountability through politicians, trustees or members. The examples in this book suggest a positive correlation between organizations that account for their performance and their contribution to the achievement of outcomes in an open, direct and largely autonomous way and their degree of strategic appetite. Public organizations can strengthen their degree of accountability in several ways, including:

Hold board meetings in public: For an organization where public confidence is essential, openness and transparency are likely to be a high priority: the UK Food Standards Agency webcasts its monthly board meetings, which the public can attend. Policy papers setting out alternative options and evidence are public. Knowing that much of their discussion will be open to public scrutiny doesn't constrain staff in their consideration of evidence. If anything, they are more keenly aware of the impact of decisions taken and of their likely public perception (http://www.food.gov.uk/aboutus/ourboard/boardmeetings/ accessed 13 August 2013).

Reporting on indicators: All public organizations report annually on income and expenditure and most report on sets of indicators beyond the organization, as well as on measures of their own performance, often using 'balanced scorecards' (a mix of financial and non-financial performance indicators, typically covering finance, customers, processes and staff development). Organizations that report more regularly and more directly to the public can help performance and also awareness of the outcomes they exist to achieve (see Chapter 7).

Autonomous governance: Making sure that the reporting on indicators and other measures by which the organization is held to account has autonomous governance is another important measure. Accountability should increase the desire and confidence to work strategically rather than weaken it. Accountability can reduce appetite if people see the indicators and performance measures as targets, and begin to game them. Political pressures to drop indicators showing either poor programme/agency performance or poor progress towards the achievement of outcomes will also affect appetite.

One way to avoid the potential gaming of indicators (that is, the tendency to report only on those indicators that are 'going in the right direction' and to fail to report – or worse still, to tamper with the measurement of – those that are going in the 'wrong direction') is to give a high degree of autonomy to the reporting body. This is often the case with national statistical agencies. The US State of Oregon set up a 'progress board' which worked independently of the Governor to monitor and report on performance and progress towards outcomes. The Scottish Government has put similar arrangements in place. In this way, while the performance of the administration and the outcomes which it wished to see achieved both remained as political as ever, the process by which progress was monitored and accounted for 'belonged' to the citizen, with a more direct and transparent relationship between officials and the citizens in this respect, contributing to awareness of desired outcomes. We discuss accountability frameworks in more detail in Chapter 7.

The role of strategy units

A strategy unit – a dedicated team of officials in an organization or at the centre of government – is widely seen as helpful in developing, communicating and implementing strategy as well as in creating strategic capability. However, such units vary enormously in effectiveness. In this section we consider the factors that contribute to a strategy unit's success or failure.

The roles of these units range from national planning (for instance, the two thousand staff of the former Turkish State Planning Office) to wide-ranging analytical work (the former UK Prime Minister's Strategy Unit) to working closely with a team of ministers on forward policy issues to horizon scanning for a government department or agency to corporate strategy reviews.

A 2002 (unpublished) review across UK government strategy units conducted by the Prime Minister's Strategy Unit found almost all strategy units gathered evidence, worked on organizational development, challenged existing strategy and did policy development work. Around half found themselves filling interim resource gaps elsewhere in the organization and running skills training for other parts of the department. Over 40 per cent did systems thinking.

The strategy units that seem to be most influential in helping their organizations to think and act strategically seem to be those:

1. with a clear responsibility for cross-cutting strategy work
2. that draw on analytical capacity both within and beyond their organizations but are not absorbed by the analytical community of the organization
3. that challenge the board and their ministers/elected officials but that retain a degree of autonomy both from the board and ministers (they are more than a 'cabinet' or private office)
4. that encourage a 'commissioning' role for the board and ministers for strategic thinking, but do not exclusively provide the work that responds to those commissions
5. that are well connected to the finance, resource and corporate planning functions of the organization, and are able to influence their work, but do not themselves do the corporate and resource planning work of the organization
6. that support staff across the organization in developing strategy, including strategic plans, and who help build their capability, but who do not 'do the work for them'.

There are as many 'DON'Ts' in the above list as 'DOs' – strategy units need to be able to provoke and inspire new thinking inside organizations; they need to be able to encourage others to work strategically; they need

> ## BOX 6.4 Specialist strategy units: the European Commission and the US National Security Council
>
> There have been many attempts to build strategic capability across governments. The European Commission's Forward Studies Unit (working directly for the President of the Commission), was set up in 1989, and was influential in developing vision and driving the policy process across the European Union during the presidency of Jacques Delors and, to a lesser extent, Jacques Santer and Romano Prodi. It was renamed the Group of Policy Advisors (GPA) in May 2000, and renamed again under President Barroso in 2004, becoming the Bureau of European Policy Advisors (BEPA). Clear sponsorship from the top, and a defined role in encouraging strategic thinking across the Directorates General of the Commission, coordinating work with the College of Commissioners, enabled the Unit to have traction. But much depends on the blend of officials in the team – some of whom subsequently became senior figures in their national governments (for instance, Alexander Stubb, subsequently a senior minister in successive Finnish governments) (Europa 2013).
>
> In the United States national security coordination is strong, with the National Security Council providing coordinated advice to the president and having a strong and clear institutional role. It was created by the National Security Act of 1947, and this statutory footing seems to have been helpful to its standing. There is no equivalent in the United States' domestic policy arena to the NSC's foreign and security role, in part because of the constitutional position of the president in the development of a domestic policy agenda, where the right of initiative rests in most cases either with Congress or with the States (White House 2013).

to focus on building capability for strategic thinking. For all these reasons large strategy units which are seen as the exclusive home of corporate planning and of major strategic work are unhelpful. But small strategy units seen as centres of expertise, of new thinking and of support to people throughout an organization can be enormously effective.

In the United Kingdom there have been many attempts to create coordinating units for strategy at a national level. In 1970 Prime Minister Edward Heath's government published a White Paper *The Reorganization of Central Government* which offered a clear rationale for a strong strategic planning function in the centre of government. ' For lack of ... a clear definition of strategic purpose under the pressures of the day to day problems immediately before them, governments are always at some risk of losing sight of the need to consider the totality of their current policies in relation to their longer term objectives ... The Government therefore propose to begin by establishing a small multi-disciplinary central policy review staff in the Cabinet Office ... the new staff will not duplicate or replace the analytical work done by departments in their own areas of responsibility.

But it will seek to enlist their co-operation in its task of relating individual departmental policies to the Government's strategy as a whole' (HM Government 1970).

The Central Policy Review Staff lasted until 1983, when it was closed by Prime Minister Margaret Thatcher.

Following the election of Prime Minister Tony Blair in the UK in 1997 a Policy & Innovation Unit (PIU) was established in the Cabinet Office, bringing in external expertise from elsewhere in government and from the private and non-profit sectors to work on projects for, typically, around six months. Following the 2001 election a parallel unit, the Forward Strategy Unit, was established in Number Ten. Although both units were nominally headed by the same person – Geoff Mulgan – their work was different; the PIU continued to work openly, the FSU more privately to the Prime Minister. In 2002 the two units merged to form the 60-strong Prime Minister's Strategy Unit (PMSU).

The Unit was successful at engaging people from across government in projects and in working closely with people in Departments and it 'exported' staff who had worked there to support strategy units in departments and agencies. The experience of those who ended up in departments with a low strategic capability was often that they were overwhelmed by the lack of institutional space to operate strategically. As we saw earlier in this chapter, building strategic capability is a complex task, and it requires several measures to be taken in parallel.

In May 2010 the newly-elected UK Coalition Government established a National Security Council (NSC) to coordinate national security strategy, chaired by the Prime Minister. Later that year the House of Commons Public Administration Committee found a lack of sustained strategic thinking outside the NSC and recommended, echoing 1970, widening its remit to encompass national strategy and take a central coordinating role. As we said at the very beginning of this book, strategy tends to come in cycles. Lessons are learned, forgotten and learned once again.

Big strategy units inevitably find themselves expected to write the strategic plan for the government or the department or agency, or to provide the analytical capability of the organization or to conduct the resource and business planning cycle, or to respond to every crisis or to fill urgent gaps in policy capability or all of these at the same time. None of these roles will build the overall strategic capability of the organization, nor is any of these roles best performed by a strategy unit. Government departmental strategy units in the UK vary in size from two staff to around 50. The larger units are, for the reasons outlined above, often the least effective or influential. They are performing a wide range of tasks or second-guessing what others are doing and have little time to do strategic thinking. At their worst these units are seen as the 'people who do strategy', and other parts of the organization can too easily then regard strategy as somebody else's job.

BOX 6.5 Turkey: state planning through a cross-government strategy unit

The State Planning Organization (SPO) was founded in 1960, setting out major national infrastructure and energy projects, producing detailed economic plans and regional development programmes. It published nine five-year plans since the first in 1963, as well as three longer-term plans, looking 25 years ahead.

This was the vision from the 2007–13 ninth five-year national development plan: *Turkey is an information society, stable and sharing the benefits of its growth equitably, globally competitive and convergent with the EU.*

Turkey has undergone a series of periods of profound political instability, including a military coup against the elected government in 1960, military intervention to force the resignation of the prime minister in 1971, a further coup in 1980 and military pressure leading to the resignation of a government in 1997. Yet economic growth ran on average at 7 per cent during the 1960s and 70s, a little lower in the 1980s and 90s, and back to an average of 7 per cent in the 2000s – one of the highest growth rates in the world.

The SPO was a technocratic organization with around 2,000 staff, drawing evidence from a wide range of expertise. It also gathered views from across the political spectrum. It acted principally as an advisor to government but reported to parliament and its plans were approved by parliament. A significant number of politicians served a part of their apprenticeship in the SPO, including former Presidents Turgut Ozal and Suleyman Demirel.

This ability to work for politicians, to serve the elected government of the day, yet to act to some extent independently of politicians and to provide a sense of continuity in periods of political instability appears to have given the SPO the scope to plan beyond the cycles of elections and military coups.

In 2011 the SPO ceased to exist as a separate body, and was absorbed into the Ministry of Development (Turkish Ministry of Development 2013).

Source: author interviews with members of the Turkish SPO.

Despite this, big strategy units can still be successful. Turkey's State Planning Organization was, effectively, a national strategy unit, and it worked between 1960 and 2011 (when it was subsumed into the Ministry for Development) as an institution in its own right, though it was less successful at building strategic capability across the other parts of the Turkish government. One of the strengths of Turkey's SPO appears to have been in its dual accountability – both to the executive and to the legislature.

It's unwise to be prescriptive, but in a large organization (as opposed to cross-government, as in the Turkish example) strategy units of between five and ten staff seem effective. Their tasks are usually well-defined. They are big enough to be able to engage across the department or agency, covering particular themes or units and working with colleagues, yet they remain small enough to bring their thinking together as a team. Big enough to be able to contribute effectively to the board's and to ministers' thinking and to the corporate and business planning processes; small enough not to have these roles seen as their exclusive domain or to be second-guessing the business of other areas of the organization. One large government agency with a chairman with private sector experience specified the role of the strategy unit he commissioned as to offer independent advice from the side, so that when business areas pitched investment opportunities, he would have a small team acting as an independent advisor that could look across the agency as a system, and show where an intervention in one area might have unforeseen consequences in another.

Ensuring the right mix of knowledge and skills is crucial in developing a dynamic team. Strategy units commonly reflect the existing strength of organizations – so a department that deals with economic issues will have a strategy unit of economists; a criminal justice agency will have a unit of social researchers; an environmental agency, a unit of natural scientists. Such homogeneity risks breeding groupthink, expert bias and lack of challenge. Organizations therefore need to try to ensure the right mix of staff. In the same 2002 Prime Minister's Strategy Unit review mentioned earlier in this chapter, it was reported that strategy units across UK government included policy specialists (64 per cent), economists and other professional analysts (55 per cent), finance professionals (55 per cent), IT experts (27 per cent), social researchers (20 per cent), HR professionals (20 per cent) and scientists in just 11 per cent of strategy units. And these skills were not necessarily mixed within each team. There are some omissions. Historians, for instance, are likely to be useful in any strategy unit and the respected head of strategy in one department saw a need for more anthropologists in her strategy unit.

An 'ideal' strategy unit might comprise:

- a social researcher
- an engineer
- a scientist
- a statistician
- an economist
- a historian
- a 'practitioner' (for instance, an operational manager or other professional).

A historian is valuable for the skills of a historian, not (necessarily) their knowledge, and because, 'The past does not repeat itself, but it rhymes' (attributed to Mark Twain).

In Chapter 3 we looked at the risks of 'groupthink'. Irving Janis puts it this way: 'Groups, like individuals, have shortcomings. Groups can bring us the worst as well as the best in man. Nietzsche went so far as to say that madness is the exception in individuals but the rule in groups. A considerable amount of social science literature shows that in circumstances of extreme crisis, group contagion occasionally gives rise to collective panic, violent acts of scapegoating, and other forms of what could be called group madness. Much more frequent, however, are instances of mindless conformity and collective misjudgement of serious risks, which are collectively laughed off in a clubby atmosphere of relaxed conviviality' (Janis 1982: 5).

Lehrer (2012) cites research that shows it is wrong to assume that technical problems can be solved only by people with technical expertise; the researcher most likely to find the answer is the one most familiar with the terms of the question. The people inside a domain – the chemists trying to solve a chemistry problem – often suffer from a kind of intellectual handicap. As a result the impossible problem stays impossible. It's not until the challenge is shared with motivated outsiders that the solution can be found. Outsider thinking means problem-solving is most effective when working at the margins of expert fields.

Strategy toolkits: benefits and pitfalls

There is no shortage of models, methodologies and toolkits available to the strategist. Indeed, they may well outnumber those who actually use them. Why might this be the case? In part because the rewards for building a strategy model or a toolkit and publishing it are greater than those for making use of such tools; in part because the level of awareness of different models and toolkits is surprisingly low. Despite working with many hundreds of officials from strategy teams across the public sector, it is only occasionally that the authors meet people who nod in recognition when we mention particular resources or toolkits. Almost all the organizational effort goes into their production, almost none to ensuring there is appetite for their use.

The benefits of models, methodologies and tools are that they can be selected and applied in a variety of ways to understand context, to clarify desired outcomes, to develop direction and to measure progress. They should be approached less like a mechanic approaches a toolkit – where a screwdriver fits a particular size of screw, a spanner a particular shape of nut – and more like an artist's palette, where a range of colours can be employed, and where they can be combined in different quantities to create new colours. What is fatal to the creation of strategic capability is the approach advocated by certain consultancy firms and business schools, who promote 'step-by-processes', 'tick-boxes', 'strategy mapping' and so on, which offer a guide to those who must develop strategy, but which have the effect of switching off instead of stimulating new thinking. It is a little like deciding to explore a city in a country you have never visited before, and choosing to take an official bus tour, blindfolded. You can honestly report back that you toured the city, but what value was there in that tour?

The relationship between elected politicians and unelected officials

One important aspect of the work of politicians – one from which administrators can find themselves largely excluded – is that of political party. All governments are in one sense coalitions – coalitions of different interests, of different political outlooks, of different constituencies of support, of a range of experiences – even where all members of the government are drawn from a single political party. Administrators aren't always aware of the different streams of thinking and personal rivalries within the governing party in a single party government and this can impede thinking, planning and acting strategically. This tension – between acute awareness on the part of politicians of distinctions in sets of values or in policy preferences between ministers and, on the part of officials, a form of (relative) institutionalized ignorance – can be eased by effective political appointees who work as publicly paid administrators, but who have overt political allegiance. Systems of political appointment vary. In the US the proportion of political appointees is high, typically around 7,000 following a presidential election and change of incumbent. In the UK it is low, at around 80. In most European countries the figure is nearer the UK figure than the US figure, though in many countries (Germany, for example) public administrators are expected to declare their party affiliation, and ministers generally try to appoint affiliated officials to the most senior jobs, while also ensuring a degree of balance at the tier below.

Formal coalitions between two or more political parties expose some of the tensions, creative or otherwise, that can remain largely hidden to officials when a single party is in government. During an election two or more parties oppose each other, expose their policy differences and contrasts in values and each has platforms or manifestos with sets of specific commitments. Following an election one way of reaching a reasonably rapid agreement on a programme of government between those competing parties is to aggregate specific manifesto commitments which are acceptable, or not wholly objectionable, to each party. This approach has advantages for the formation of a coalition government but potential drawbacks for strategy-making, given that there can be irreconcilable trade-offs within a government programme, and the focus of the strategic capability of government can be directed at resolving trade-offs instead of setting direction.

Coalition formation is fraught in many countries. An example from Denmark: 'It is important to stress that having a programme is not the same as having a strategy. All parties have a programme, but not all parties are equally skilled at developing, thinking and acting strategically. Similarly, the best strategies need not be founded in a party programme. It may be precisely the freedom and/or innovation inherent in the strategy that makes the difference' (Lindholm and Prehn 2007: 27–8).

In Germany departments often focus narrowly on the demands of their own minister; administrators are often themselves members of the minister's party and can be keen to emphasize their loyalty not only to his or her programme but to the elements of the government programme identified with the political party of which they are themselves a member. 'In practice the chancellor's ability to set policy is greatly affected by the balance of power ... it is becoming increasingly difficult under these conditions to form a governing majority at the national level ... because the German system places a premium on stability, it tends to produce stable rather than powerful governments. Accordingly, change in Germany is more likely to consist of piecemeal reforms than radical shifts in policy' (Glaab 2007: 63–4).

Coalitions can sometimes avoid these difficulties. By developing strong strategic capability within government as a whole and by sharing that strategic capability with political parties it is possible for officials to work more effectively with politicians in shaping the programme of new administrations around a coherent set of outcomes that offer line of sight to the system as a whole. But coalition governments can also be the product of compromise, focusing on 'piecemeal reform'.

In a democracy politicians have legitimacy which unelected officials lack – in other words they provide the 'authorizing environment' for public strategy. Officials look to ministers, secretaries of state, councillors, mayors, presidents and prime ministers not only for that authorization or legitimation, but also for guidance, leadership, or simply for signals and hints about the direction of strategy and policy. Sometimes they will be given whole strategies by the politicians – for instance in the form of a manifesto, a coalition agreement, a programme of government or a major speech – sometimes they will be given nothing at all. The relationship between elected and unelected officials is what sets the tone for strategic thinking, planning and action. Sometimes arguments are made that call the relationship into question, particularly focusing on suspicions that officials are too ready to try to subvert

BOX 6.6 It's a coalition agreement: but is it strategic? Finland, the UK and the Netherlands

Coalitions bring coalition agreements – a programme for government, usually intended to last four or five years. These agreements tend to open with a preamble setting out the approach the coalition will take to government. This would, one might think, be an ideal opportunity for a statement of strategic intent. But because coalition agreements often attempt to obscure inherent tensions between parties with a statement of overall purpose that is at a sufficiently high level to make this possible, they rarely succeed in being strategic.

The 2007 Finnish general election resulted in a 'blue–green' coalition of four parties: 'The underlying values of the new blue–green Government are a balance between man and nature, responsibility and freedom, caring and rewarding, and education and competence' (Finnish Government 2007).

The 2010 UK general election resulted in a coalition between the centre-right Conservative Party and the centrist Liberal Democrats. 'We share a conviction that the days of big government are over; that centralisation and top-down control have proved a failure. We believe that the time has come to disperse power more widely in Britain today; to recognize that we will only make progress if we help people to come together to make lives better ' (United Kingdom Government 2010).

The 2012 Dutch general election resulted in a coalition agreement between the largest parties, the centre-right VVD (People's Party for Freedom and Democracy) and the centre-left PvdA (Labour Party). 'One of the coalition parties wants to guard against a government that gets in the way. The other wants to guard against a government that leaves people to their fate. Together, we choose a government that sees people not primarily as consumers but as citizens. Citizens who will shape the future of the Netherlands both individually and collectively (Netherlands Government 2012). The Coalition Agreement's title was not auspicious – it was called 'Building Bridges'.

Perhaps parties entering into coalitions need to have the K'iche (Mayan) quote mentioned in Chapter 1 in mind: 'We did not put our ideas together. We put our purposes together. And we agreed, and then we decided' (Diez Pinto 2004: 79).

the political direction set by elected politicians, or to assert the superiority of technocratic processes over the legitimate deployment of ideology. There is also, as we examined in Chapter 4, a respectable argument in favour of 'muddling through', and muddling through can sometimes be a politician's preferred method of operation in any context. While muddling through is unlikely to ever be the strategist's preferred approach, it is sometimes the context in which they are obliged to operate.

Unelected officials operating in the public strategy field need to understand and be sensitive to the politician's desire to keep options open and to have their individual mandate for the exercise of power recognized. There is not much point in running for office and winning it, whether as a ward councillor who becomes a council leader or as a Member of Parliament or a National Assembly who becomes a minister or as a president who forms an administration if, when that politician arrives in office, they find that the strategy of the town or region, of the department or nation has already been fixed for ten or 20 years ahead. The whole reason why that politician knocked on doors, gave speeches in cold and empty halls on Monday nights, agreed to argue for a platform of policies advocated by the political party they joined was so that the ideas in which they passionately believe would have a chance of becoming reality. It was so that their vision for their town, region or country, their vision for health care or education or crime reduction or alternative energy would be realized. And they can then find, on winning power, that their own officials are telling them that it's all already been decided; that the 'Vision 2030' is the product of the best research; that it enjoys widespread popular support; that the last minister or council leader, that the last administration was all for it; that it was the result of a major strategic review involving all parties, all stakeholders, that evidence was gathered, international comparisons were made. What was the point in winning 4,532 votes more than the other candidate if you cannot influence anything? What is the point in democracy?

On the face of it this is an argument for trying to keep officials away from making strategy and for restricting them to a role supporting politicians in their early days in office either to give form and reality to a platform or manifesto or to help them to shape a set of ideas into a coherent strategy. But strategy cannot work that way. It needs officials with understanding, appetite and capability to think, plan and act strategically. Politicians who wish to act strategically need to find themselves working in organizations where working strategically is the norm. That means that strategies will already exist, they will be evidence-informed, forward-looking and familiar to people working in the organization and in the wider operating environment. Major strategies can, of course, be devised with support from politicians across the political spectrum. The Jamaican National Development Plan (Jamaica Government 2009) has a foreword from the Governor-General, the Prime Minister and the Leader of the Opposition. But even these broadly-supported strategies will not be immutable, because good strategy is ever-changing. Good strategy is responsive and adaptable to the changes outside the organization, and one significant change is that those who were once outside the organization take charge of it. Strategy is a compass, not a tightrope or even a map. A new captain can set a new course. The ship is hers to command and she has a reasonable expectation that her officers will not only know the basic principles of steering, sailing and rowing but are also familiar with the uses of a compass.

Politicians are usually interested in achieving long-term goals for society, but that interest can be diminished in several ways in addition to the obstacles identified in Chapter 4. The 'machine' itself saps energy and interest; the demands of the media are hungry and immediate; pressure from legislators, lobby groups and the public is constant; meetings take all the time that could be spent on thinking about longer-term goals and planning for their achievement. Senior officials often enter public service for reasons similar to politicians, though generally with a preparedness to serve rather than to lead and generally with a less clearly-defined set of political values and goals than those entering politics. But many of the problems that afflict politicians afflict unelected public servants too.

The key to correcting for this tendency to be overwhelmed by pressing concerns is to focus on increasing the capability of leaders to act strategically. An effective way of prompting reflection in leaders, one that distances them from their day-to-day concerns, is to ask (perhaps complementing a Delphi survey across the organization) what they would like to be remembered for from their time with the organization. This puts leaders in an alternative psychological space, one in which they are freed from the expectation that they must defend and promote existing policy lines, allowing them to take the perspective of a disinterested onlooker or impartial spectator.

Most people will be constrained by the 'lens of now', but many politicians reach elected office precisely because they show strategic leadership – they see possibilities beyond the immediate, they articulate new and different approaches to dilemmas and frame those in terms of goals that others can support, and they can often be very good at detecting bias. Governments and other organizations in the public sphere must nurture and support those qualities, both in their elected and unelected officials. Support, development and training for politicians in strategic thinking is no less important than training in media handling, campaigning or in tabling legislation, yet it is routinely overlooked.

Conclusion: create the appetite and the rest will follow

Strategic appetite is the key to creating an organization that prepares for the future and that proves resilient in the face of the unexpected, while identifying ambitious but realizable desired outcomes for the wider system in which it operates. The means to create this appetite are well within the reach of any organization. The creation of appetite is a subtle rather than a difficult task. It takes leadership and it takes enthusiastic participation. One cannot exist without the other.

The ideal conditions for the creation of appetite include: a leadership that is keen to set strategic direction, that is giving the right signals to its own staff and those beyond that it is serious about strategy; that shows a consistent interest in the future and that puts some institutional systems in place to help foster both supply and demand of strategic analysis within the organization. An organization that welcomes challenge and the questioning of assumptions, and uses its own staff and people from outside the organization to maintain challenge, is likely to foster more strategic appetite, as will an organization that has a strong sense of accountability and works to build on the usual avenues of accountability to increase its sense of responsibility to the public. People in the organization who have the desire to create public value, and some sense of mission or broader outcomes than the simple efficiency of the organization itself are the builders of strategic appetite.

With these elements in place it is possible to start building practical (not just theoretical) capability by embarking on a process of strategy-creation. The nature of the process will vary. It may be a corporate process involving every member of the organization through a process to create new strategic direction; a policy project process taking a particular issue or set of issues and working with a team drawn from within and beyond the organization to find a course to the future, identifying goals and setting direction. It may be a social process, broad, drawing in large sections of the community at local, regional, national or international level to set a new course through a set of issues, from marine fishing policy to care for the elderly, from sustainable consumption to climate change.

In each case the process will entail similar stages, but all who are involved must be able to see how each stage informs the other, and understand the process as something that is systemic rather than merely a series of 'milestones' in a project plan.

Chapter 7

Delivering Strategically: Performance and Accountability for Results

Developing a strategy is easy – if a strategy is a speech, a poster on a wall, a report to a legislature, a resource plan. You can create a document that looks impressive, talks convincingly about the future and describes the changes that a government or agency will work to bring about. But the test of whether a strategy works is whether it achieves desired outcomes, in other words, whether it delivers results – and to know whether it is delivering results, the strategy needs to be *measured*. The issue of measurement is not a mere technical detail in strategy-making. Planning for measurement and evaluation of the strategy from the outset shows people – employees, funders, service users, politicians and public – that you are serious about the strategy.

Good strategies have good measures – a clear and strong measurement framework is a sign of healthy design, of a determination to make the strategy work in practice, and a willingness to be held to account.

We looked at accountability generally in Chapter 3 in terms of securing a mandate for public strategy, and the authority, legitimacy, accountability and trust that needs (Figure 3.1). In Chapter 6 we looked at accountability for achievement of outcomes. Here we look at the following features of a good measurement frameworks, which

1. measure outcomes, not merely the use of resources (inputs) or levels of activity
2. use indicators of progress, so that it is easy for the board or for politicians or the public to monitor progress over time
3. use proxy measures where these are useful
4. use some lead indicators, not just lag indicators
5. use a limited number of measures and indicators, so that the whole measurement framework is easy to understand
6. avoid targets and other forms of measurement that are likely to be 'gamed'.

There's more detail on these later in this chapter ('Outcomes, indicators and performance measures').

172

It follows that a *bad* measurement framework will run to dozens of pages of fine detail of targets showing '100 per cent' accuracy rates, or '92 per cent customer satisfaction rates'. They will be laden with figures about 'staff utilization' or 'productivity' that will be impossible to compare between different parts of the business or even from one time period to another. Sadly, such measurement frameworks are not uncommon. They tend to reflect a culture where staff feel obliged to show that 'everything is fine', regardless of reality.

The first step in translating a process of strategic thinking and development into action is to ensure that there is a clear vision in place which contains stated outcomes that are amenable (perhaps with some adaptation) to measurement. Once a vision is in place, the organizational mission statement does its job in aligning the activities of the organization to the achievement of the desired outcomes described in the vision statement.

Building a vision of the desired future

Vision without action is a daydream. Action without vision is a nightmare.

Japanese proverb

Public organizations can get into difficulty creating strategic vision. This happens for two main reasons. Firstly, when they don't use a strategic process to create their vision, then the vision isn't based in analysis or understanding of the context in which they operate, and is simply a piece of 'blue skies' thinking. This produces a vague assemblage of desirable activities or generic phrases instead of a set of relevant and valuable desired outcomes. Secondly, they may adopt the approach of corporate strategy and focus entirely on the organization and barely at all on economic or social outcomes, overlooking the public value it is the purpose of their organization to create. This is manifested in published vision statements full of language about what 'we' the organization will do, instead of about the outcomes the organization exists to achieve.

Richard Rumelt (2011) points out that bad strategy is not the absence of strategy but a list of goals and aspirations that don't identify the problems that the organization will need to overcome to achieve them. Good strategy by contrast is underpinned by a detailed diagnosis identifying leverage points in the system, aimed at fixing the disease, not treating the symptoms.

A vision should describe the outcomes the organization exists to achieve, not the undertaking of activities or even the provision of services, particularly when other organizations from the public, non-profit, or private sectors often provide the services. It is primarily the job of the public agency to enable others to achieve outcomes as much as it is for the agency itself to achieve them. If the vision doesn't identify desired outcomes its effect is inevitably going to be limited. What's more, because outcomes are often motivating and meaningful to employees and others who work with the public organization, not articulating them is likely to hamper the operational capabilities of the organization.

Six pointers for the creation of a vision as part of a public strategy are:

Scope. The vision should distinguish between those elements in the world 'out there' that the organization cannot change, and those that it can aspire to shape.

Provenance. The organization should be able to explain every statement in the vision pointing to analysis of drivers and trends or features of modelling or scenarios which justify what is in the statement.

Internally consistent. The vision should not be full of unresolved tensions or inexplicable trade-offs – for instance 'people make informed choices about what they eat' and 'people no longer choose to eat sugary, fatty or salty food' is a resolvable tension, but some explanation needs to be offered for why, given choice, people make the 'right choice'.

Outcomes-based. Vision statements in the public domain should be free of sentences beginning 'we will' … because such statements inevitably refer to activities that the organization will perform. The vision is about the external world, and should be expressed as a series of desired outcomes.

Plausible and **credible**. This does not (necessarily) mean that vision statements need to be probable, but they do need to be possible and believable. A catastrophic asteroid strike on planet Earth is not probable (soon), but it is plausible. Humans, in our present form, living forever (that is, never dying) is both improbable and implausible.

Public value. The vision must demonstrate why life will be better for others and should capture the legitimacy offered by stakeholders and the authorizing environment and the political desire inherent in a public strategy.

National and state visions

Many countries have a national vision that encapsulates a set of goals that a government or that successive governments and citizens work to achieve. Like any vision, to be meaningful and worthwhile they need to abide by the pointers above. Former Namibian President Sam Nujoma expressed the purpose of national vision as follows: 'A national vision is

BOX 7.1 Malaysia, Abu Dhabi, Jamaica: three approaches to national visions

In 1991 then Malaysian Prime Minister Mahathir Mohamed set out his Vision 2020 for Malaysia:

> Malaysia should not be developed only in the economic sense. It must be a nation that is fully developed along all the dimensions: economically, politically, socially, spiritually, psychologically and culturally. We must be fully developed in terms of national unity and social cohesion, in terms of our economy, in terms of social justice, political stability, system of government, quality of life, social and spiritual values, national pride and confidence. (Wawasan 1991)

This vision became formalized in Malaysia's National Economic Development Plan. But the vision was seen by some as a Western capitalist template. The Consumers' Association of Penang had this to say: 'The National Vision Policy (NVP) 2020, with national unity as its overriding objective ... but [the national vision] is rooted in the tunnel vision of Western capitalist development ideology, which regards human beings as essentially economic creatures. While paying lip service to pursuing environmentally sustainable development and cultivating a tolerant and more caring society, the NVP's main goals are industrialisation, economic growth, increased productivity and production of wealth' (Consumers' Association of Penang 2002).

The government of Abu Dhabi, following extensive scenario planning work, formulated this as the vision for the emirate:

> Abu Dhabi as a sustainable, diversified, high value-added economy that encourages enterprises and entrepreneurship and well integrated in the global economy leading to better opportunities for all. (Abu Dhabi 2011)

In 2009 the Government of Jamaica published its national development plan 'Vision 2030', with a national vision supported by a set of outcomes which could, in turn, be measured and reported on. There had been previous national development plans, but they had been 'government-owned' and achieved little. The 2009 plan was intended to be different – produced following wide engagement across the political spectrum with NGOs and citizens. At its centre is this vision:

'Jamaica, the place of choice to live, work, raise families, and do business.'

Its foreword carried endorsement from the Governor-General, Prime Minister and Leader of the Opposition, emphasizing its intended longevity and it has since withstood a change of government in the December 2011 general election (Jamaica 2009).

a perception of the future, which reveals and points to something new, beyond what is already available and accessible. The goal of our Vision is to improve the quality of life of the people of Namibia to the level of their counterparts in the developed world by 2030. In order to get there we need a framework that defines clearly where we are today as a nation, where we want to be by 2030 and how to get there. Defining this framework in operational terms is visioning' (Namibian Government 2004: 9).

Strategies without visions are unlikely to succeed, because the vision should encapsulate the desired future, the outcomes within the future that the strategy articulates and the actions needed to make those actions come about. Confusing or unrealistic visions are worse than useless, as are visions without an accompanying statement of the actions needed to bring them about.

Ministry and agency visions

Ministries and agencies need visions in the same way countries need national or regional visions, to set direction for the organization. These must still look *outwards*, because they are describing a set of conditions the ministry or the agency will help to create. They are distinct from the organizational mission that describes the actions the organization itself will take to help bring those conditions about.

The dangers of poor visions are just as great at this level as at national level. The risk is that they focus inwardly on the organization or agency and don't pay sufficient attention to the change in the world 'out there'. This seems to happen because

- those who construct the vision conflate the purpose of vision with the organizational mission
- the vision doesn't pay enough attention to the context within which the organization operates, now and tomorrow
- the vision isn't forward-looking
- there's no rigour or evidence – it comes from 'board awaydays' or consultants and amounts to 'wishful thinking'
- the vision is insufficiently relevant to the enterprise; it could apply to any organization – clichés like 'world class' and 'centre for excellence' are a warning sign
- the vision contains no desired outcomes to inform the goals, which the policies of, and actions undertaken by, the organization – usually in collaboration with others – will work to achieve.

Organizations can avoid these problems if they use the scenario process as the building blocks of their vision. Visions developed from scenarios will be based on evidence, because all of the future operating scenarios will be (or should have been) plausible. The approach is to look at what things are common to all the scenarios (and the scenarios will make the organization aware of the aspects that are unique to individual scenarios). If they all show, for instance, that energy costs will rise and that average working age of the population is increasing, then the vision can acknowledge that by beginning:

In a future where energy costs are rising and where people are working longer ...

But the vision can then make statements of **choice** about how the **world will be.** Because scenarios are not predictions, it is legitimate to select features from each of the potential future worlds that scenarios represent and to show only those that would be present in a desired or **preferred** future.

Identifying desired outcomes

Having created a vision that is compelling, credible and rich in desired outcomes, the next step is to disaggregate the vision to produce specific

---

BOX 7.2 Oregon: from vision to outcomes

The US state of Oregon was one of the first jurisdictions in the world to adopt an outcome measurement and accountability framework, in 1989, with the state legislature creating a directly accountable board to work with the Governor and other elected officials to agree a vision and a set of desired outcomes for the state and then to report regularly to the people of Oregon on progress (Tryens 2004). It set a goal of improving the economy, environment and communities of Oregon over 20 years. A second 'Oregon Shines' vision was created in 1997 and a third vision in 2007. In 2009 the Oregon Progress Board fell victim to deep spending cuts in the Oregon state budget.

The 1997 'Oregon Shines II' programme included this as its strategic vision:

A prosperous Oregon that excels in all spheres of life

Supported by three goals:

Quality jobs for all Oregonians; Engaged, caring and safe communities; Healthy, sustainable surroundings

Each objective was supported by up to six objectives; each of these measured by around a dozen benchmarks and hundreds of key performance measures (Oregon 2008).

policy outcomes for government to work with other agencies and with citizens to achieve. Having clear desired outcomes is perhaps the single most crucial element in any strategic process.

Organizational mission

So far we've talked about understanding the context, and arriving at a vision expressed in terms of outcomes. The mission, on the other hand, describes what the organization (agency, department, city administration) does to make change happen. The vision, the overarching outcome, may need to be achieved by a number of agencies, all with missions that in aggregate will achieve the wider vision.

Unless the organization has thought about the future (for example using scenarios) to develop a clear, outward-looking vision, an organizational strategy is like a bullet fired by someone wearing a blindfold: dangerous and arbitrary in its effect. It is hardly surprising that organizations that

---

BOX 7.3   Singapore's prisons: strong mission

The Singapore Prison Service (SPS) has been unusually successful at reducing reoffending. Between 1998 and 2007, the recidivism rate dropped significantly from 44.4 per cent to 26.5 per cent and, for the 2010 release cohort, had fallen further to 23 per cent (2013 statistics). Crucial to this transformation was a strategy that shifted from a focus on incarceration to rehabilitation. The original (1997) mission at the heart of this was:

> We aspire to be captains in the lives of offenders committed to our custody. We will be instrumental in steering them towards becoming responsible citizens with the help of their families and the community. We will thus build a secure and exemplary prison system. (Leong 2010)

Note the link created between the organization and the outcomes the organization will achieve, working with others. The SPS aims to achieve two main outcomes: 'for prisoners to become responsible citizens, with the help of their families and the community'; and 'to build a secure and exemplary prison system'. The process of creating the new strategy began in 1999. More than 800 staff were engaged in the process. The Singapore Prison Service had no stated mission at the beginning of the process. The strategy was seen as 're-thinking the prison's purpose for existence' – echoing the public value approach of Mark Moore, and it was clear that it expressed a meaningful change in direction for all those who worked for the SPS. Although there is a good deal of 'we will ...' language in the mission, the connection is made between the agency and the world beyond the agency (Singapore Prison Service 2013).

haven't worked on outcomes end up producing poor mission statements. This is not just found in the public sphere; plenty of private sector organizations don't have meaningful mission statements. Brews makes the point: 'A statement like "Our mission is to be the highest quality provider of XYZ in ABC markets" does not contain any creative fiction. Nor does it provide any insights into the future products, services or solutions that are to be developed. As a result it is a stagnant, uninspiring platitude that is unlikely to stir employees, shareholders – or customers' (Brews 2005: 6).

Where the vision for the business lacks any outcomes – where everything is a performance measure – it can be hard to shape a meaningful mission to support it and for those working in the business to understand how they are to add value, let alone to show imagination in doing so. A prior description of the desired end-state is helpful, for instance: 'People choose our products because they are always the latest design; they are widely-recognized as environmentally-friendly and they appeal to young and old alike.' This then enables the mission to include some description of how the business will achieve the vision.

Other problems arise in both the corporate and public spheres when the mission statement is too generic. 'You find a mission statement that could apply to all your competitors: to be market leader in the quality delivery of xyz services to ABC consumers worldwide. Carefully crafted over months of intensive debate, the statement is accompanied by other "stretch" goals and desired firm attributes ... but now, you discover, quite unhelpful when real strategy is needed' (Brews 2003: 35).

The difficulty Brews outlines is that the mission statement is, once again, doing far less than it should to help motivate the employees of the company to work innovatively to achieve anything at all. This is just as common a problem in government, where phrases like 'world leader' or 'centre for excellence', while reflecting ambition, should act as warning signals of lazy, generic thinking and lack of analysis of the future services, outcomes and civic goods that the organization exists to create. Good mission statements are specific to the work of the organization and the line of sight from the outcomes in the vision through to the activities of the organization needs to be clear.

The most successful companies have missions or core purposes that make a statement about what they exist to achieve, not merely how successful they will be in respect of their competitors.

Other corporations, however, make the mistakes described by Brews, for instance, ICI:

> The ICI Group's vision is to be the industry leader in creating value for customers and shareholders through market leadership, technological edge and a world competitive cost base.

BOX 7.4 Corporate mission statements

Here are some typical corporate mission statements:

Merck: To discover, develop and provide innovative products and services that save and improve lives around the world.

(Merck 2014)

Wal-Mart: To save people money so they can live better

(Wal-Mart 2014)

John Lewis Partnership: The happiness of all [our] members [employees], through their worthwhile and satisfying employment in a successful business.

(John Lewis Partnership 2014)

Until 1997 ICI had adopted a different strategy , embodied in a different mission statement:

ICI aims to be the world's leading chemical company, serving customers internationally through the innovative and responsible application of chemistry and related science.

Through achievement of our aim, we will enhance the wealth and well-being of our shareholders, our employees, our customers and the communities which we serve and in which we operate.

As Kay (2010) argues this second, earlier mission statement is notably less laden with jargon and more meaningful. It tells ICI's employees and customers quite a lot about the company and their role in it. The change in mission statement coincided with a change in the company's fortunes. A poor mission statement in itself is unlikely to have been responsible for ICI's misfortunes, but it may have been a signifier of poor leadership:

The company embarked on an extensive programme of acquisitions and disposals that failed in every respect, including that of creating shareholder value. The share price peaked in 1997, a few months after this new strategy was announced. The decline thereafter was relentless. In 2007 ICI ceased to exist as an independent company. The responsible application of chemistry not only created a better business than did the attempts at creating value: it also created more value. (Kay 2010: 20)

Drucker points out that it's not a leader's charisma that matters but the leader's mission, which has to be operational otherwise it's just good intentions, and has to be simple: 'Almost every hospital I know says, "Our mission is health care." And that's the wrong definition, the hospital does not take care of health; the hospital takes care of illness. You and I take care of health by not smoking, not drinking too much, going to bed early, watching our weight and so on. The hospital comes in when health care breaks down. An even more serious failing of this mission is that nobody can tell you what action or behavior follows from saying: "Our

---

BOX 7.5 Mission statements from national revenue services

Here are some examples of mission statements from national revenue services:

US Internal Revenue Service (IRS):

> *Provide America's taxpayers top quality service by helping them under-stand and meet their tax responsibilities and by applying the tax law with integrity and fairness to all.*
> (United States Inland Revenue Service 2014)

New Zealand Revenue Service:

> *To provide quality tax and social policy services to the Government for all New Zealanders. We aim to maximise compliance with New Zealand's tax and social policy legislation through education, quality service and appropriate enforcement.*
> (New Zealand Inland Revenue Department 2014)

Spanish Revenue Service:

> *Better Together (Así Mejoramos Todos – thus we improve for all).*
> (Spanish Revenue Service 2014)

South African Revenue Service:

> Vision .... *an innovative revenue and customs agency that enhances economic growth and social development, and supports our integra-tion into the global economy in a way that benefits all South Africans.*
>
> Mission: *Collect all revenues due. Ensure optimal compliance with tax and customs legislation. Provide a customs service that will optimise revenue collection, protect our borders and facilitate legitimate trade.*
> (South African Revenue Service 2014)

mission is health care"' (Drucker 1995: 4). Drucker cites the simple and (most people thought) too obvious statement that the mission of an emergency room is *to give assurance to the afflicted.*

A mission statement has to focus on what the institution really tries to do so that everybody in the organization can say: 'this is *my* contribution to the goal'. A mission should not try to encompass everything the organization tries to do as if it is a landfill site, showing how difficult and extensive its remit is. A good mission statement is succinct, clear and meaningful to the organization's employees and to the world beyond, it makes reference to the outcomes the organization exists to achieve (generally articulated separately in a vision of the desired future) and itself describes the activities the organization will engage in to support their achievement.

Outcomes, indicators and performance measures

Leaders and managers in the public sector need to be absolutely clear about the difference between vision, mission, outcomes, objectives, indicators and performance measures. One of the main reasons why some public institutions produce little public value is because of a fixation on activity, and on the consumption of inputs (money, people's time) to produce outputs (letters, reports, arrests, examinations), sometimes to the exclusion of attention on publicly valuable outcomes or results.

So let's be clear about terminology.

In the example in Figure 7.1 more heart bypass operations can be carried out, but they don't necessarily produce less coronary heart disease or longer lives. That depends in part on how well the operations are conducted and in part on how many people need the treatment. The desired *outcome* is that people live longer (or, better still, that people live healthily longer). A system that conducts lots of heart bypass operations might even be a form of 'failure demand', in which the output of operations is a product of more and more people needing such operations. It would naturally be better if such operations weren't necessary at all – because of low prevalence of coronary heart disease. Many health services might be better understood as illness services. They provide treatment for illness (a publicly valuable service) but they can be poor at promoting health (potentially an even more publicly valuable service).

We need to be as clear as we can be about the distinctions between inputs, outputs, intermediate outcomes and ultimate outcomes (see Figure 7.1). Many countries show how their national vision translates into a set of outcomes and in turn into objectives and indicators that can then be monitored and through which governments can be held accountable, *both for their own programmes and for the outcomes produced by organizations, communities and citizens outside government.* The first

FIGURE 7.1   *Inputs, activities, outputs, intermediate outcomes and ultimate outcomes – their meaning and measurement*

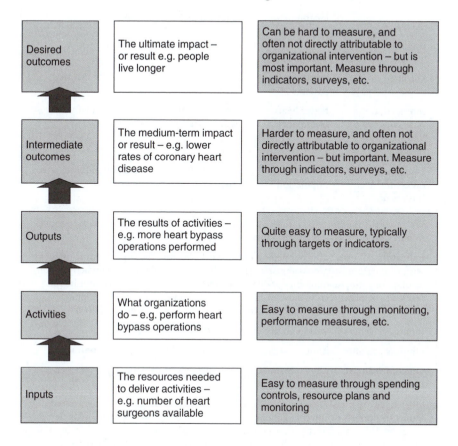

stage in this is to specify the outcomes the government seeks to achieve, through others.

Let's look at a number of examples of policies and programmes where measurement of outcomes (or results) is hard to do, but important.

Measuring the number of people who use a drug rehabilitation centre is easy. It's progressively harder to measure

- the quality of the treatment
- whether users successfully complete treatment
- whether users stay off drugs for more than a year
- whether they are able to contribute to society fully (free of crime, free of health problems, contribute to family life, economically active).

Yet the hard things to measure are the ones that matter in public policy, in health, criminal justice, education, housing, employment, defence and

TABLE 7.1 Types of measurement and terminology

	Health	Education	Crime
Inputs	number of doctors	teachers	police
Outputs	number of patients seen	number of exams passed	number of arrests made
Intermediate outcomes (or 'intermediate results')	better heart treatment	better qualified school leavers	more successful convictions
Ultimate outcomes (or 'results')	healthy population	children fulfil their potential	safe communities, free of crime

We generally measure the efficiency of an organization's use of inputs and production of outputs through **performance measures.**

Indicators tell us what is happening in the world beyond the organization. We will wish to measure progress against a set of indicators to help us know whether intermediate or ultimate outcomes are being achieved – these may or may not be the result of the organization's use of inputs and production of outputs. **Aligning performance to the achievement of outcomes is the key to strategic delivery.**

Inputs are generally within an organization's control (spend, employ).

Outputs are often within an organization's control (direct, regulate, contract).

Outcomes almost always rely on others (e.g. behaviour of patients, of children and their parents, of neighbours, of taxpayers).

Objectives are usually designed to help the organization align the sequence from inputs to outputs to intermediate and ultimate outcomes, for example 'reduce unsuccessful convictions'; 'increase exam pass rates'. Sometimes achievement of these objectives is supported by specific **targets** – but targets often distort effort, particularly where they are poorly aligned with outcomes. We will look at that problem later in this chapter.

so on. It's relatively easy to measure whether prisoners get training opportunities in prison, but progressively more difficult to know whether they

- find work on leaving prison
- are still in employment a year after leaving prison
- are housed on leaving prison
- have housing one year after leaving prison
- are in good health a year after leaving prison
- are able to engage in family life on leaving prison
- continue to have a good quality of family life a year after leaving prison.

BOX 7.6 Results Based Management: a global effort to measure outcomes

The Canadian federal government introduced evaluation of policy imple-mentation in the 1970s, and successively strengthened management accountability frameworks through the 1990s and 2000s. Canada's government is one of the best known for encouraging and promoting 'Results Based Management' (RBM), also adopted by a number of UN bodies. One of the keys to successful Results Based Management is to be clear about the results being sought and to have a clear hierarchy of outcomes, from activities to outputs to intermediate and ultimate outcomes (Canada Treasury Board 2013).

Results Based Management is now a standard approach to managing the performance of programmes in the developing world through devel-opment aid. The United Nations Development Programme (UNDP), the Organization of Economic Cooperation and Development (OECD) and a range of national development aid agencies adopt RBM. Its strength is the standardization of terminology, and a recognized and (in theory) outcomes-focused approach to the delivery of public management programmes (UNDP 2002).

The RBM approach recommends:

formulating objectives
identifying indicators
setting targets
monitoring results
reviewing and reporting results
evaluating
using performance information to drive improvement.

Weaknesses of RBM include that it can be adopted a little mechanistically, or seem imposed upon a country or a programme without sufficient consideration of context; it can be too focused on 'counting what can be measured' instead of measuring what really counts; it can become caught up in the gaming of targets (see later in this chapter); and (the biggest prob-lem of all) that it can be devised in the absence of a broad strategy.

It's these more difficult things that affect likelihood of reoffending most directly. It's also hard to measure areas where government has least control, so public sector managers may take correspondingly less interest in them.

At the time of writing, there is interest in the idea of governments offering 'payment by results' to either private companies or charities for the achievement of defined outcomes in a field – for instance employ-ment services, or prisoner rehabilitation, or adult social services. In a distinct but associated development, interest in 'Social Impact Bonds' is increasing. SIBs seem to promise a way of encouraging private investment in the achievement of public outcomes, releasing capital, particularly to charities and other forms of social enterprise, and, if they can transfer the financial risk to the (private sector) holder of the bond without government ultimately underwriting the risk, protecting those who deliver the services from the risk (typically NGOs, often charities) of not meeting the outcomes defined as 'successful results' by government.

'Payment by results' needs robust measurement and a culture where there's no 'gaming' (that is, placing disproportionate effort into the appearance of meeting a particular target, neglecting other vital aspects of the programme).

What gets measured gets done, but what matters doesn't get measured. Hubbard claims there's nothing that can't be measured: 'a costly myth ... permeates many organizations today: that certain things can't be measured. This widely held belief is a significant drain on the economy, public welfare, the environment and even national security. "Intangibles" such as the value of quality, employee morale, or even the economic impact of cleaner water are frequently part of some critical business or government policy decision. Often an important decision requires better knowledge of the alleged intangible, but when an executive believes something to be immeasurable, attempts to measure it will not even be considered. As a result decisions are less informed than they could be. The chance of error increases. Resources are misallocated, good ideas are rejected, and bad ideas are accepted. Money is wasted. In some cases life and health are put in jeopardy. The belief that some things – even very important things – might be impossible to measure is sand in the gears of the entire economy. All important decision makers could benefit from learning that anything they really need to know is measurable' (Hubbard 2010: Preface xii).

Gaming is often insidious and sometimes even well-intentioned. The people in government, government agencies and city administrations are human. They want to do well and be seen to do well. They measure things they do well, and may not measure the things going less well, especially where those 'aren't our fault' or 'are beyond our control'. Mark Friedman (Friedman 2005) observed this tendency to measure what we can measure instead of what we ought to measure and noted how it impedes our ability to understand the effect of policies and programmes (which is distinct from understanding whether they are running efficiently or not), and how it can have the effect of distorting the behaviour of public managers and employees towards worrying only about the performance of programmes with too little attention to whether they do any good at all.

Friedman makes a distinction between outcome measures on the one hand and performance measures on the other. He calls the first set of measures 'population accountability' and the second 'performance accountability'. 'What is accountability? Accountability is a relationship between persons or groups, where one is responsible to another for something important. The superintendent is accountable to the school board for the success of the children in the school system. The teen pregnancy task force is accountable to the community for reducing the rates of teen pregnancy. Accountability means that it matters if we succeed or fail. It matters if things get better or worse ... Results Accountability has two components: population accountability and performance accountability. In population accountability a group of partners takes on responsibility for the well-being of a population in a geographic area. In performance accountability a manager or group of managers takes responsibility for the performance of a program, agency or service system. These two kinds of accountability have been badly confused over the last 50 years or more' (Friedman 2005: 6).

Confusing outcomes with performance causes problems:

1. People managing organizations think that it isn't worthwhile developing indicators to measure outcomes because achievement of the outcome isn't wholly attributable to the performance of the government programme or agency.
2. People managing organizations try to develop performance indicators to measure achievement of the outcome, conflating the two measures. This causes problems of attribution and obliges staff to make incorrect assumptions about cause and effect. It can also squeeze out an understanding of how the system operates and the role of citizens as co-producers of outcomes.
3. People working in organizations and stakeholders lose confidence in the accountability measures or indicators because they tell them neither about the performance of their organization or programme or about achievement of the outcome.
4. People leading organizations and politicians become preoccupied with measuring performance and overlook the need to measure outcomes.

It's easy to talk about the efficiency of programmes and hard to explain their effectiveness. When a government says it has increased spending – an input – on a programme by 50 million pounds, dollars or euros it can sound impressive.

It's also easy to talk of outputs – more police, more operations, more or faster rail journeys made.

It's just as convincing to speak about activities – number of cases being handled, time spent on delivering treatment, safety checks on railway signals.

It's less convincing, and can sound vague, to speak of communities that are safer, more law-abiding, more able to protect each other in a neighbourly way; it can sound unconvincing when politicians point to the success of communities where people exercise more regularly and eat more healthily and consequently need less hospital care; less convincing to speak of communities where fewer and shorter car journeys are taken because places of work, schools and places to shop are nearby. Yet these are the outcomes that matter. The most successful political leaders understand this (think of Kennedy's 1968 speech in Chapter 3) and find ways of communicating about outcomes in inspiring ways. And the most able public managers are able to find ways to measure outcomes.

Outcome or population accountability indicators measure the gross effect of government interventions *together with* the actions of other agencies, including those of professionals, voluntary organizations, of citizens and of their families.

By contrast, performance indicators measure the performance of specific programmes and agencies.

Mark Friedman makes clear that it is helpful to understand the difference between measuring:

1. How much service is delivered (which measures quantity of input).
2. How much effect is delivered (which measures quantity of output).
3. How well a service is delivered (which measures the quality of effort).
4. How much quality of effect is produced (which measures the quality of outcome).

It is important to measure all four of these, but (4) is much tougher to measure than (1), but is also the most important thing to measure (Friedman 2005: 68).

If government indicators can become targets, and if those working in the system feel that they must 'improve the indicator', governments must mitigate this with a strategic framework that shows those working in the system the 'line of sight' through inputs, activities, outputs and objectives through to the outcomes in the vision.

Perverse behaviours fuelled by indicators aren't improbable. Targets set or followed without attention to outcomes cause profound problems. This happened in the UK's National Health Service. In early 2000 in hospitals up and down Britain investigations were under way into complaints from patients awaiting treatment for 18 months and more. In many cases they weren't on the waiting lists. Ministers had set the Department of Health the task of bringing down waiting lists for inpatient treatment from a maximum of 18 months to six months or less in five years, by the end of 2005. A lack of attention to outcomes meant that the Department's strategy focused on performance to the neglect of the wider and long-term effects of particular policies.

By late 2001 the UK National Audit Office found 6,000 patient records had been manipulated, including deletion and suspension from the waiting lists, the direct result of Health Service managers so determined to avoid breaching the 18-month maximum waiting time that they neglected the outcome of people being made well (National Audit Office 2001). In a number of cases patients on the waiting list approaching the 18-month maximum had letters from their local hospitals asking when they were going on holiday, which suggested to the innocent patient a high-quality personalized service. The hospital wrote shortly before they were due to go on holiday with a date for their operation while they were away. In some cases the notification arrived when the patient was already on holiday. Patients not only missed their operation but were suspended from the waiting list for non-attendance. This helped the hospital to avoid breaching the 18-month target, but didn't contribute to the overall outcome, nor build trust and legitimacy for the National Health Service. This is one drawback of targets, where people feel doing a good job is meeting the target while missing the point – although there are examples of targets that can work by allocating resources to what matters if accompanied by sanctions designed to stop manipulation of indicators. Having clearly defined outcomes helps put targets in the context of what the organization is trying to achieve.

Similar problems occur in any policy field. Imagine a government outcome for the criminal justice system that *crime and fear of crime are reduced* and a specific target for the criminal justice system that *80 per cent of crimes detected lead to prosecution within six months of detection*. An output target would be, for a particular jurisdiction, 80,000 crimes prosecuted successfully as opposed to 65,000 the previous year. Assume the total number of crimes detected has remained at 100,000 in each of the two years in question. Assume that the government agencies involved have responded to the target and achieved it. The output is clear and measurable. Has the outcome been achieved? On one measure, clearly not: crime has not declined, it has remained the same. Has *fear* of crime declined? That would be measurable. It might have done; people might be reassured to see the criminal justice system working more effectively. But it is equally likely that people would be concerned to see so many more prosecutions; they might think that crime is getting worse, whatever the statistics say.

It goes without saying that you have to be reasonably sure there is a strong correlation between your inputs, activities, outputs and intermediate outcomes, in other words, that your interventions are informed by evidence and evaluation. You might test whether an input contributes to an outcome and check that the effect is more than a casual correlation, and ideally whether there are any counterfactuals – that is, would the outcome have happened in any case, without the intervention by the organization? An example might be a government that claims its economic interventions generated economic growth, yet without the intervention growth would have been higher (the counterfactual).

Measuring outcomes

Clear sets of indicators show whether a government or agency is achieving its strategy – whether it is moving from the desired outcomes expressed in its vision to the achievement of those outcomes. Indicators are 'neutral' – they are there to help to *measure* and *monitor* the achievement of outcomes. Targets, on the other hand, play a role in *managing performance*, and are examined in the next section. The best indicators have arrows showing performance improving, stable or worsening, as in *Scotland Performs* and Virginia's *Virginia Performs* (examined briefly in Chapter 3). The analysis behind that broad assessment is usually in graphic form (Scotland Performs 2013; Virginia Performs 2013).

The Scottish Government has adopted an approach similar to Virginia's. Arriving with a clear view of the outcomes they wanted to achieve, SNP (Scottish Nationalist Party) Ministers in May 2007 took office as a minority administration. The accountability system, 'Scotland Performs', mapped the 'line of sight' from the overarching purpose right down to specific indicators, like those of its Virginian counterpart. The emphasis was on how Scotland was performing rather than on how the government was performing, as the outcome framework aligns the public sector and society in partnership, bound by a unifying purpose and set of outcomes.

Rather than ministers for departments, having ministers for outcomes encouraged collaborative working towards common goals. The 32 elected Scottish local authorities had expected the usual reams of prescriptive guidance from the centre showing how they should achieve the outcomes. It took some while to recognize that it was for them to decide how best to achieve them in their areas.

A system of government that focused on such broad outcomes inevitably raised questions about how accountability and risk were aligned, particularly when the outcomes required the involvement of the entire public sector and Scottish people. Scotland Performs and the focused national outcomes and indicators helped monitor how successfully the government has been in striving towards its desired outcomes.

While the accountability system adopted by the Scottish Government showed a mixed picture in terms of progress over the four-year life of the administration, the SNP minority government won a sweeping victory in the 2011 Scottish parliamentary election – a vindication, some would argue, for adopting a strategic approach, with clear purpose, transparency about policy choices and high levels of accountability for the achievement of outcomes.

'Baskets' of measures blend measures of inputs, activity (useful for measuring productivity) and outputs, coupled with indicators that help show whether outcomes are being met. Baskets of measures need a few 'lead' indicators – offering early warning signs that things may be going

FIGURE 7.2 *Virginia Performs Scorecard*

The Virginia Performs Scorecard, like a number of others from US states and cities (and the Scottish Government), shows in clear graphic form the performance of different programmes using arrows as follows (Virginia Performs 2013):

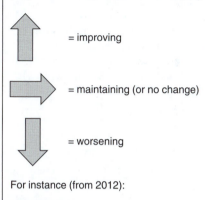

= improving

= maintaining (or no change)

= worsening

For instance (from 2012):

Economy

Business Climate

Business Startups

Employment Growth

Personal Income

Poverty

Unemployment

Workforce Quality

'RAG' ratings (red-amber-green) are a common way of showing progress towards outcomes, with green representing 'success' and red 'failure'. One form of gaming is the desire to see all of the indicators moving from red to green (so the 'neutrality' of the measurement is compromised). Using arrows, as tends to be preferred in the US, instead of 'RAG' ratings seems to reduce the problem of gaming (Scotland Performs 2013).

BOX 7.7 China: baskets of performance measures

Since the early 1990s, China's municipalities have used increasingly sophisticated baskets of measures to monitor the performance of their local economies and of their public services.

In the 1990s the emphasis tended to be on use of resources, and measures were skewed towards inputs, like mushroom production, or numbers of pigs; and levels of activity, like numbers of new businesses.

By the mid-2000s measures were more typically sets of indicators, a basket mix of inputs, outputs, indicators of outcome, of proxies and of lead as well as lag indicators, as below.

Harmonious society construction:

Index of new village construction
Urban residents income index
Income index for rural residents
Index of educational development
Development index for public health
Rate of social security coverage
Rate of registered unemployment
Index of public safety
Satisfaction rate for public safety

This basket of nine measures for social cohesion ('harmonious society construction'), is matched by baskets for sustainable development, progress in modernization and administration by law (Burns and Zhiren 2010).

off track, or are going particularly well, as well as 'lag indicators', giving the recent historical position. Proxy measures – measures that sit apart from the things being directly measured, but that in some way represent it, can also be useful, and are often the most useful 'lead' indicators. We looked at lead indicators in the context of forecasting in Chapter 5. For instance, brick sales are a lead indicator of growth in the construction industry, which doesn't otherwise show up for a year or more. But brick sales are not a proxy. The opening of coffee shops in a previously depressed area of a city may both be a lead indicator of house price growth and a proxy measure of that growth.

Organizational alignment and 'line of sight'

Having done all the hard work of creating a strategy informed by evidence, with scenarios of the future, a vision with clear desired outcomes and a relevant organizational mission, and having established indicators to monitor progress in achieving outcomes and a system of performance measurement, the organization must align its resources to delivering the strategy. That doesn't always happen. It should be a matter of concern if spending allocations or numbers of staff don't change between different areas of activity before and after a new strategy. If the organization recruits and trains for the same capabilities after it adopts a new strategy, an alarm should sound. You would also expect to see some change in organizational processes and structures with a new strategy. It should engender a series of changes in the organization which drew it up, and often in other organizations, too. This is not only necessary as an obvious practical means of implementing the strategy, but also a clear signal to those who work in the organization and to other organizations and to citizens that the strategy is real, not simply an empty gesture.

Critchley observes, in the context of order emerging from chaos in complex adaptive systems, 'Much conventional management theory speaks of the need for alignment, but contrary to this received wisdom, it is through misunderstanding, contention and a certain amount of messiness that novelty (and hence innovation) emerges' (Critchley, *Strategy as a Social Process*, in Verity 2012: 169).

There's a vital need for diversity of thinking in strategy formulation on the one hand and, on the other, the need to organize a place or institution in such a way to make it a reality once you have a strategy (which is what we call alignment). If you don't do the former you get mindless conformity and decay; if you don't do the latter you get whimsy and 'faffing' (ineffectual activity).

Targets: their uses and misuses

Used judiciously, targets can help people to be clear about what their activities are expected to achieve in terms of improved performance. In the context of a well-designed strategy people will see how the improved output in turn contributes towards the achievement of an outcome, usually alongside the efforts of other agencies, public, private and non-profit social enterprise, and the behaviours of citizens themselves. But all too often targets distort behaviour and focus efforts on performance in a way that misaligns with the achievement of outcomes.

There's a story of a boiled sweet factory in the 1980s, not far from Moscow, that had a target for the number of sweets it produced each week. In an attempt to ensure that the targets were met, the ministry of planning monitored sweet production not by relying on the factory's reported production but by measuring the number of sweet wrappers ordered and used. Most people who later bought the sweets at their local shops barely noticed that they had two wrappers. Perhaps they assumed that there was a fault on the machine that put the wrappers on the sweets, rather than surmising that the double-wrapped sweets enabled half the factory's production to be sold on the black market without wrappers.

Targets have their place. But targets must be used in an accountable system where alignment to the outcomes that the organization exists to achieve is clear. Without that alignment gaming of targets becomes commonplace. Because targets can be gamed they can be accompanied by sanctions in a 'targets and terror' culture. Hood (2006) identifies different types of target gaming: the 'ratchet effect' is where the expected tendency of target-setters to fix next year's targets as an incremental advance over last year's results causes the managers of production units to restrict performance; the 'threshold effect' is where people reduce the quality or quantity of their performance to just what the target requires, and there is output distortion by manipulating reported results.

Hood notes the eagerness of managers to accept 'good news' performance data at face value without putting scarce resources into probing those numbers, leading to no anti-gaming strategy. He adds that some see target gaming as the product of 'blaming, bullying, non-transparent [organizational] cultures' in public service delivery organizations. But many of the antidotes identified by those respondents tended to focus on limiting opportunities to game the system by low-trust measures to check up on or constrain the gaming options rather than changing motivation by active measures, to reduce bullying and blaming.

Alfie Kohn describes in *Punished by Rewards* (1999) how paying children to increase literacy rates meant that the payment became the goal, and reading became the chore that got in the way of the outcome of increasing literacy rates.

What makes the difference between good targets and bad ones? In part it's leadership, and in part the visibility of the alignment between targets, measures and outcomes. Targets don't work when they are confused with measures. Measures of progress to outcomes are helpful and essential; targets for inputs and outputs are not – so targeting arrests, or targeting the number of parking tickets issued, are perverse incentives that lead to behaviours that won't help you achieve outcomes.

Organizations see targets as a way of influencing individual performance, a means of changing the behaviour of staff. If we accept that most people want to do a good job they may manipulate the data the organization uses to assess how well they are doing their jobs. They may feel they are doing a good job but the organization doesn't measure what matters and there are no clear outcomes. The role of public-facing staff can be where the shoe rubs – staff don't know whether they are working in the interests of the public or in the interests of their manager.

Targets can work well when they prioritize activity in ways that mean the leaders of the organization resource the area. A target can give the area prominence. It puts it on the agenda at board meetings, and attracts resource. For example, when UK ministers declared in 2004 they were going to halve hospital acquired infection rates for MRSA (Methicillin-resistant *Staphylococcusaureus*), the rates of MRSA did indeed halve over time. Hospitals now celebrate, for example, '300 days without an infection case'. But you can't prioritize everything, and it's all too easy to confuse targets with measures.

Targets don't produce quality. For example, answering telephone calls quickly and effectively is an indication of a quality organization. If you make that indicator a target, it won't produce a quality organization. It confuses the by-product or indicator of a quality organization with what contributes to a quality organization. You can't mandate quality, you have to devolve the power to deliver quality. If you derive your measures from the purpose of the organization, in terms of creating public value, and put measures in the hands of staff, you achieve performance you wouldn't achieve with targets, if you also address the bullying and blaming Hood identifies.

Understanding these areas as complex adaptive systems rather than machines where you can pull a lever in one place and something predictable happens in another can inform the approach to targets. Managers who work in the public sphere talk about 'levers of change', about 'policy instruments', about 'roadmaps' and 'cogs' and 'dashboards' and 'flagships' and 'trajectories' and 'pilots' and 'rollouts' and so on and on – the language of machines and those who operate them litters public management. The prevalence of the metaphor of the machine is likely to have arisen because in the industrial era of the 20th century machinery became synonymous with efficiency. These quasi-industrial terms are intended to act as useful analogies – but what most people understand to be a complex system doesn't work like a machine at all. We need to ask whether it is helpful for us to use such language at all.

Using language that creates or embeds unhelpful constructs in our minds can be damaging; we see the world through a distorting lens and as a result behave in a way that is inappropriate for our environment. An economy, a town, a relationship between two countries, life within a family – all of these are complex, ever-changing and often unpredictable systems. As we examined in Chapter 5, the use of the language of the machine, of which targets are the most obvious component, can encourage us to think, plan and act as if the system of government, and – more importantly – of the society that government responds to and shapes, really does behave like a machine. We become victims of the conceptual framework we have created for ourselves. Chapman described this phenomenon and its causes in *System Failure*. 'The essential aspect of [the complex adaptive system] approach is that the human-activity system needs to be approached in terms that are quite different from the normal, linear mechanical framework used. This difference has been graphically illustrated by Plsek, who compares throwing a stone with throwing a live bird. The trajectory of the stone can be calculated quite precisely using the laws of mechanics, and it is possible to ensure that the stone reaches a specified destination. However it is not possible to predict the outcome of throwing the live bird in the same way, even though the laws of physics ultimately govern the bird's motion through the air. As Plsek points out, one approach is to tie the bird's wings, weight it with a rock and throw it through it. This will make its trajectory (nearly) as predictable as the stone, but in the process the capability of the bird is completely destroyed' (Chapman 2004: 51).

The tied bird metaphor is helpful to bear in mind when creating targets. Is the target something that encourages the system to use its qualities in a way that helps to achieve the outcome, or is it likely to shackle that system? Targets can, if designed without due thought to their behavioural impacts, distort performance, obscure the pursuit of desired outcomes and diminish public value.

If we intervene in a certain part of the system with a particular policy, we still can't be certain how all parts of the system will respond, even if we have reasonable confidence in how the group or groups, or organizations or processes we are attempting to change the behaviour of, will respond. We always need to understand that unintended consequences will flow from any action we undertake. It is necessary to observe these consequences, to learn from them and to adapt appropriately. We will never be able to control any system fully. Once we have understood this we can begin to work more effectively and – perhaps a little counter-intuitively – are likely to be able to exert far more influence over the system than when we were constrained by our input–activity–output, target-led model.

In an author interview in 2008 with James Smith, at the time the Chairman of Shell UK, he described this approach to government as 'supply-push' and characterized a more strategic approach as being 'demand-pull'. He said: 'You can't push on a string. When government notices that pushing on a string doesn't work, it thinks that it can push on a rope instead. But you can't push on a rope either.'

This comment echoes Plsek's observation (quoted by Chapman) that placing a bird feeder strategically might be more likely to induce the behaviour we wish from a bird than trussing it up, tying a stone to it and hurling it through the air. What we seek is not merely incentivization, but also an understanding of how the bird will behave and why it is likely to behave that way. If we can develop our understanding we are likely to be able to learn from the behaviour of the bird and adapt our responses so that they are more appropriate when influencing other birds. We are also less likely to assume that a cat behaves exactly as a bird behaves, because we will apply the same systemic approach – observing, learning, adapting, acting – to the cat as we do to the bird.

Seddon goes further: 'There is no value in having a target, since it is an arbitrary number; by its nature it will drive sub-optimisation (distortion) into a system, allowing parts to "win" at the expense of the whole. It is, however, vital to know how the system actually performs – its capability. This gives a real as opposed to an arbitrary number' (Seddon 2008: 97).

Sir Michael Barber, when head of UK Prime Minister Tony Blair's Delivery Unit, placed targets in particular contexts (Barber 2007). He defined three phases of public service reform:

- *Awful to adequate.* When services are awful people exit where they can.
- *Average to good.* People grumble.
- *Good to great.* People believe in, are engaged with and committed to good services.

If the government is investing money in public services in the first phase, it will want a return on that investment and it can be appropriate to set targets. In the second phase you'll need competition to increase productivity. Barber points out that you cannot mandate excellence in the third phase, you have to unleash it.

As Barber argues: in the first stage of reform (awful to adequate) the intervention has to be top down; in the second stage of reform (adequate to good) you regulate, build capacity and capability using quasi-market incentives; in the third stage of reform (good to great) you grow better services by offering greater equity, and building public confidence through continuous improvement. The role of government in this phase is to enable and incentivize. You can mandate awful to adequate but you must unleash good to great. The phases move from strategic partnership to public engagement to co-production.

Good to great requires a shift of emphasis from money and staff to quality and consistency. Change and capability will require quasi-market devolution, transparency and regionalization. Where should power lie? It needs to shift from government to the institution that the professional works in, not from government to the professional. Barber holds that professionals and managers should drive this phase, which needs to be evidence-driven, not picking and choosing. You can personalize services only when they are reliable and have good systems.

Targets can work only in a system of accountability, where the capability of the system and the outcomes the system is trying to achieve are both understood and monitored. At least some of the negative effects of target-setting can be mitigated and even overcome by a clear strategic framework that offers clear visibility from inputs through activities and outputs to the desired outcomes, and that understands the inherent and the potential capability of the system.

Conclusion: meaning it

We've shown in this chapter that you should start with the wider context before you identify outcomes, and only then settle your mission (what the organization will do) once you have the vision (what the organization will seek to achieve).

Words matter because meaning matters. How we frame something colours how people understand it: the term *machinery of government* creates a potentially misleading construct of how government works. If we describe a tax as an *inheritance tax* it frames it quite differently from a *death tax*, and while these two expressions may be describing the same thing, they frame understanding in quite different ways; similarly, those who are *anti-abortion* often frame their argument as *pro-life*. George Lakoff's *Don't Think of an Elephant* theorizes that the Democrats lost the 2004 US presidential election because Republicans were better at using language to frame the issue – usually meaning you need to say what you are in favour of, not what you're against. Republicans talked about 'tax relief' rather than 'tax cuts', because the former suggests that tax is an affliction (Lakoff 2004). The manner in which we conceive of our world and of potential worlds matters a great deal, for that understanding will have a direct impact on what we consider to be both feasible and desirable to create.

The words we choose to describe desired outcomes will affect the nature of the system of organizations and individuals expected to achieve the outcome – in other words, capability is shaped by aspiration. For the efficiency of programmes to be known, then they must be measured accurately. But it is even more important to measure the progress towards the achievement of desired outcomes, even when the impact of any programme on the desired outcome may be marginal. Without measuring both outputs and outcomes there cannot be genuine accountability. One of the reasons we need strategy is to create alignment between targets, objectives and outcomes, to understand the system as a whole and how we can influence it and to help it to perform in a way that creates public value.

Chapter 8

Imagination, Curiosity and Strategic Judgement

Wise strategy requires analysis and judgement. What is strategic judgement? It's more than a 'safe pair of hands' – the leader who never takes a risk is the one who has no strategy, who can't set a direction or build a vision of the future, because these involve the exercise of judgement and therefore carry the risk of making the 'wrong judgement'. We consider what leads to 'wrong' and 'right' judgements in this chapter, by looking at the idea of judgement and its exercise from various angles. But if wise strategy needs a risk-taker, it does not need a wild risk-taker who sets a bold vision and pursues it without anyone following.

Does this mean leaders should be somewhere between the two stereotypes of the cautious 'mule', stubbornly digging in their feet, and the over-imaginative 'rabbit', ready to run down holes? In practice, we are likely to look for the better qualities of both the mule and the rabbit. We want caution, but with an openness to possibility, a weighing of the risks and the benefits, a seeing through of all possibilities, a keen interest in evidence, a strong sense of curiosity and an attentiveness to the views of others and what we see in the world around us.

Judgement and sensemaking

Strategic judgement relies on understanding systems and how they work, but it's difficult to do this from within, you have to stand outside the system. In this chapter we'll examine what helps that ability to 'stand outside' an issue and look afresh, and consider what we can learn from progress in the last couple of decades in understanding how we think. Our brains are reflexive; as just one part of the environment they shape it and are shaped by it, not only through evolution taking generations, but by affecting the way our own genes are expressed and inherited (see, for example, Virtue *et al.* undated). Improved technologies (described by Camerer *et al.* 2005) monitor the microscopic changes in blood flow in different areas of the brain to reveal much about the way we think and respond. The new knowledge this provides is finding its way from academia into popular science writing. It would be an omission when so much of strategy is based on strategic thinking and judgement, if we did

199

not pay regard to developments in neuroscience and psychology, because these advances give us important insights into how we think and exercise judgement. Psychology is significant because 'The future is psychological territory, the place we project our hopes, fears, dreams and expectations' (Tibbs 1999: 1).

In Chapter 3 we drew out the significant difference between strategy in the public sector and strategy in the private sector. Although private sector innovation changes our lives, broadly, corporate strategy aims for a 'best fit' between an enterprise and the wider world in which it operates, so that it will survive and prosper. Public sector strategy by contrast specifically seeks to change the future, by adapting the environment itself, and those within it, into one where citizens flourish.

Strategic judgement relies on attentiveness. As we saw in Chapter 5, the kind of attention we pay alters what we find. In public strategy, we are bringing new worlds into being, and our knowledge of how the brain processes information will play a part in what we find.

We saw in Chapter 5 that Pierre Wack was selected by Shell for its scenario work because he was a compelling storyteller. Stories are a powerful means of explaining change and transmitting knowledge. For more than 50 thousand years, long before the invention of writing, they have been the way humans have passed information between generations. This has a flip side. Getting locked into plausible stories can override judgement. Our brains fill in the gaps (Virtue *et al.*) and string together fragmented facts to create a story that resolves ambiguity and complexity – a story that may make sense of the world, at least provisionally, and also provides the basis of memory (Schank 1995). It's hard to let go of a narrative that gives those facts coherence, in retrospect or prospect. Strategic judgement engages with compelling stories that convince people that change is within their grasp. Humans tell stories to capture heart and mind. They provide a sense of change that we can picture. They can raise aspirations. Their language should resonate. Plausible stories can be more powerful than evidence:

> Let's take the CEO who announces to her staff that they must all strive to 'maximize shareholder value' ... Contrast the 'maximize shareholder value' idea with John F Kennedy's famous 1961 call to 'put a man on the moon and return him safely by the end of the decade' ... Had John F Kennedy been a CEO, he would have said, 'Our mission is to become the international leader in the space industry through maximum team-centred innovation and strategically integrated aerospace initiatives.' Fortunately, JFK was more intuitive than a modern day CEO; he knew that opaque, abstract missions don't captivate and inspire people ... it was a brilliant and beautiful idea – a single idea that motivated the actions of millions of people for a decade. (Heath and Heath 2008: 21)

Author Philip Pullman tells us that stories are important because 'they entertain and they teach; they help us both enjoy life and endure it. After nourishment, shelter and companionship, stories are the thing we need most in the world' (Pullman, undated). This attests to the value of being able to communicate and explain a strategy as a plausible story, although we need to be aware of the downside risk of our ability to weave simple stories to explain unrelated events when formulating strategy, in what Taleb calls the 'narrative fallacy: our need to fit a story or pattern to a series of connected or disconnected facts' (Taleb 2011: 303).

But strategy demands more than stories, we want people who can make sense of the world and that's where strategy gives political leaders a framework more rigorous than mere dreams of a better future, more objective than doctrine alone can offer, more balanced than either the lessons of history or the sobering effect of daily events and more far-sighted than the fleeting approval of public opinion. Strategy gives the public officials whose job it is to put the wishes of politicians into practice a discipline in which that becomes possible, with judgement.

We need to apply judgement to strategy, but what is judgement, and is it an individual, or organizational, strength? The intuition on which we base judgement is knowledge that we haven't acquired by reasoning. It relies on automatic processes not easily accessible to conscious awareness. Kahneman and Klein (2009) conclude that the quality of intuitive judgement depends on heuristics (automatic rules of thumb, the mental and cognitive processes we use to navigate life). The reliability of these short cuts depends on the regularity of the environment in which we make a judgement, the opportunity to learn those regularities and on ample feedback. If an environment is regular enough to provide valid cues and good feedback, expert intuition can develop (Kahneman and Klein: 523–5).

Kahneman and Klein approve Simon's definition of skilled intuition: 'the situation has provided a cue: The cue has given the expert access to information stored in his memory, and the information provides the answer. Intuition is nothing more and nothing less than recognition' (Simon 1992: 155). Kahneman and Klein find the model of intuition as recognition helpful in demystifying intuition: 'The process by which the paediatric nurse recognizes that an infant may be gravely ill is not different in principle from the process by which she would notice that a friend looks tired or angry or from the way in which a small child recognizes that an animal is a dog, not a cat' (Kahneman and Klein: 520). They explain that true experts know when they don't know and switch from effortless intuition to careful reasoning when there are cues that an intuitive judgement could be wrong, which may result in a different strategy. This ability to recognize a novel challenge is authentic expertise. Automatic processes – whether cognitive (reacting with reason) or affective (reacting with emotions or gut feel) – are the default mode of brain

operation. 'They whir along all the time, even when we dream, consti-
tuting most of the electro-chemical activity in the brain. Controlled
processes occur at special moments when automatic processes become
"interrupted", which happens when a person encounters unexpected
events, experiences strong visceral states, or is presented with some kind
of explicit challenge in the form of a novel decision or other type of problem' (Camerer *et al.* 2005: 18). The learning for strategic thinking, where
fast feedback on outcomes may be delayed, is that we need to make the
considerable effort to unpack and evidence our intuitions, or to test them
on a small scale without assuming success will be replicable in different
contexts.

Certainty is one way heuristics can lead to biases that affect our judgement. 'Certainty is the greatest of all illusions: whatever kind of funda-
mentalism it may underwrite, that of religion or of science, it is what the
ancients meant by "hubris". The only certainty, it seems to me, is that
those who believe they are certainly right are certainly wrong'
(McGilchrist 2009: 460). In Chapter 4 we looked at the Abilene Paradox
and Harvey's reference to Hamlet as an example of someone who can't
make up their mind. That's usually seen as a bad thing, but not when it
keeps possibilities open in a way that is useful. Hamlet shouldn't have
been frozen by his doubts; he should have been freed by them. Adelman's
biography of economist Albert Hirschman (Adelman 2013) notes
Hirschman 'always feared that orthodoxy and certainty excluded the
creative possibilities of doubt (Adelman 2013: 13). He distinguished
doubt and uncertainty. 'Doubt is not the same thing as uncertainty ...
Uncertainty means that you think you may be wrong; doubt means you
are not sure you know. The first makes you less confident; the latter does
not' (Adelman 2013: 116). He saw doubt as creative where it allows for
alternative ways to see the world.

All science is provisional. Philosopher Hilary Lawson sees the world
not as a fixed reality but something 'open'. Through closure we form
what we take to be reality. He argues that it is only through closure
that we are able to successfully intervene in the world. Scientific theories of how things work are a story that works until a new story renders
it obsolete. Nothing is fixed. 'Through the process of closure the character of openness is hidden but it is also through closure that reality is
realized. Each closure provides something that we did not have previously, and at the same time obscures the openness from which that
something was realized. Closure can be seen therefore to be in part a
loss, an obscuring of openness, in the same way that catching sight of
the face in the dots is also the loss of the other things that those collection of dots might have been. Yet without this loss we would have nothing' (Lawson 2001: 7).

Concepts precede their observation and must be tested before they
can be determined to be 'true'. Even then, our idea of truth is likely to

change. Black holes in space were imagined before they were observed; the *idea* of wormholes through the fabric of space exists, but wormholes have not yet been observed or established by scientists to be true; they might never be observed – to the human mind wormholes simultaneously exist and do not exist which, in the case of wormholes in space, is satisfyingly apposite. Atoms were conceptualized many thousands of years ago but they did not exist – or not to the observable satisfaction of the human mind – until observations made in the 19th century; the structure and behaviour of atoms only began to be better understood with Rutherford's experiments in the early part of the 20th century. Under observation by Bohr our understanding of the construction of an atom changed. Under further observation by Schrödinger, that understanding changed again. If we believe in observable reality then it is not the construction of the atom that has changed, but human understanding of the atom that has adapted. If this is true of atoms then how much truer it must be of all else we think we know. This is the kind of expertise the strategic thinker seeks – questing, adaptive; a challenging form of expertise that is capable of tearing the fabric of all we know.

Herbert Simon put it this way: 'The term "factual premise" does not mean an empirically correct statement but a belief, that is, an assertion of fact. The assertion may or may not be supported by evidence, and such evidence as exists may be out of greater or lesser validity. Human decision-making uses beliefs, which may or may not describe the world as it really is. We call such belief, whether true or false, "factual premises"' (Simon 1997: 69).

In 1934 Karl Popper held that scientific theory, and human knowledge generally, is hypothetical, generated by the creative imagination in order to solve problems that have arisen in specific cultural settings. No number of repeatable scientific experiments can prove a scientific theory but a single counter-example is decisive. In other words, you can't prove something scientifically is true; you can only prove it false (Popper 2002, first published 1935).

In public strategy we must be on guard against making toxic assumptions that reduce uncertainty – openness – to something we feel we can cope with, instead of embracing uncertainty head on and dealing with it through policies to deliver our strategic intent that will remain resilient under a range of circumstances, rather than being optimized only for the 'official' view of the future.

Karl Weick (Weick 1995) introduced the term 'sensemaking' to organizational theory to help structure the unknown. It's one of four leadership capabilities advocated by the MIT Sloan School of Management (along with visioning, relating and inventing). People in organizations try to make sense of their environment by creating an internal abstraction of reality. This means reality is not something outside the organization, but is constructed by people within it using rational models that avoid ambiguity and complexity. These models acknowledge and structure the unknown, the ambiguous and the complex, and help the development of strategic judgement.

Sensemaking involves coming up with plausible understandings and meanings; testing and refining our understandings or abandoning them in favour of new ones that better explain a shifting reality. Sloan recognizes people are constrained by their own environment and leaders should pursue opinions that differ from their own and adopt multiple perspectives.

Sensemaking, like strategy, calls for courage, bravery and doggedness because, as we suggested in Chapter 6, advocating change can be a lonely and unpopular task. The leader who demonstrates that an organization's strategy has not been successful, for example, may clash with those who want to keep the image of achievement alive.

Imagination and curiosity

'We believe the 9/11 attacks revealed four kinds of failures: in imagination, policy, capabilities, and management ... It is therefore crucial to find a way of routinizing, even bureaucratizing, the exercise of imagination.'
Final Report of the National Commission on Terrorist Attacks Upon the United States, Chapter 11 (2004)

'On all sides there was a failure of imagination to appreciate the scale of the fragilities and their potential consequences. No-one could quite bring themselves to believe that in our modern financial system the biggest banks in the world could fall over. But they did.'
Sir Mervyn King, Governor of the Bank of England, 2 May 2012
BBC *Today* Lecture

We said in Chapter 5 that strategic thinking needs imagination. What circumstances favour the exercise of imagination? Taleb advises that you maximize the serendipity around you – by going to cocktail parties. He's talking of making connections between random pieces of information. Schwartz advises reading specialist magazines from fields you might otherwise have no interest in. This all speaks to the curiosity Panksepp (Panksepp 2004) tells us is innate, and essential to a strategy-maker.

McGilchrist explains that both hemispheres of the brain process the same information, but do it in very different ways. The left hemisphere processes information linearly, the right hemisphere in parallel. We, and other animals, find ourselves in two minds as in his illustration of a bird pecking seed against a background of grit:

- birds use their left hemisphere (right eye) to give narrow, focused attention to what they already know is of importance (the seed among the grit)
- they keep their right hemisphere (left eye) vigilant broadly for predators or friends
- the left hemisphere fixes the world as a mechanical model and discounts anything that does not fit with it
- the right hemisphere offers the context essential to understanding and change.

(McGilchrist 2009: 26–7)

Undue reliance on the left hemisphere carries the risk that we try and fit reality to our model of the world. In particular, the left hemisphere confabulates: it constructs stories in order to make sense of isolated pieces of information, sometimes in evidently preposterous ways when not mediated by the right hemisphere. Public servants are often selected primarily for intellectual, rather than creative, ability. This favours the kind of thinking in the left hemisphere, where short and direct pathways between brain cells are optimized for rapid decisions. Those in the right hemisphere 'meander' and take longer to process thoughts, but make unexpected connections along the way. Focus is important but not when it leads to tunnel vision at the expense of situational awareness. A good strategy – and good judgement – rely on the accurate observation of evidence and of patterns, coupled with a view of context and the wider system. In McGilchrist's analysis, each hemisphere is working together, each serving the other in harmony, guarding against the vocal left hemisphere drowning out the voiceless right hemisphere.

Ramachandran says 'The coping strategies of the two hemispheres are fundamentally different. The left hemisphere's job is to create a belief system or model and to fold new experiences into that belief system. If confronted with some new information that doesn't fit the model, it relies on Freudian defense mechanisms to deny, repress or confabulate – anything to preserve the *status quo*. The right hemisphere's strategy, on the other hand, is to play "Devil's Advocate" to question the *status quo* and look for global inconsistencies' (1999: 136). Thiele summarizes 'We must find ways to stimulate the novelty-receptive right hemisphere of the brain, lest the left side carry through its conformist mandate of rationalizing and legitimizing expectations, habits and prejudices' (Thiele 2006: 158).

We said in Chapter 4 that if we could predict the future we would be unable to change it. We might extrapolate into the near future and be proved right if no discontinuity occurred, and we might be able to be reasonably certain about predicting some things, for example the number of people aged 20 in 20 years' time, because they are already born. Scenario thinking (Chapter 5) is helpful not only because it changes the way people think – instead of imagining the future as more of today (the default position), scenarios present alternative futures. Because they synchronize what would otherwise be individual perspectives into collective ones, these become shared stories that meld evidence ('left brain thinking') with context, and ideas of the future ('right brain thinking'). Scenarios, presented as sets of different potential futures, encourage rather than suppress different perceptions, and these are essential in forming strategic judgement. In the example of 20-year-olds in 20 years' time, scenarios will take fuller account of migration, of pandemics and other plausible (if not probable) events, than will our 'prediction'.

Pisapia and others (Pisapia 2009) describe the cognitive skills that enable leaders to use their imagination to make strategic judgements. Their research looked at the way students preparing for school leadership roles at four universities in the United States, Malaysia, Hong Kong and Shanghai use mental skills to acquire knowledge, manipulate ideas, and process new information and beliefs and measured three such skills: reframing; reflection; and systems thinking.

Reframing situations so they become clearer and more understandable. A conscious effort to switch attention across multiple perspectives to generate new insights and options for action (see next section).

Reflecting and developing theories of practice which guide actions, as described by Senge (2006). The first level is technical reflection, which is concerned with examining the efficiency and the effectiveness of means to achieve certain ends. The second level, practical reflection, involves examining not only the means but also the ends, questioning the assumptions and the actual outcomes. The third level is critical reflection, which considers the moral and ethical issues – the social compassion and justice along with the means and the ends, encompassing the first two levels.

Systems thinking/thinking in more holistic ways. We looked at systems thinking in Chapter 5.

Pisapia's research found these skills did not vary from country to country because of Western and Eastern cultural norms. The skills were found in all locations and the variance in their use was more a function of age and gender than location.

The skills Pisapia identifies help see events and problems in terms of concepts, which are useful ways of thinking effectively about problems. Pisapia says strategic thinkers work from a mental model of the complete system. As explained in Chapter 5, where we stand determines what we see, and what we pay attention to alters what we find. The ability to interpret and make meaning of discrete and seemingly unrelated events is a hallmark of today's (and perhaps any day's) successful leader. In 2006,

Pisapia noted that leaders who find themselves in messy, chaotic, complex environments often fail because they are trained in and rely upon a linear thinking mindset that does not work in situations characterized by ambiguity and complexity.

Reframing

McGilchrist (2009), Ramachandran (1999) and others show that our left hemispheres fit events to a schema or 'frame' of how the world works that people use to navigate life. Sometimes there's a tension between what we know and what we experience, causing 'cognitive dissonance' – we rationalize or reassess our position to resolve the ambiguity of holding contradictory positions. Occasionally we find ourselves in wholly new frames, such as the end of the Cold War between East and West (following the fall of the Berlin Wall in 1989) or the accession of China to the capitalist World Trade Organization in 2001 after a couple of decades of opening up its economy, in what is often described as capitalism with Chinese characteristics, or state capitalism.

Tversky and Kahneman(1981) showed that the way in which you frame a question affects the answer you get. Similarly, Gall (Gall 2002) says that if you cannot change the system, reframe the system. You can try to change the structure of a system so that people think, feel and behave differently but if you can change the mental model in people's heads you may not need to do anything physical to the system itself. Gall explains that the understanding of a system is a metaphor. The new frame is also a metaphor. Creative reframing is the art of substituting useful metaphors for limiting metaphors to conceptualize the system differently. Reframing doesn't solve a problem – the problem may or may not exist in the new frame – but the decisions people make are different because they flow from a different appreciation of the system.

Gall uses several real examples and a deliberately simplified example to demonstrate his point: 'a jet pilot whose plane breaks through the clouds on approach to a strange airport at an unfamiliar destination. The pilot is suddenly faced with the problem of putting down the plane on a runway fifty feet long and half a mile wide. As we have previously noted, until the pilot solves the meta problem of restating his problem in solvable terms, he will experience some frustration ... Clearly, the airport system, existing OUT THERE in the form of concrete runways, tower, personnel, etc., does not change one iota as the pilot ponders his dilemma. But in the moment when the pilot reorganizes his perception of the system – when he revamps the model of the universe IN HERE, inside his own head – in that moment his problem is resolved. What is needed is a new model – in this case achieved by simply rotating the old model by ninety degrees' (Gall 2002: 182).

Schön and Rein (1994) discuss frames as an approach to intractable policy controversies resistant to resolution by appeal to evidence, research or reasoned argument. They point out that reason ends up taking sides rather than building bridges of rational persuasion from one side to another and contest the view that the world of officials is one of action, but thinking is the world of scholars (because thinking is essentially a withdrawal from action), recommend collaboration (194–5) and claim that competent practitioners can reflect on policy from a position within it (165). They note that contemporary sociologist Joseph Gusfield has written that 'the clinician, the practitioner, the official cannot afford to stand outside the frameworks within which action occurs, to examine their institutions and beliefs as only one of among a number of possible worlds' because they would have to give up commitment to a single set of beliefs indispensable to effective action (Schön and Rein 1994: xiii). Schön and Rein recommend challenging one's own frame by reflecting on frames of others. 'It is plausible that when scientists or policy makers are caught up in conflict their ability to reach agreement depends on their learning to understand one another's point of view. In order to do this, however, each party would have to be able to put in terms of his or her own frame the meaning of the situation as seen by the other in terms of *the other's frame*. The antagonists might then create a reciprocal, frame reflective discourse' (Schön and Rein: 45).

The frames that shape policies are often tacit and we don't recognize them when developing strategy. Our unconscious mental frames come into play when looking with the temporal dimensions, which we looked at in detail in Chapter 4. Pollitt's rich analysis (Pollitt 2008) reviews leading texts on time from Barbara Adam and Helga Nowotny to show clock time established dominance during the machine age, and examined three main types of time – electronically networked temporality, clock time, and the time of living and social processes (Pollitt 2008: 60–1). The 'time is money' equation of capitalism replaces unquestioned assumptions of linear clock time with an understanding that perspectives on time are themselves culturally constructed and conditioned and can vary between groups, contexts and activities (Pollitt 2008: 111).

Frames may also be path dependent. Griffin (1974) claims Abraham Flexner's landmark 1910 study *Medical Education in the United States and Canada* skewed US medical education in favour of drugs from 1913 onwards. It identified inadequacies in medical education and proposed sweeping changes including strengthening courses in pharmacology and the addition of research departments at all qualified medical schools, so that the selection process attracted researchers in pharmacology. 'This has resulted in loading the staffs of medical schools with men and women who, by preference and training, are ideal propagators of the drug-oriented science that has come to dominate American medicine' (Griffin 1974: 267).

We sometimes find our frames challenged, for example by artists like Paul Klee or Pablo Picasso who prompt us to see familiar landscapes in new ways. And as McGilchrist puts it (McGilchrist 2009: 28), the way we perceive an object like a mountain depends on whether we regard it as a prospector, a climber or someone who admires the view. In strategy work, standing back and recognizing the frame we are in, and whether alternative frames compete (for example 'people are naturally competitive versus people are naturally collaborative'), or are compatible ('people are evolved both to compete and to collaborate'), is difficult but rewarding. Inayatullah (2004) offers a way of approaching this in his causal layered analysis model, which uses a layering approach to explore frames, and once you have named the frames, lets you 'flip' them to make inflection points (where the frame might change) evident. This helps tease out uncertainties dependent on significant shifts in values, discourse and cultural meaning. Its four frames are: litany; system; worldview; and metaphor. The most visible level is the litany that looks at the quantitative trends, for example 'overpopulation', and what people are saying about such issues (politicians, experts, journalists, the person in the street). The system layer identifies the systems which underpin that view of the world: which drivers of change push in this direction; what institutions support it; what laws and regulations frame it; what historical events and turning points are evoked by its advocates; who gets heard and the counter-trends which might weaken this system; who – and what – gets marginalized and who is not heard at all. Beyond this layer is the prevailing worldview which summarizes this, and following that the cultural metaphors connected to that worldview, the emotive stories that may see people as creative resources rather than a problem or alternatively as 'other'. Insight comes from understanding the layers more deeply, and the connections between them. 'Inflecting' the worldview and metaphor statements means you can retrace a journey back through the layers to understand what driving forces would be needed to make any 'taken for granted' frames different.

Recall Pierre Wack, of the Shell scenarios in Chapter 5. He makes the point that forecasting works in stable environments. But in fluid and turbulent environments – which must include public strategy where you are 'inventing the future' – you need to recognize, confront and embrace uncertainty as a structural element of the environment. Causal layered analysis may help you steer clear of the risk of framing the future in your current mental model, letting you reframe it – reflect on it, generate insight and recognize the fragile (and sometimes toxic) assumptions you make to negotiate the world *as it currently is*. Otherwise you are steering a ship by its wake; driving using the rear-view mirror, or 'muddling through'.

All this shows we can do things in our daily lives to foster the exercise of imagination and to reframe problems. The imaginative brain is also the brain that is most likely to be able to exercise strategic judgement.

Errors of omission

We spoke about errors of omission in Chapter 4 in the section on group-think. Progress isn't possible without change, and effective change needs strategy. Absence of an implementable strategy that will deliver a future vision is, perhaps, the greatest omission of all. Both Art Kleiner (2008) and Richard Rumelt (2011) have written persuasively on this, with Kleiner saying: 'In all too many companies the numbers were used to make people look good or to reinforce the comforts of a complacent position. People from the CEO on down lost sight of the purposes of their enterprises. They fixed their attention on the trappings of the rituals instead: the business plans, job descriptions, quarterly results, and performance appraisals, all of which had originally meant nothing in themselves. These decision makers had cornered the market on "know how", said the architect and visionary Buckminster Fuller, but they lacked "know why"' (Kleiner 2008: 10).

Fuller had plenty of stories on which he based this claim. Again and again during his long life as an inventor and would-be entrepreneur, he had seen the 'numbers' lead to corporate decisions that didn't make sense – decisions that undermined not just outsiders but the company's own long-term interest.

For companies this decoupling of purpose and strategic vision from the planning and resourcing that make a company's strategy a reality can be calamitous. The company can go bust, destroying its potential to create value and costing people their livelihoods.

In the public domain it's even more serious. A government that fails, whether at agency, city or at national level, can destroy the prospects not just of one company but of many companies, not just the livelihoods of many people, but of almost all its people. As we have seen in this book, governments that fail often fail for lack of strategy – for lack of an essential idea of where the city or country is heading, of why it should be heading there, and for lack of the organizational ability to start in that direction. Sometimes a lack of strategy seems harmless enough – places can thrive for a while just 'muddling through', especially when times are good. But in times of crisis the lack of strategy is like a hole below the waterline where water has trickled in unnoticed, perhaps for years.

Governments, agencies, city administrations that simply 'mind the shop', holding office but not setting any direction, simply responding to events as they occur, adopting different tactics depending on the circumstances of the day, can survive and even seem to thrive. Sometimes governments without a sense of direction can present themselves as refreshingly free of dogma. But these governments store up problems for the near future. Tough issues are 'cans that are kicked down the road', because there is no vision, no mission, no plan and no story to make sense of the problems that keep bubbling up, and no way to get ahead of the running tide of those problems. Energy security, water shortages or flooding, transport infrastructure, youth unemployment, regional development, cyber-security, counter-terrorism: each one will throw up surprises, each one will need its own response, and each response will – unsurprisingly – be uncoordinated with all the other responses. Administrations without strategy hold office but struggle to exercise power because they are unable to set direction. But it is never too late to begin to transform their fortunes by adopting the strategic approach – the approach we have described in this book.

Warren Bennis wrote about leadership throughout his career, starting in the early 1960s, but his interest accelerated after he spent seven years as president of the University of Cincinnati, applying the lessons of leadership. This experience taught him a number of important things about leadership: managers were people who do things right, while leaders do the right thing. He came to believe, as Buckminster Fuller did, that organizations needed people not just with 'know how' but also with 'know why' (Fuller 1995). Knowing why is essential to the exercise of strategic judgement. In this model each component is crucial in creating a 'virtuous cycle' of increased strategic capability. Strategic appetite is itself, of course, a product of many pre-existing conditions. Appetite, in turn, plays a crucial role in contributing to a strategy process in public organizations seeking to achieve outcomes.

Top managers have achieved their position by exercising judgement that has proved successful – in *The Puritan Gift* (Hopper and Hopper 2009), the Hopper brothers show the value of the judgement of executives with a lifelong experience of a sector, steeped in knowledge of an industry as opposed to a trend for regarding companies as financial enterprises that can be run by financial experts or professionalized mangers interested only in a short-term return on capital.

Look at your own strategy – if there is one. Does it require 'three miracles' to be delivered? In Chapter 5 we saw how Pierre Wack showed Shell executives that their favoured scenario would need three miraculous things to happen if it were going to come about.

Does your strategy tackle the detail of your trickiest issues? Richard Rumelt says that having a list of goals and aspirations and saying 'make it so' won't deliver if the organization hasn't identified what problems it will need to overcome to achieve them.

And do you have a sense of purpose? Herbert Simon said: 'purposiveness brings about an integration in the pattern of behaviour, in the absence of which administration would be meaningless; for, if administration consists in "getting things done" by groups of people, purpose provides a principal criterion in determining what things are to be done' (Simon 1997: 3). Strategy brings purpose, but if you find you have no sense of purpose, you are certain to find that you have no strategy.

Conclusion

Strategy in the public realm means organizing with a sense of purpose, by understanding future capabilities and the policies that will be needed for delivering outcomes beyond the organization for the common good. Purposive endeavours create a collective, or public, value at some point in the future – schools, universities, libraries and health services. Public strategy identifies and shapes the future, it creates a narrative and plan that will carry people with it from the start to whichever plausible future has been imagined. It understands what it is trying to achieve or the system it is trying to improve. Being clear about the purpose of an activity changes it to an action capable of achieving a meaningful result, for instance, not simply carrying out safety inspections but making industry safer. That action must be accountable. It needs a mandate (the authorizing environment) for its social mission and the operational capability to deliver it if it is to gain legitimacy for the outcomes it seeks to deliver.

There's little in the literature on strategy specifically for those working on making strategy for the common good. Often they have to rely on corporate or military texts. But public strategy is different in its aim of creating better futures and lives ('changing the future'), not just adapting to whichever future comes about with optimal performance and profitability ('surviving the future'). The competitive dimension, which is all important in commercial strategy, doesn't dominate in the same way in public strategy, other than in seeking greater productivity and efficiency. Governments and public organizations more usually collaborate to secure outcomes for those they serve. Public strategy combines the best of public and private resources to deliver social goals working with other actors in complex systems to deliver shared objectives. A public organization, whether a government, a non-profit social enterprise or a charity, must always try to achieve outcomes that sit beyond the success of the organization itself.

The choice for governments is not between problem-solving and identifying and pursuing desired outcomes but adopting both a goal-seeking and problem-solving approach. Problem-solving approaches on their own are 'whack a mole' strategies where each time a problem (the adversary) is 'whacked' it pops up again somewhere else. This approach is as bad as the wishful thinking strategies that need three miracles before they can come about.

Getting people to take enough interest in the future means appreciating where human psychology favours the lens of now, groupthink and expert bias. It must resist the trap of simply muddling through.

Runciman (2013) writes that democracies tend to learn from their mistakes that they can survive them, leading to the false belief that they can muddle through anything. We need particular techniques to address what are, in the context of long-term thinking, the human frailties that conspire to make us think that we need worry about the future only in the future. These include the 'three waves' that connect analysis of today, tomorrow and the distant future: drawing attention to the drivers of change; trend analysis; and using scenarios to open up thinking.

Building strategic appetite means leaders being clear to everyone about the outcomes they seek and having a clear understanding of the relationship and distinction between missions (or core purposes); inputs and activities; outputs; intermediate outcomes; and ultimate outcomes and the vision they support, together with the line of sight that connects all of these, and the accountabilities and measurement of them, recognizing that the rational responses to measures create perverse incentives.

Strategy needs to ask why, not just how, and use techniques like reflection and causal layered analysis to surface the frames of thinking that may trap us. It feeds on imagination and the circumstances that favour its exercise. Albert Hirschman never gave up on the ability to imagine life differently, better. He would often tell his readers (Adelman 2013: 14) that a solution to the world's problems lay not so much in some technical discovery as in the power of imagination.

Public strategy in the 21st century

This may not be a time when hierarchies are giving way to networks – there will always be a need for final authority in any institution. Yet it is a time when increasing information flows are making hierarchies more unsettled and less durable. It's a time when 'command and control' can't be as effective as it once was; a time when it takes too long for decisions to make stately progress up and down a chain. It's a time when hierarchies are looking and acting more like networks.

This is a time when, because the resources needed to achieve desired outcomes are decentralized, they don't behave predictably. It's a time when publics are more empowered, connected, self-confident and self-directed. It's a time when it's harder to shape change and expect it to stick, when our worldview is one of complexity, digital technology, systems and networks (Green 2010). For good social, technological and economic reasons, it's becoming harder to tell apart the public and private realms. It's a time when boundaries that were once relatively clear are blurred.

This is the world in which we have to rethink public strategy, a world where strategy is not just essential but intensely practical because it provides ways of thinking that don't assume that tomorrow will be 'more of the same'. Plans optimized for today's environment but that are not shaped by strategy become anachronisms in tomorrow's world. Our aim in this book has been to offer those who want to understand the public sphere the confidence to take a strategic view by showing what that means, and how to spot the gaps – whether in personal practice or in the organizations in which they work.

Strategic analysis and planning techniques are often made to look complicated. People can advocate one way above others. The point throughout this book is that strategy is not merely a management tool, nor a formula that answers every question – it is a way of thinking, helping us to understand possible futures and to shape the one we seek. Effective strategy uses many lenses: political, economic, environmental, social, technological and scientific. It needs a combination of approaches, where the process is as important as the product because the thinking it stimulates produces new insights which are the real product. Producing a corporate plan doesn't make a strategy, although unfortunately creating it can subsume all strategic effort.

Strategy that is seen as 'belonging to the board' or, worse still, to the 'strategy unit' will often seem irrelevant to day-to-day work. A strategic process should involve a range of people from within the organization and beyond it. This takes time and effort, but is essential if the strategy is to help people understand what the organization is trying to achieve and to motivate them to get there. When a public organization doesn't have a strategy with a clear vision, it risks its functional strategies (HR, IT, marketing) filling the vacuum. The organization can end up being driven by its information technology strategy, for instance, instead of its IT strategy being shaped to advance the organization's strategic vision.

The futures analysis that strategy depends on can seem irrelevant when it doesn't recognize immediate pressures. Yet it is equally useless if it does no more than tell people what they can already see for themselves. Even the best analysis will be unheard if it doesn't offer resilience in the short term as well as an understanding of the long term. It must anticipate the unexpected and encourage intelligent opportunism to help steer around unforeseen obstacles while preserving the long-term direction (as long as continued analysis shows this long-term direction is still relevant). We saw that strategic analysis works best when presented in three 'waves' that help understanding of the short, medium and long term. This will help create the necessary organizational appetite for strategic thinking, and encourage ministers and boards to demand it. Without appetite, strategic thinking happens only by chance, under the radar or on an *ad hoc* basis. Unofficial strategic thinking may be better than none, but its outputs will be accidental rather than a systematic part of governance. Where there is no demand for strategic thinking we will often see little more than an accumulation of documents and initiatives.

Leaders of organizations can be encouraged to become 'strategic commissioners' when they are convinced that future-focused strategy translates into successful policy delivery, and when they see that a strong strategy offers the best frame of reference for dealing with the short term as well as the long term. Leaders must, in turn, foster a culture that questions assumptions and challenges groupthink if they wish to embed the strategic thinking expected of leaders.

The public sector has plenty to learn from the corporate sector, especially about resilience and responsiveness to demand, but the business of governments is to create public value, which goes beyond the delivery of products and services (although that may be an important part of what they do). When the public sphere tries to do no more than copy from the corporate sector we may fail to identify and set out the changes in society that all governments exist to achieve. We've stressed the importance for public sector organizations of a vision of the outcomes they seek to achieve, that should go beyond the delivery of services or products because the creation of public value depends upon changes in society at large – especially of public attitudes – as well as the performance of government and its agencies. We should carefully examine whether our public organizations are helping outcomes to be achieved – which may not be through anything like the current service design or, indeed, any service design at all.

We've shown strategy needs to offer a 'line of sight' or 'golden thread' up and down an organization to connect activity to purpose. Strategy is most useful when it identifies desired outcomes, shapes the policies that help to achieve those outcomes and enables and encourages delivery of the outcomes. The links between the organization's core purpose and vision, its desired outcomes, its policies and programmes and its strategic delivery plans and goals must be explicit to all in the organization and to its stakeholders. Outcomes that are widely understood and supported motivate everybody to achieve them, acting as building blocks of a narrative everyone can understand. Measuring the achievement of outcomes, and ensuring proper accountability through those measures, is what turns strategy into a tangible reality, although we must always guard against the likelihood that targets will breed perverse behaviours.

Often it will be clear to an organization or institution that things in the outside world are changing and these will dominate the direction it is taking. In health care, it's a commonplace that demand upon finite resources is growing, for reasons that are self-evident (longer living populations; medical advances; a fundamental shift to catering for chronic, not acute, illness; a rising interest in wellbeing). But the response to these demands is uncertain and should be shaped strategically. Will the future direction of health care increase or reduce inequality? Will it take the mechanical, electronic, biological or genetic path, or combinations of all of these? What infrastructure will these developments require

– the building of large operating theatres or small rooms where a pharmacist injects stem cells? In addition to obvious challenges there will be inevitable surprises that can catch us out if we haven't primed our thinking. Scenarios are a way of identifying and organizing uncertainty. We have seen how surfacing uncertainty through trend analysis can sensitize people within the organization to alternative futures and the signals that show which future might be coming about.

We outlined the need for leaders to embrace and confront uncertainty, to use it to seek the right questions, not give in to the temptation to discount it because it's not in their control. Pierre Wack makes the point that forecasting works in stable environments but that in fluid and turbulent environments – which must include public strategy where you are 'inventing the future' – you need to recognize, confront and embrace uncertainty as a structural element of the environment (Wack 1985: 73). Steer clear of the risk of framing the future in your current mental model, reframe it, reflect on it, generate insight and recognize the silent or toxic assumptions made to negotiate the world as it currently is. Are we, in the question in the title of a chapter in Peter Senge's *The Fifth Discipline*, 'Prisoners of the system, or prisoners of our own thinking?' (Senge 2006: 27).

We touched on the thesis that the strategic role of leaders – one that sets them apart from managers who have the answers to solvable tame problems – is to seek goals by finding the questions to ask when dealing with wicked problems. As with all generalizations this distinction may be too stark and we have argued that everyone in the organization must involve themselves in formulating and implementing strategy, but a principal responsibility of leaders is to expect and commission strategic thinking.

We looked at strategic judgement and the circumstances in which it is reliable. The executives who have reached the top of their organization having 'grown up' in a particular industry have generally achieved that position by exercising their judgement successfully using their deep domain expertise. The Hoppers (Hopper and Hopper 2009) argue for the strategic value of this judgement, contrasting it unfavourably with those who see companies as financial enterprises best run by financial professionals looking only for a short-term return on capital. There's inevitably a risk where professionals have a vested interest in the *status quo* where their expertise is valued. Should a tax agency be run entirely by tax inspectors, an airline by pilots or oil companies by geologists? Almost certainly not. A strategy process should guard against expert bias, but it would be a mistake if we didn't incorporate valuable domain knowledge in the formulation of strategy.

Finally we looked at the role of imagination and the factors that favour it, taking note of the reflexive relationship between the brain and the kind of physical environment we are in, and how our thinking changes as that varies. We looked at advances in neuroscience that show how the two hemispheres of the brain process the world in distinctly different ways, constantly combining the worlds that their two different kinds of attention create. The left hemisphere is a closed system perfectly suited to operating in, even creating, a bureaucratic world with a narrow, sharply focused, and fragmented attention to detail. It sees things with a clarity that helps us negotiate the already known, fixed, static, isolated, de-contextualized and generic. The right hemisphere offers context; it maintains broad, open, vigilant alertness, on the look-out for things that might differ from expectations. It sees a changing, evolving, interconnected, implicit, living world, never fully grasp-able, never perfectly known. Although the left hemisphere is more convincing because it deletes what doesn't fit, to make itself consistent and compelling, the right is absolutely essential to providing the broader context.

Not least important in the exercise of imagination is the strategy process itself. Scenario thinking is the 'safe harbour' for the exercise of imagination, stimulated by the rigour of trend analysis and testing, or creating, a bold vision for building public value. We saw in the Honda City example that an ambition should not be so narrow as to constrain, and that the purpose may change over time (as for the Tennessee Valley Authority). Today some of the biggest American car manufacturers are discussing whether their future may be as mobility providers rather than building and selling cars, in response to a decline in car ownership among young Americans living different lifestyles from those of their parents. English poet Robert Browning (1812–89) wrote 'a man's reach should exceed his grasp, or what's a heaven for?' A strategy for delivering public value will probably need ambitious goals. But ambition is not enough. A strategy that's no more than a pipedream – that omits the gritty detail of plans to address the fundamental barriers to its achievement – is a bad strategy because it skips over pesky details such as problems (Rumelt 2011: 4–6). A good strategy is not just a narrative of the future – yet it won't deserve to be called a strategy without a compelling narrative, as we saw when we looked at the power of stories in Chapter 8.

Becoming a strategist

Some people, it is said, are naturally strategic. Others, naturally unstrategic. While it is probably true that some people have biases in favour of long-term thinking and others in favour of short-term thinking (in part for the reasons we explored in Chapter 8), it is worth considering what predisposes a person to learn about strategy.

Learning about strategy calls for an interest in the theory and history of strategy as well as an eagerness to apply strategic approaches, including those explored in this book. It requires the ability, innate or acquired, to reflect on, and gain insight from, its application to develop good strategic practice. In this, of course, strategy is like most other areas of learning. But there are a number of challenges for the study of strategy. These include:

- The literature on strategy often compares 'porcupines with pears', whether (as we explored in Chapter 3) because of the differences between commercial and public strategy, or because of the differences in context from place to place or from time to time. It seems that the 'sensemaking' ability to find patterns in apparently dissimilar things is very important for the strategic learner.
- There is no prevailing agreement on a 'theory of strategy'. As we have explored throughout this book, there are many approaches, and many are legitimate. There are certain features without which no public strategy can deserve to be described as strategic: public strategy must be forward-looking, outward-looking, purposive and concerned with the creation of public value. But these features do not alone create a comprehensive theory of strategy. In this sense good strategic learners are more likely to be foxes (or, perhaps, jackdaws) than hedgehogs – picking up useful morsels of learning from many experiences.
- Openness to insight is essential in strategic learning. This is hardly unique to the field of strategy, but strategy does require the reframing of familiar issues, the ability to narrow complex sets of issues sufficiently to make them amenable to understanding and change, but not to narrow them so far that they fall into the 'problem–solution' paradox, which quickly leads into 'whack a mole' territory, with superficial solutions that simply store up new problems. In this sense strategic learning needs wisdom. Can a person learn to be wise? We would argue that the answer to that question is 'yes', and (at the risk of circularity) being strategic is part of the journey to wisdom.

There are also sets of challenges in strategic practice. While the well-known strategic consultancies often produce good work, challenge and best practice, they can sometimes apply rote solutions to problems. This arises in part from incentives to narrow issues to the point where they are amenable to solution, but it is also a feature of left-brained thinking, identifying something observed as a 'match' to something already known, and being reluctant to explore the unknown and gain what might be the crucial insight that will enable reframing and the creation of a new strategy.

Another danger in strategic practice is the eagerness to drive towards a strategy without engaging enough of the right people in the process. This means involving sceptics as well as supporters, being open to 'heresies', ensuring that a clear mandate is maintained, not only from above but also from those who will have to carry out the strategy and those who will be affected by it. Giving everyone enough involvement and a voice in the strategy process is time-consuming and often unglamorous work. But it is vital in good strategic practice.

The building of strategic institutions depends on the creation of strategic appetite, as we explored in Chapter 6. One of the most intriguing challenges of all in strategy is how to institutionalize strategy once the appetite has been created. We have found very few examples of institutions that have maintained strategic appetite for longer than 40 or 50 years. Much more commonly an institution will operate strategically for five to ten years before reverting to 'muddling through'. It seems that strategy operates on a cycle, as we suggested at the very beginning of the book. Perhaps 'strategic renewal' is healthy and, in any case, unavoidable.

Strategy, the indispensable discipline

For something indispensable, strategy can be treated with surprising carelessness in government. Worse still, some governments argue that they have all the strategy they need. For politicians of this persuasion, strategy is something best left to a small coterie in the Prime Minister's or President's or Mayor's office. They don't worry about strategy or strategic thinking as a capability across government because they may not understand strategy as a capability. Some may cling to dogma as their only guide. Some may see strategy as a political threat, with the capacity to challenge prior ideologies or to annex resources to 'technocratic projects' that enjoy a life of their own, beyond the electoral cycle of political control. Some confuse a published plan, a set of manifesto promises or a speech with the process of strategy, and then seem surprised when the puff of intention is carried away on the first strong breeze of reality.

It is hard to imagine a successful business deciding that they have had all the strategy they can take. Successful businesses care about the future, they worry about competitors, they monitor the performance of their most profitable products and services and they invest in new products and services, accepting the risk this entails. They understand that without some failures there can be no success. Successful businesses also look at how the world is changing around them. Yet governments, particularly when times are tough, can tend to hunker down and seek to retrench and consolidate at precisely the moment when retrenchment and consolidation are most perilous for the welfare of their economies and societies. This reaction arises, in part, because political and administrative leaders have too little confidence in government's ability to construct and deliver effective public strategy. That lack of confidence is understandable, given the rocky record of strategy, the uneven and sometimes non-existent levels of strategic capability in government and the constraints and complexities of operating in a global economy. It is understandable, but it is not forgivable. The job of governments is, above all else, to ensure the resilience and endurance of their cities and nations. It follows, therefore, that good governments have a responsibility to encourage and strengthen strategic capability among both their political class and among the bureaucratic class that supports them.

Strategy is not an insurance policy. It does not allow governments to hedge bets and prepare for every possibility. One of the reasons that some politicians are allergic to strategy is because of the priesthood of futurists, self-styled strategic thinkers and 'horizon scanners' who can sometimes prognosticate about the future in ways that seem divorced from the immediate realities of decision-making. While politicians will often talk about making 'tough choices' and making 'the right decisions for the long term', in practice most political decisions have to be sustainable in the short term. The job of strategy is not to look above or over the short-term realities, but to see through those demands and to make sure that the short term is connected in a meaningful way to the long term.

Strategy relies on making choices about what matters, about where a nation or city or area of policy is heading. Rumelt (2011: 61) says that in the early 1990s the Digital Equipment Corporation became irrelevant because its leaders 'avoided the hard work of choice, set nothing aside, hurt no interest groups or individual egos, but crippled the whole'. A good strategy allows leaders to pay attention to the things that really do matter and to not waste energy on the things that do not. A realistic strategy, with an effective plan for its delivery, will help leaders to spend time on the areas where their efforts can make a difference, instead of on futile initiatives that make no difference at all. Leading change means getting things done, and paying individual attention to the issues that make a tangible difference to achieving a successful outcome.

This capability to see through to the long term, to understand and cope with uncertainty, to articulate a vision and win legitimacy and support for it, to develop plans that people can work to implement and to hold oneself to account for the results of a strategy is what we mean by 'strategic capability'. But it is not inherent or universal or easy. It needs practice, hard work, the use of certain tools and approaches and the ability to make connections between seemingly disparate things. A system view, not a compartmentalized view, helps, though often our response to complexity is the reductionist approach of breaking things down in the hope it makes them more manageable. Above all strategy needs insight – the insight that goes with being prepared to look at old problems with a fresh eye, to listen to lone voices as well as the crowd, to look at history not as a stately progression of events that were somehow predetermined and knowable but as, in Philip Roth's words, 'the tyranny of the unforeseen'. Strategically capable people know that the only way to steer a way through the future is to be prepared to take the tiller – but also to encourage others to take the tiller, too.

What of public strategy-making in the 21st century? We've warned of the perils of prediction but strategy-makers will have to grapple with problems like diminishing availability of food, water, energy and land as well as reframing issues like biodiversity, inequality, wellbeing, population growth, infrastructure, intergenerational equity, conflict and ideas on what constitutes efficiency. The fundamental question 'what is progress, and how do we achieve it?' is likely to be re-examined in the near future. Along the way strategic understanding will be helped by knowledge from new fields, like biomimicry or genomics. Public strategy will be shaped by advances that have taken place in the last two or three decades in understanding how people think and behave.

Governments can do many things but they can't do everything, and they will have to make choices. That needs a sense of what they want to achieve – in other words, of *strategic intent* – the framework in which they can make the decisions, test factual premises, take risks, understand failures and build success. Strategy provides a coherent framework for policy-making and for delivery. Without it governments are condemned to the worst variety of 'muddling through'. A business that muddled through would, sooner rather than later, go bust or be acquired by a business better able to create value from it. Governments cannot afford to muddle through.

Governments have yet another responsibility, even beyond the solemn responsibility of providing resilience for the states and cities they govern. For, as we discussed earlier in this book, it is not enough for governments to simply *survive* the future. The point of public strategy is both to build resilience and to *change the future* for the better. Because we do not know what the future will bring we are liberated to imagine it and, by imagining it, begin the process of creating it. Leadership, strategic thinking and bold execution are the instruments of successful strategies – strategies that transform lives for the better, that build great cities, that can send people to the moon, that extend lifespans, that defeat tyrannies and that one day may find sustainable ways to produce unlimited energy, secure food supplies and safe communities for all who live on the planet, and that might even land humans or our genetically modified progeny on distant planets orbiting other suns. If we can imagine it we can make it true, and to make it true we need strategy to take us there.

Further Reading

1 Introduction: Strategy – Everywhere and Nowhere

For an exploration of public policy-making in the 'post bureaucratic age' Elaine Kamarck, a White House staffer under Vice President Gore, explores the emerging issues in an engaging way, focusing particularly on the increasing demands on governments by a more networked citizenry (Kamarck 2007). She considers the role of governments with fewer traditional levers to pull in helping to create markets to achieve socially desirable outcomes. Henry Mintzberg's *The Rise and Fall of Strategic Planning* (Mintzberg 1994), while focusing mainly on the corporate world, offers a compelling tour of the world of strategy-making and its pitfalls. Mintzberg exposes many common misconceptions about strategy, and questions the value of the role of formal strategy processes – certainly those that result in suppressing rather than encouraging insight.

2 Public Strategy

University of Minnesota-based John Bryson offers an essential handbook for how to do strategic planning in the public sphere, with many tools and examples as well as clear explanations of theory (Bryson 2011). Paul Joyce (Joyce 2000) provides a similarly practical introduction to public strategy-making from a UK perspective. Charles Hampden-Turner (Hampden-Turner 1990) explores the power of strategic thinking, advocating openness to possibility and detailing the traps of narrowing problems to the point where they are amenable to solution but also irrelevant. The dilemma, and the human response to dilemma, is all important in innovation. Nonaka and Takeuchi's *The Knowledge-Creating Company* (1995) contrasts the conceptual split between mind and body in Western thinking, dating back to philosopher Descartes (1596–1650), with the integration of mind and body in the East, showing how this affects thinking and practice. It is worth reading for increasing our self-awareness of the way in which culture may affect how we approach strategy.

3 Corporate Strategy and Public Strategy

Mark Moore's *Creating Public Value* (Moore 1995) is a 'must read' for an understanding of the importance and distinctiveness of strategy-making in the public sphere. This book, although written in 1995, seems to grow in relevance year by year. Archon Fung (Fung 2006) is a leading authority on participative democracy – and the importance of public accountability in lending legitimacy to public action.

4 Barriers to Strategic Thinking

Peter Hennessy is an outstanding and entertaining observer of the UK political scene, and his many books chronicle the tensions, failures and occasional successes as 'events' and a propensity for muddling through get the better of strategic intent, including *Muddling Through: power, politics and the quality of government in post-war Britain* (Hennessy 1996).

5 Thinking Strategically: Methods and Approaches

There are many fascinating and useful books on scenario planning. One of the best known authors in the field is Kees van der Heijden, whose many practical books on scenario planning include *The Sixth Sense* (Heijden *et al.* 2002). Gill Ringland's *Scenario Planning* (2006) is another useful and practical guide to the various scenario planning techniques.

6 Acting Strategically: Building Strategic Appetite

Getting an organization behind a strategy is tough and depends on the ability to engage people at all levels. David Macleod and Chris Brady's *The Extra Mile* (Macleod and Brady 2008) is full of wisdom and practical examples of how to do that. Understanding the competing interests and personalities in the political process is vital to creating strategic capability. John Kingdon's *Agendas, Alternatives and Public Policies* (Kingdon 2003) provides a conceptual framework firmly rooted in the realities of policy-making to help guide a way through political complexity.

7 Delivering Strategically: Performance and Accountability for Results

The best designed delivery plans, even those that are well-funded, strongly mandated and with clear accountability reporting, can fail. Few books explain why that is so as clearly as *Implementation: how great expectations in Washington are dashed in Oakland, or Why it's amazing that Federal programmes work at all* (Pressman and Wildavsky 1973) – as apposite today as when it was first published.

8 Imagination, Curiosity and Strategic Judgement

Clumsy solutions for a Complex World (edited by Verweij and Thompson 2006) shows, in a series of incisive essays, why the same solutions are deployed as ineffectively as ever on the same problems with – predictably – the same results, and examines the mental framing that underpins this behaviour. Narrative fallacies mislead us, yet narrative is a powerful way of conveying strategy and ambition. John Yorke's *Into the Woods* (2013) shows the role of story in human lives, how and why storytelling grips us, the common elements of structure in every story and the role of desire in animating us. A good strategy must inspire, but Richard Rumelt (2011a) shows it has to do more than urge us forward toward a goal or vision; it has to honestly acknowledge the challenges we face and provide the approach to overcoming them.

Bibliography

Abu Dhabi Government (2011) *Economic Vision 2030*, http://www.upc.gov.ae/template/upc/pdf/abu-dhabi-vision-2030-revised.pdf (accessed 3 November 13).

Adam, Barbara (2004) *Time*, Cambridge, Polity Press.

Adelman, Jeremy (2013) *Worldly Philosopher: The Odyssey of Albert O. Hirschman*, Princeton, Princeton University Press.

Afghanistan COIN (Counter Insurgency) Dynamics, http://www.theguardian.com/news/datablog/2010/apr/29/mcchrystal-afghanistan-powerpoint-slide; http://msnbcmedia.msn.com/i/MSNBC/Components/Photo/_new/Afghanistan _ Dynamic_Planning.pdf (accessed 28 September 2013).

Ainslie, G. (1992) *Picoeconomics*, Cambridge, Cambridge University Press.

Allison, Graham T. (1980) *Public and Private Management: Are they fundamentally alike in all unimportant respects?*, http://cstl-cla.semo.edu/walling/Public%20Private%20Mgt.pdf (accessed 9 August 2013).

Aristotle (c335 BCE) Politics, http://classics.mit.edu/Aristotle/politics.1.one.html (accessed 7 September 2013).

Asch, S.E. (1955) 'Opinions and Social Pressure', *Scientific American*, 193(5): 31–5.

Ashby, W. Ross (1956) *An Introduction to Cybernetics*, London, Chapman & Hall.

Axelrod, Robert and Cohen, Michael D. (1999) *Harnessing Complexity: Organizational Implications of a Scientific Frontier*, New York, Free Press.

Baghai, M., Coley, S. and White, D. (1999) *The Alchemy of Growth*, London, Orion Business.

Bahrain Government, Economic Development Board (2013) *Bahrain Vision 2030*, http://www.bahrainedb.com/en/EDBDocuments/EDB%20-%20Vision%202030%20-%20May%202013.pdf (accessed 3 November 2013).

Barber, M. (2007) *Instruction to Deliver*, London, Politicos.

Baumgartner, Frank R. and Jones, Bryan D. (1993) *Agendas and Instability in American Politics*, Chicago, University of Chicago Press.

Beckhard, R. and Harris, R. (1977) *Organizational Transitions: managing complex change*, Reading, MA, Addison-Wesley.

Beinhocker, Eric (2007) *The Origin of Wealth: Evolution, Complexity, and the Radical Remaking of Economics*, London, Random House Insight.

Bell, C. (1992) *Ritual Theory, Ritual Practice*, Oxford, Oxford University Press.

Benington, J. and Moore, M.H. (2011) *Public Value, Theory and Practice*, Basingstoke, Palgrave Macmillan.

Bentley, A., Earls, M., O'Brien, M.J. and Maeda, J. (2011) *I'll Have What She's Having: Mapping Social Behavior*, Cambridge, MA, MIT Press.

Bentley, T. and Wilson, J. (2003) *The Adaptive State*, London, Demos.

Berlin, Isaiah (1953) *The Hedgehog and the Fox: An Essay on Tolstoy's View of History*, London, Weidenfeld & Nicolson.

Beveridge, William (1942) *Social insurance and allied services*, London, HMSO.

Bichard, M. (1999) *Performance Management Civil Service Reform – A Report to the Meeting of Permanent Heads of Departments*, Sunningdale, 30 September–1 October 1999, Cabinet Office, London 5 http://www.enap.gov.br/downloads/ec43ea4fcivilservice_publicmanagement.pdf (accessed 25 January 2014).

Bozeman, Barry (1987) *All Organizations are Public: Comparing Public and Private Organizations*, San Francisco, Jossey Bass.

Brand, Stewart (1999) *The Clock of the Long Now: Time and Responsibility*, New York, Basic Books.

Brews, P. (2003) 'Star Trek Strategy: real strategy at work', *Harvard Business Review*, 14(3), Autumn Edition: 35.

Brews, P. (2005) 'Great Expectations: strategy as creative fiction', *Harvard Business Review*, Autumn Edition: 6.

Bryson, J.M. (2011) *Strategic Planning for Public and Non-profit Organizations* (4th edn), San Francisco, Jossey-Bass.

Burns, J. P. and Zhiren, Z. (2010) 'Performance Management in the Government of the People's Republic of China: Accountability and Control in the Implementation of Public Policy', *OECD Journal of Budgeting Volume 2010/2*, Paris, OECD.

Camerer, C., Loewenstein, G. and Prelec, D. (2005) 'Neuroeconomics: How neuroscience can inform economics', *Journal of Economic Literature*, XLIII, March: 9–64, http://www.hss.caltech.edu/~ camerer/JELfinal.pdf (accessed 16 August 2013).

Cameron, D. (2007) Speech to Young Foundation, http://www. conservatives.com/News/Speeches/2007/11/David_Cameron_From_government_to_people.aspx (accessed 1 September 2013).

Camillus, J. (2008) 'Strategy as a Wicked Problem', *Harvard Business Review*, May.

Campbell, S., Benita, S., Coates, E., Davies, P. and Penn, G. (2007) *Analysis for policy: evidence based policy in practice*, London, HM Treasury, Government Social Research Unit, www.gsr.gov.uk.

Canada Treasury Board Secretariat (2013) *Results Based Management Lexicon*, http://www.tbs-sct.gc.ca/cee/pubs/lex-eng.asp, (accessed 3 November 2013).

Capra, F. (2002) *The Hidden Connections: A Science for Sustainable Living*, London, Flamingo.

Chapman, J. (2003) 'Thinking out of the machine', in Tom Bentley and James Wilsdon (eds) *The Adaptive State*, London, Demos.

Chapman, J. (2004) *System Failure: Why governments must learn to think differently* (2nd edn), London, Demos.

Checkland, Peter (1981) *Systems Thinking*, Systems Practice, Chichester, John Wiley and Sons.

Clark, P. and Neill, S. (2001) The Value Mandate: Maximising Shareholder Value Across the Corporation, New York, AMACOM American Management Association.

Clarke, Arthur C. (2000) *Fountains of Paradise*, London, Gollancz.

Clarke, Arthur, C. (1945) Letter to the February 1945 edition of *Wireless World* magazine can be found at: http://lakdiva.org/clarke/1945ww/ (accessed 10 July 2013).

Clements, B (1997) 'The Real Plan, Poverty and Income Distribution in Brazil', *Finance and Development*, IMF, September: 44–6.

Collins, J. and Porras, Jerry (1994) *Built to Last: Successful Habits of Visionary Companies*, London, Random House Business Books.

Consumers' Association of Penang (2002) *The lack of vision of the National Vision Policy*, http://www.socialwatch.org/book/export/html/10798 (accessed 3 November 2013).

COSATU (2013) Congress of South African Trade Unions (2013) *Mangaung and the second phase of the transition: discussion document for the COSATU CEC 25–27 February 2013*, http://www.cosatu.org.za/docs/discussion/2013/NDPcritiquesummary.pdf (accessed 13 October 2013).

Curry, A. and Hodgson, A. (2008) 'Seeing in Multiple Horizons: Connecting Futures to Strategy', *Journal of Futures Studies*, 13(1), August: 1–20.

Diez Pinto, E. (2004) *Vision Guatemala 1998–2000: Building Bridges of Trust*, Guatemala, Magna Terra Editores.

Dowdy, John (2000) *Targeting Improved Performance*, Public Services Productivity Panel, HM Treasury, London 3, http://www.slideshare.net/Jackie72/targeting-improved-performance (accessed 25 January 2014).

Drucker, Peter (1999) *Management Challenges for the 21st Century*, Oxford England, Elsevier

Drucker, Peter F. (1995) *Managing the Non-Profit Organization*, Oxford, Butterworth-Heinemann.

Economic Development Board of Singapore (2013) www.edb.gov.sg (accessed 13 October 2013). (The EDB website has a useful history of the development of strategy in Singapore at http://www.edb.gov.sg/content/edb/en/about-edb/company-information/our-history.html.)

Eisenhower, D. (1957) 14 November 1957 speech to the National Defense Executive Reserve Conference in Washington, DC, http://www.presidency.ucsb.edu/elections.php (accessed 7 Sept 2013).

Eldredge, N. and Gould S.J. (1972) 'Punctuated equilibria: an alternative to phyletic gradualism', in T.J.M. Schopf (ed.) *Models in Paleobiology*, San Francisco, Freeman Cooper: 82–115. Reprinted in N. Eldredge *Time Frames*, Princeton: Princeton University Press 1985: 193–223.

Energy Information Administration (May 2003) *International Energy Outlook 2003*, Washington, US Department of Energy, www.eia.doe.gov (accessed 7 September 2013).

Ereaut, G. (2012) 'Strategy and Discourse', in J. Verity *The New Strategic Landscape: Innovative Perspectives on Strategy*, Basingstoke, Palgrave Macmillan.

Europa (2013) *About the Bureau of European Policy Advisers*, http://ec.europa.eu/bepa/about/.

Finnish Government, April 2007 (2007) Government Programme of Prime Minister Matti Vanhanen's Second Cabinet, Helsinki, http://valtioneuvosto.fi/tietoarkisto/aiemmat-hallitukset/vanhanenII/hallitusohjelma/en.jsp (accessed 7 September 2013).

Fishkin, J.S., He, B., Luskin, R.C. and Siu, A. (2010) 'Deliberative Democracy in an Unlikely Place: Deliberative Polling in China', *British Journal of Political Science*, 40(2): 435–48.

Fontaine, P. (2000) *A new idea for Europe: The Schuman declaration 1950–2000*, http://eeas.europa.eu/delegations/georgia/documents/virtual library/07_new_idea_for_europe_en.pdf (accessed 20 October 2013).

Fortune 500 www.money.cnn.com/magazines/fortune/fortune500/ (accessed 2 September 2013).

French National Security Strategy (2013) *The French White Paper on defence and national security*, http://www.gouvernement.fr/sites/default/files/fichiers_joints/livre-blanc-sur-la-defense-et-la-securite-nationale_2013.pdf (accessed 13 October 2013).

Friedman, M. (2005) *Trying Hard is Not Good Enough*, Bloomington, Indiana, Trafford Publishing.

Fuller, Buckminster (1995) *Grunch of Giants*, Santa Barbara, California Buckminster Fuller Institute: 2.

Fung, A. (2006) 'Varieties of Participation in Complex Governance', *Public Administration Review*, December.

Gall, J. (2002) *The Systems Bible*, Walker, Minnesota, The General Systemantics Press.

Gates, Bill (1995) *The Road Ahead*, New York, Viking.

Gawande, Atul (2008) *Better: A Surgeon's Notes on Performance*, London, Profile Books.

Gibson, William (2003) *Pattern Recognition*, London, Viking.

Glaab, M. (2007) 'Strategy and Politics: the Example of Germany', in T. Fischer, G.P. Schmitz and M. Seberich (eds) *The Strategy of Politics*, Gütersloh, Bertelsmann Foundation: 63–4.

Global Business Network (1990) *Mont Fleur Scenarios*, Emeryville, CA, Deeper News/Global Business Network.

GlobeScan (2010) *Climate Concerns Decline Since Copenhagen Summit: Global Poll*, http://www.globescan.com/news_archives/cancun_radar/ (accessed 3 November 2013).

Green, Josephine (2010) *From Pyramids to Pancakes*, commentary at http://thedx.druckerinstitute.com/2010/11/of-pyramids-and-pancakes/ (accessed 19 October 2013).

Greenaway, J. (1998) 'Policy Learning and the Drink Question in Britain 1850–1954', *Political Studies XLVI*, Political Studies Association, Oxford, Blackwell: 906.

Griffin, G. Edward (1974) *World without Cancer: The Story of Vitamin B17*, California, American Media.

Grint, Keith (2008) *Wicked Problems and Clumsy Solutions: the Role of Leadership, Clinical Leader*, 1(II): December, BAMM Publications.

Hallsworth, M. (2011) *System Stewardship*, London, Institute for Government, http://www.instituteforgovernment.org.uk/sites/default/files/publications/System%20Stewardship.pdf (accessed 10 July 2013).

Hampden-Turner, C. (1990) *Charting the corporate mind: from dilemma to strategy*, Oxford, Blackwell.

Haque, M. Shamsul (2009) 'New Public Management: Origins, Dimensions and Critical Implications', in *Public Administration and Public Policy Vol. I* edited by Krishna K. Tummalaaytex in *Encyclopedia of Life Support Systems* (EOLSS), Developed under the Auspices of the UNESCO, Eolss Publishers, Oxford UK, http://www.eolss.net.

Harvey, J.B. (1974) 'Is Agreement ever a Problem? The Abilene Paradox: The Management of Agreement', *Organizational Dynamics*, 3(1), Summer: 63–80.

Heath, Chip and Heath, Dan (2008) *Made to Stick*, London, Arrow Books Random House.

Heffernan, M. (2011) *Wilful Blindness: Why We Ignore the Obvious at Our Peril*, London, Simon & Schuster.

Heijden, K. van der, Bradfield, R., Burt, G., Cairns, G. and Wright, G. (2002) *The Sixth Sense: accelerating organizational learning with scenarios*, Chichester, John Wiley.

Henrich, J., Heine, S.J. and Norenzayan, A. (2010) 'The weirdest people in the world?', *Behavioral and Brain Sciences*, 33: 61–83.

Hennessy, P. (1996) *Muddling Through: power, politics and the quality of government in post-war Britain*, London, Victor Gollancz.

HM Government (1970) *The Reorganization of Central Government*, London, HMSO: 13–14.

Home Office (2002) *Entitlement Cards and Identity Fraud: A Consultation Paper*, London, The Stationery Office.

Hood, C. (1991) 'A Public Management for All Seasons', *Public Administration*, 69 (Spring): 3–19.

Hood, C. (2006) 'Gaming in Targetworld: The Targets Approach to Managing British Public Services', *Public Administration Review*, 66(4): 515–21.

Hopper, K. and Hopper, W. (2009) *The Puritan Gift*, London, I.B. Tauris.

House of Commons Public Administration Select Committee (2010) *Who does UK National Strategy? First report of Session 2010–11 HC 435*, London, The Stationery Office: EV39.

House of Commons (2004) *Review of the Intelligence on Weapons of Mass Destruction* ('The Butler Review'), http://www.archive2.official-documents. co.uk/document/deps/hc/hc898/898.pdf (accessed 20 October 2013).

Hubbard, Douglas W. (2009) *The Failure of Risk Management: Why it's broken and how to fix it*, London, John Wiley.

Hubbard, Douglas W. (2010) *How to Measure Anything: Finding the Value of Intangibles in Business*, Hoboken, New Jersey, John Wiley.

Hutter, Jim (2009) 'Groupthink and the Invasion of Iraq', Paper presented at the annual meeting of the Midwest Political Science Association 67th Annual National Conference, The Palmer House Hilton, Chicago, IL, 2 April.

Inayatullah, Sohail (2004) 'Causal Layered Analysis: Theory, historical context, and case studies', in Sohail Inayatullah (ed.) *The causal layered analysis (CLA) reader*, Taipei, Taiwan, Tamkang University: 1–52.

Intergovernmental Panel on Climate Change (2007) *IPCC Fourth Assessment Report: Climate Change 2007*, http://www.ipcc.ch/publications_and_data/ ar4/syr/en/spms1.html (accessed 3 November 2013).

Ipsos-Mori (2013) *The Most Important Issues Facing Britain Today*, http://www.ipsos-mori.com/researchpublications/researcharchive/ 2905/Issues-Index-2012-onwards.aspx?view=wide (accessed 22 November 2013).

Jamaica (2009) *Vision 2030 Jamaica National Development Plan*, http://www.vision2030.gov.jm (accessed 3 November 2013).

Janis, Irving L. (1972) *Victims of Groupthink: A psychological study of foreign policy decisions and fiascoes*, Boston, Houghton Mifflin.

Janis, Irving L. (1982) *Groupthink: Psychological Studies of Policy Decisions and Fiascos*, Boston, Houghton Mifflin.

Jefferson, M. (2012) 'Shell Scenarios: what really happened in the 1970s and what may be learned for current world prospects', *Technological Forecasting & Social Change*, 79: 186–97.

John Lewis Partnership (2014) http://www.johnlewispartnership.co.uk/content/cws/resources/faqs/general.html (accessed 24 January 2014).

Johnson, G. and Scholes, K. (1999) *Exploring Corporate Strategy* (5th edn), Harlow, Pearson Education.

Joyce, P. (2000) *Strategy in the Public Sector: a guide to effective change management*, Chichester, John Wiley.

Kahane, A. (2012) *Transformative Scenario Planning: working together to change the future*, San Francisco, Berrett-Koehler.

Kahane, A., Le Roux, P. and Maphai, V. (1997) 'The Mont Fleur Scenarios', *Deeper News*, 7(1), Emeryville, CA, Global Business Network, http://www.universitiesuk.ac.uk/aboutus/whatwedo/PolicyAnalysis/UKHigherEducation/Futures/Documents/MontFleurScenarios.pdf (accessed 3 November 2013).

Kahneman, D. (2011) *Thinking, Fast and Slow*, London, Allen Lane.

Kahneman, D. and Klein, G. (2009) 'Conditions for Intuitive Expertise: A Failure to Disagree', *American Psychologist*, 64(6): 515–26.

Kamarck, E. (2007) *The End of Government... as we know it: Making Public Policy Work*, Boulder, CO, Lynne Rienner Publishers.

Kaplan, R. and Norton, D. (1996) *The Balanced Scorecard: Translating Strategy into Action*, Cambridge, MA, Harvard Business School Press.

Kay, J. (2007) 'The Failure of Market Failure', *Prospect Magazine*, 137, August.

Kay, J. (2010) *Obliquity: Why Our Goals Are Best Achieved Indirectly*, London, Profile.

Kennedy, Robert F. (1968) Speech to University of Kansas 18 March1968, http://www.jfklibrary.org/Research/Research-Aids/Ready-Reference/RFK-Speeches/Remarks-of-Robert-F-Kennedy-at-the-University-of-Kansas-March-18-1968.aspx (accessed 2 September 2013).

King, Anthony and Crewe, Ivor (2013) *The Blunders of our Governments*, London, Oneworld Publications.

King, Martin Luther (1963) 'I have a dream' speech, in Brian MacArthur (ed.) *The Penguin Book of Twentieth Century Speeches* (1999), London, Penguin: 327–32.

Kingdon, J.W. (2003) *Agendas, Alternatives and Public Policies* (2nd edn), London, Addison-Wesley Educational.

Kleiner, Art (2008) *The Age of Heretics: A History of the Radical Thinkers Who Reinvented Corporate Management* (J-B Warren Bennis Series) San Francisco, Jossey-Bass.

Kohn, Alfie (1993) *Punished by Rewards: The Trouble with Gold Stars, Incentive Plans, A's, Praise and Other Bribes*, Boston, Houghton Mifflin.

Kurzweil, Raymond (2006) *The Singularity is Near*, London, Gerald Duckworth.

Lakoff, George (2004) *Don't Think of an Elephant: Know Your Values and Frame the Debate*, White River Jct, Vermont, Chelsea Green Publishing Co, First Printing edition.

Lawson, Hilary (2001) *Closure: A Story of Everything*, London, Routledge.

Lazaroff, M. and Snowden, D. (2006) 'Anticipatory Models for Counter Terrorism' in *Emergent Information Technologies and Enabling Policies for*

Counter-Terrorism, ed. Robert L. Popp and John Yen, Hoboken, New Jersey, John Wiley & Sons.

Lehrer, Jonah (2012) *Imagine: How Creativity Works*, Edinburgh, Canongate.

Leong, L. (2010) *The Story of Singapore Prison Service: from custodians of prisoners to captains of life*, Singapore, Civil Service College.

Lewig, K., Scott, D., Holzer, P., Arney, F., Humphreys, C. and Bromfield, L. (2010) 'The role of research in child protection policy reform: a case study of South Australia', *Evidence and Policy*, 6(4): 461–82, Bristol, The Policy Press.

Light, P. (2002) *Government's Greatest Achievements: From Civil Rights to Homeland Defense*, Washington, Brookings Institution Press.

Lindblom, Charles E. (1959) 'The Science of Muddling Through', *Public Administration Review*, 19: 79–88.

Lindblom, Charles E. (1979) 'Still Muddling, Not Yet Through', *Public Administration Review*, 39(6), November–December.

Lindholm, N.R. and Prehn, A. (2007) 'Strategy and Politics: The Example of Denmark', in T. Fischer, G.P. Schmitz and M. Seberich (eds) *The Strategy of Politics*, Gütersloh, Bertelsmann Foundation: 27–8.

Lipsky, M. (1980) *Street-Level Bureaucracy: Dilemmas of the Individual in Public Services*, New York, Russell Sage Foundation.

Luft, J. and Ingham, H. (1950) *The Johari window, a graphic model of interpersonal awareness*, Johari Window created by Joseph Luft and Harry Ingham in 1955. Proceedings of the western training laboratory in group development (Los Angeles: UCLA).

Lunn, P. (2008) *Basic Instincts: Human Nature and the New Economics*, London, Marshall Cavendish.

Macleod, D. and Brady, C. (2008) *The Extra Mile: how to engage your people to win*, Harlow, FT Prentice-Hall.

Maddison, A. and Wu, H.X. (2008) 'Measuring China's Economic Performance', *World Economics*, 9(2), April–June.

Manski, C. (2003) *Partial Identification of Probability Distributions*, New York, Springer-Verlag.

Mant, A. (1997) *Intelligent Leadership*, London, Allen & Unwin.

Maslow, Abraham H. (1966) The Psychology of Science, Chapel Hill, Maurice Bassett.

McGilchrist, Iain (2009) *The Master and His Emissary: The Divided Brain and the Making of the Western World*, New Haven, Yale University Press.

McQueen, Alison (2005) 'A Groupthink Perspective on the Invasion of Iraq', *International Affairs Reviews*, 14(2), Fall.

Meadows, Donatella (1999) *Leverage Points Places to Intervene in a System*, The Sustainability Institute at http://www.sustainer.org/pubs/Leverage_Points.pdf (accessed 7 September 2013).

Merchant, Nilofer (2012) *11 Rules for Creating Value in the Social Era*, Cambridge, MA: Harvard Business Review Press.

Merck (2014) https://www.merck.com/about/Merck%20Vision%20Mission.pdf (accessed 26 January 2014).

Minztzberg, H. (1994) *The Rise and Fall of Strategic Planning*, Hemel Hempstead, Prentice-Hall Europe.

Mintzberg, H., Ahlstrand, B. and Lampel, J. (1998) *Strategy Safari*, New Jersey, Prentice-Hall.

Modis, Theodore (1992) *Predictions: Society's Telltale Signature Reveals The Past And Forecasts The Future*, London, Simon & Schuster.

Modis, Theodore (1998) *Conquering Uncertainty*, New York, Business Week Books.

Moore, M. (1995) *Creating Public Value: strategic management in government*, Cambridge, MA, Harvard University Press.

Moore, M. (2003) *The Public Value Scorecard: A Rejoinder and an Alternative to 'Strategic Performance Management in Non-Profit Organizations' by Robert Kaplan*, Harvard, MA, The Hauser Centre for Nonprofit Organizations, Kennedy School of Government, Harvard University: 4–5.

Mueller, Dennis C. (2003) *Public Choice III*, Cambridge, Cambridge University Press.

Mulgan, G. (1997) *Connexity: how to live in a connected world*, London, Chatto & Windus.

Mulgan, G. (2007) *Ready or Not? Taking Innovation in the Public Sector Seriously*, London, NESTA.

Mulgan, G. (2009) *The Art of Public Strategy: Mobilizing power and knowledge for the common good*, Oxford, Oxford University Press.

Mulgan, G., Reeder, N., Aylott, M. and Bo'sher, L. (2010) *Social Impact Investment: the challenge and opportunity of Social Impact Bonds*, London, The Young Foundation.

Namibian Government (2004) *Namibia Vision 2030*, Windhoek, Office of the President.

Nathan, S.A., Devlin, E., Grove, N. and Zwi, A.B. (2005) 'An Australian childhood obesity summit: the role of data and evidence in "public" policy making', *Australia and New Zealand Health Policy*, 2: 17.

National Audit Office (2001) *Inappropriate Adjustments to NHS Waiting Lists*, London, The Stationery Office.

National Audit Office (2010a) *Managing Major Projects*, London, The Stationery Office.

National Audit Office (2010b) *Reorganising Central Government*, London, The Stationery Office.

National Commission on Terrorist Attacks on the United States (2004) *The 9/11 Commission Report Final Report* Chapter 11, http://www.gpoaccess.gov/911/pdf/sec11.pdf (accessed 7 September 2013).

Netherlands Government (2012) *Coalition Agreement: Building Bridges*, http://www.government.nl/government/coalition-agreement (accessed 3 November 2013).

New Economics Foundation (2008) *Co-production: A manifesto for growing the core economy*, London, New Economics Foundation.

New South Wales Government (2013) http://www.dlg.nsw.gov.au/dlg/dlghome/documents/Circulars/13-39.pdf (accessed 13 October 2013).

New Zealand Inland Revenue (2014) http://www.justice.govt.nz/ publications/global-publications/d/directory-of-official-information-archive/directory-of-official-information-december-2001/alphabetical-list-of-entries-1/i/inland-revenue-department (accessed 24 January 2014).

New Zealand National Library (2011) *Annual Report July 2010–January 2011*, http://www.dia.govt.nz/pubforms.nsf/URL/NLNZ-Annual-Report-2011.pdf/$file/NLNZ-Annual-Report-2011.pdf (accessed 20 October 2013).

New Zealand National Library (2007) *New Generation National Library: Strategic Directions to 2017*, http://natlib.govt.nz/files/strategy/Strategic_Directions_to_2017.pdf (accessed 20 October 2013).

NISTEP (Japan National Institute for Science and Technology Policy) (2010) *NISTEP REPORT No.145 Contribution of Science and Technology to Future Society Summary on the 9th Science and Technology Foresight*, http://www.nistep.go.jp/achiev/ftx/eng/rep145e/pdf/rep145e.pdf (accessed 3 November 2013).

Nokia (2013) http://www.nokia.com/global/about-nokia/about-us/about-us/ (accessed 13 October 2013).

Nonaka, Ikujiro and Takeuchi, Hirotaka (1995) *The Knowledge-Creating Company: How Japanese Companies Create the Dynamics of Innovation* (7th edn), Oxford University Press.

Nowotny, Helga (1994) *Time: the modern and postmodern experience*, Cambridge, Polity Press.

Nugent, N. (2006) *The Government and Politics of the European Union* (6th edn), Basingstoke, Palgrave Macmillan.

OECD (2013) *Better Life Index – Germany*, http://www.oecdbetterlifeindex. org/countries/germany/ (accessed 20 October 2013).

Oregon, State of (2008) *Oregon Shines III*, The Oregon Progress Board.

Osborne, D. and Gaebler, T. (1992) *Reinventing Government: How the Entrepreneurial Spirit is Transforming the Public Sector*, New York, Penguin.

Panksepp, Jaak (2004) *Affective Neuroscience: The Foundations of Human and Animal Emotions*, Oxford University Press.

Parker, S., Paun, A., McClory, J. and Blatchford, K. (2010) *Shaping Up: A Whitehall for the Future*, London, Institute for Government.

Pascale, R., Sternin, J. and Sternin, M. (2010) *The Power of Positive Deviance: How Unlikely Innovators Solve the World's Toughest Problems*, Cambridge, MA, Harvard Business School Press.

Perez, C (2002) *Technological Revolutions and Financial Capital: The Dynamics of Bubbles and Golden Ages*, Cheltenham, Edward Elgar Publishing Ltd (see also Perez, C. (2009) *Technological revolutions and techno-economic paradigms*, http://hum.ttu.ee/tg/ (accessed 3 August 2013).

Peters, B. Guy and Pierre, John (1998) 'Governance without Government', *Journal of Public Administration Research and Theory*, April: 223–43, http://bush.tamu.edu/pa-archive/JPART8-2.223-243.pdf.

Pew States (2008) A useful website full of comparative information about US states, http://www.pewstates.org/uploadedFiles/PCS_Assets/2008/Grading-the-States-2008.pdf (accessed 20 October 2013).

Pfeffer, J. and Sutton, J. (1999) *The Knowing–Doing Gap: How Smart Companies Turn Knowledge into Action*, Cambridge, MA, Harvard Business School Press.

Pisapia, John, Sun-Keung Pang, Nicholas, Hee, Tie Fatt, Lin, Ying and Morris, John D. (2009) 'A Comparison of the Use of Strategic Thinking Skills of Aspiring School Leaders in Hong Kong, Malaysia, Shanghai, and the United States: An Exploratory Study', *International Education Studies*, 2(2), May: 46–58, www.ccsenet.org/journal/index.php/ies/article/download/1682/1627? (accessed 27 September 2013).

Poister, Theodore (2003) *Measuring Performance in Public and Nonprofit Organizations*, San Francisco, Jossey-Bass.

Pollitt, C. (2008) *Time, Policy, Management: Governing with the Past*, Oxford, Oxford University Press.

Popper, Karl (2002) *The Logic of Scientific Discovery*, London, Routledge Classics.

Porter, M. (1980) *Competitive Strategy*, New York, The Free Press.

Pressman, J. and Wildavsky, A. (1973) *Implementation: how great expectations in Washington are dashed in Oakland, or Why it's amazing that Federal Programmes work at all*, Oakland, University of California Press.

Pullman, P. (Undated) http://www.randomhouse.com/features/pullman/author/qa.php (accessed 4 November 2013).

Ragnitz, J. (2009) 'East Germany Today: Successes and Failures', in *CESifo DICE report 4/2009*, Oxford, Oxford University Press: 51–8 and at http://www.cesifo-group.de/ifoHome/publications/docbase/details.html?docId=14567033 (accessed 20 October 2013).

Ramachandran, V.S and Blakeslee, S. (1999) *Phantoms in the Brain: Human Nature and the Architecture of the Mind*, London, Fourth Estate.

Ringland, G. (2006) *Scenario Planning* (2nd edn), Chichester, John Wiley.

Rittel, H. and Webber, M. (1973) 'Dilemmas in a General Theory of Planning', *Policy Sciences*, 4: 155–69, Amsterdam, Elsevier Scientific Publishing Company. Reprinted in N. Cross (ed.) (1984) *Developments in Design Methodology*, Chichester, John Wiley, 135–44.

Rohter, Larry (2010) *Brazil on the Rise*, New York, Palgrave Macmillan.

Roth, P. (2004) *The Plot Against America*, London, Jonathan Cape.

Rumelt, Richard (2011) *Good Strategy Bad Strategy: The difference and why it matters*, London, Profile Books.

Rumelt, Richard (2011a) 'The Perils of Bad Strategy', *McKinsey Quarterly*, http://www.mckinsey.com/   insights/strategy/the_perils_of_bad_strategy (accessed 4 November 2013).

Runciman, David (2013) *The Confidence Trap: A History of Democracy in Crisis from World War I to the Present*, Princeton, Princeton University Press.

Safire, William (2004) 'On Language: Groupthink', *New York Times Magazine*, 8 August.

Saint-Exupéry, Antoine de (1950) *The Wisdom of the Sands*, Boston, Houghton Mifflin (first published as Citadelle in 1948, three years after Saint-Exupéry's death in a flying accident).

Salagnik, Matthew J., Peter Sheridan Dodds, Duncan J. Watts (2006) 'Experimental Study of Inequality and Unpredictability in an Artificial Cultural Market', *Science*, 311: 854–56.http://www.princeton.edu/~mjs3/salganik_dodds_watts06_full.pdf (accessed 25 January 2014).

Sandel, M. (2009) *Justice: What's the right thing to do?*, London, Allen Lane.

Schank, Roger C. (1995) *Tell Me a Story: Narrative and Intelligence*, Evanston Illinois, Northwestern University Press.

Schein, E. (1996) *Strategic Pragmatism: The Culture of Singapore's Economic Development Board*, Cambridge, MA, MIT Press.

Schön, Donald A. and Rein, Martin (1994) *Frame Reflection: Toward the Resolution of Intractable Policy Controversies*, New York, Basic Books.

Schwartz, Peter (1996) *The Art of the Long View*, New York, Currency

Doubleday.

Schwartz, P. (2004) *Inevitable Surprises: thinking ahead in a time of turbulence*, New York, Gotham Books.

Scotland Performs (2013), http://www.scotland.gov.uk/About/Performance/ scotPerforms (accessed 3 November 2013).

Scottish Executive (2006) *The Futures Project – Trend Analysis Papers*, Edinburgh, The Scottish Executive, http://www.scotland.gov.uk/Resource/ Doc/923/0029756.pdf (accessed 20 October 2013).

Seabright, P. (2012) *The War of the Sexes: How Conflict and Cooperation Have Shaped Men and Women from Prehistory to the Present*, Princeton, Princeton University Press.

Seddon, J. (2008) *Systems Thinking in the Public Sector: the failure of the reform regime and a manifesto for a better way*, Axminster, Triarchy Press.

Seksel, K. (2002) *Report to the NSW Department of Local Government on Breed Specific Legislation Relating to Control of Dangerous Dogs*, http://dogbitelaw.com/images/pdf/NSW_BSL_Report.pdf (accessed 10 July 2013).

Senge, Peter M. (2006) *The Fifth Discipline*, London, Random House Business Books.

Sennett, Richard (2012) *Together: The Rituals, Pleasures and Politics of Cooperation*, London, Allen Lane.

Shanteau, J. (1992) 'Competence in experts: The role of task characteristics', *Organizational Behavior and Human Decision Processes*, 53, 252–62.

Shell (2014) *Scramble or Blueprint?* http://www.shell.com/global/future-energy/scenarios/videos/video.html (accessed 9 March 2014).

Shirane, R., Smith, K., Ross, H., Silver, K.E., Williams, S. and Gilmore, A. (2012) *Tobacco Industry Manipulation of Tobacco Excise and Tobacco Advertising Policies in the Czech Republic: An Analysis of Tobacco Industry Documents*, http://www.plosmedicine.org/article/info%3Adoi%2F10.1371 %2Fjournal.pmed.1001248 (accessed 20 October 2013).

Simon, H. A. (1997) *Administrative Behavior* (4th edn), New York, The Free Press.

Simon, H.A. (1992) 'What is an explanation of behavior?', *Psychological Science*, 3: 150–61.

Singapore Prison Service (2013) *Mission, vision and values*, http://www.prisons. gov.sg/content/sps/default/aboutus/vision_mission.html (accessed 3 November 2013).

Snowden, David J. and Kurtz, Cynthia F. (2006) *Bramble Bushes in a Thicket*, Cognitive Edge, http://cognitive-edge.com/library/more/articles/ (accessed 11 July 2013).

South African National Planning Commission (2012) *South African National Development Plan – 2030: Our Future – Make it Work*, http://www.info. gov.za/issues/national-development-plan/ (accessed 13 October 2013).

South African Revenue Service (2014) http://www.saembassy.org/south-africa-revenue-service/ (accessed 24 January 2014).

Spanish Revenue Service (2014) http://www.agenciatributaria.es (accessed 24 January 2014).

Staley, D.J. (2010) *History and Future: Using Historical Thinking to Imagine the Future*, Lanham, MD, Lexington Books.

Stanford, M. (1986) *The Nature of Historical Knowledge*, Cambridge, Blackwell.

Sun Tzu (2006) The Art of War, Minneapolis, Filiquarian Publishing LLC.

Sunningdale Institute (2008) *Engagement and Aspiration: Reconnecting Policy Making with Front Line Professionals*, Sunningdale, Cabinet Office.

Surowiecki, J. (2005) *The Wisdom of Crowds*, New York, Knopf Doubleday Publishing Group.

Swift, Jonathan (1726) *Gulliver's Travels*, London, Penguin (2012)

Taleb, Nicholas Nassim (2011) *The Black Swan: The Impact of the Highly Improbable*, London, Allen Lane.

Tetlock, Philip (2005) *Expert Political Judgement. How Good Is It? How Can We Know?*, Princeton, Princeton University Press.

't Hart, Paul (1994) *Groupthink in Government: a study of small groups and policy failure*, Baltimore, Johns Hopkins University Press.

Thiele, L.P. (2006) *The Heart of Judgment: Practical Wisdom, Neuroscience, and Narrative*, Cambridge, Cambridge University Press.

Tibbs, Hardin (1999) *Making the Future Visible: Psychology, Scenarios, and Strategy*, http://www.hardintibbs.com/wp-content/uploads/2009/10/future-landscape-tibbs-a4.pdf (accessed 7 September 2013).

Truman Library (1947) Text from Secretary of State George C. Marshall's 5 June 1948 speech outlining the need for European Recovery, http://www.trumanlibrary.org/whistlestop/study_collections/marshall/large/documents/index.php?documentdate=1947-06-05&documentid=8-7&pagenumber=1 (accessed 20 October 2013).

Truman Library (1947) Text from the European Recovery Programme Basic Document of 31 October 1947, http://www.trumanlibrary.org/whistlestop/study_collections/marshall/large/documents/index.php?pagenumber=2&documentdate=1947-10-31&documentid=6-3 (accessed 20 October 2013).

Tryens, J. (2004) *Using indicators to engage citizens: the Oregon Progress Board experience*, www.oecd.org/site/worldforum/33832894.doc (accessed 3 November 2013).

Turkish Ministry of Development (2013), http://www.mod.gov.tr/en/SitePages/mod_aboutus.aspx.

Tversky, Amos and Kahneman, Daniel (1981) 'The Framing of Decisions and the Psychology of Choice', *Science*, new series, 211, 4481, pp. 453–8.

United Kingdom National Security Strategy (2010), https://www.gov.uk/government/publications/the-national-security-strategy-a-strong-britain-in-an-age-of-uncertainty (accessed 13 October 2013).

United Kingdom Government (2010) The coalition: our programme for government, https://www.gov.uk/government/uploads/system/uploads/attachment_data/file/78977/coalition_programme_for_government.pdf.

UNDP (2002) *Results Based Management Concepts and Methodology*, http://web.undp.org/evaluation/documents/RBMConceptsMethodgyjuly2002.pdf (accessed 3 November 2013).

United States Commission on National Security/21st Century (1998–2001) *Road Map for National Security: Imperative for Change. The Phase III Report of the U.S. Commission on National Security/21st Century*, Washington, January 2001, Library of Congress.

United States Commission on National Security/21st Century (1999) *New World Coming: American Security in the 21st Century*. Supporting Research and Analysis. The Phase I Report on the Emerging Security Environment for the First Quarter of the 21st Century.

United States Department of Defense (1993–2010) *Quadrennial Defense Reviews*, Washington, www.defense.gov.qdr (accessed 10 July 2013).

United States Inland Revenue Service (2014) http://www.irs.gov/uac/The-Agency,-its-Mission-and-Statutory-Authority (accessed 24 January 2014).

United States National Security Strategy 2010 (2010) *National Security Strategy*, www.nssarchive.us/NSSR/2010.pdf (accessed 13 October 2013).

United States Senate (2004) Report of the Select Committee on Intelligence on the U.S. Intelligence Community's Prewar Intelligence Assessments on Iraq, http://www.intelligence.senate.gov/108301.pdf (accessed 20 October 2013).

Valerdi, R. (2011) 'Convergence of Expert Opinion via the Wideband Delphi Method: An Application in Cost Estimation Model', *21st Annual INCOSE International Symposium*, Denver, CO, 20–23 June, http://lean.mit.edu/downloads/cat_view/99-presentations/73-conference-papers/589-2011-conference-papers (accessed 7 September 2013).

Verity, J. (2012) *The New Strategic Landscape: Innovative Perspectives on Strategy*, Basingstoke, Palgrave Macmillan.

Verweij, M. and Thompson, M. (eds) (2006) *Clumsy Solutions for a Complex World: Governance, Politics and Plural Perceptions*, Basingstoke, Palgrave Macmillan.

Virginia – Council on Virginia's Future (2003), http://www.future.virginia.gov/aboutUs/history/legislation.php (accessed 20 October 2013).

Virginia Performs (2013), http://vaperforms.virginia.gov/Scorecard/ Scorecard atGlance.php (accessed 20 October 2013).

Virtue, S., Haberman, J., Clancy, Z., Parrish, T. and Beeman, M.J. (undated) *Neural Activity During Inferences*, http://groups.psych.northwestern.edu/mbeeman/documents/CBR_Manuscript_ss.pdf (accessed 18 August 2013).

Wack, Pierre (1985) 'Scenarios, Uncharted Waters Ahead', *Harvard Business Review*, September–October.

Walmart (2014) www.stock.walmart.com/faqs/ (accessed 24 January 2014).

Watts, Duncan J. (2011) *Everything is Obvious: How Common Sense Fails*, London, Atlantic Books.

Wawasan (1991) *The Way Forward – Vision 2020* (Malaysia Government Vision as set out by President Mahathir Mohamed), http://www.wawasan2020.com/vision/ (accessed 3 November 2013).

Weick, Karl E. (1995) *Sensemaking in Organizations*, California, Sage Publications Inc.

White House (2013) National Security Council, http://www.whitehouse.gov/administration/eop/nsc/ (accessed 3 November 2013).

Whyte, William H. (1952) *Groupthink*, March, Fortune magazine, http://features.blogs.fortune.cnn.com/2012/07/22/groupthink-fortune-classic-1952/ (accessed 25 January 2014).

Whyte, William H. (1956) *The Organization Man*, Simon & Schuster University of Pennsylvania Press; new edition 2002.

Wilson, H. (1986) *Memoirs: 1916–64*, London, Weidenfeld & Nicolson.

World Economic Forum (2007) *The Kingdom of Bahrain and the World:*

Scenarios to 2025, http://www.weforum.org/reports/kingdom-bahrain-and-world-scenarios-2025 (accessed 3 November 2013).

Yorke, J. (2013) *Into the Woods: A Five Act Journey into the Story*, Penguin, London.

Yukihide, H. (2013) *Halting Japan's Scientific Slide*, http://www.nippon.com/en/currents/d00059/ (accessed 3 November 2013).

Zhou, Wei (2012) 'In Search of Deliberative Democracy in China', *Journal of Public Deliberation*, 8(1): Article 8, http://www.publicdeliberation.net/jpd/vol8/iss1/art8 (accessed 10 July 2013).

Index